Maurice E. Rosen

# TWENTY-FIVE YEARS
## 1892–1916

# TWENTY-FIVE YEARS

## YEARS

### 1892-1916

BY

VISCOUNT GREY OF FALLODON, K.G.

*WITH THIRTY-TWO ILLUSTRATIONS
FROM PHOTOGRAPHS*

VOLUME I

NEW YORK
FREDERICK A. STOKES COMPANY
MCMXXV

THIS BOOK HAS BEEN WRITTEN
IN INTERVALS OF QUIET AT HOME IN THE COUNTRY DURING
THE LAST TWO YEARS. THERE MY WIFE READ OVER TO
ME THAT PORTION OF THE MS. THAT I HAD WRITTEN
EACH DAY. IN THIS WAY THE FORM AND EXPRES-
SION OF THE ORIGINAL DRAFT WERE OFTEN
GREATLY IMPROVED BY HER SUGGESTION
OR CRITICISM. WITHOUT HER CON-
STANT HELP AND ENCOURAGE-
MENT THE WORK WOULD
NEVER HAVE BEEN DONE.

# CONTENTS

## VOLUME I

x CONTENTS

# CONTENTS

# ILLUSTRATIONS

# INTRODUCTION

IT is of vital importance to the world that there should be a true account of the events that led up to the Great War: without this there can be no right understanding of the causes of the war; and without such understanding nations will not perceive how to avoid the recurrence of another and greater disaster. It has therefore seemed a duty for one who had been long and intimately concerned in pre-war diplomacy to give his narrative of events, his interpretation of them, and the impression produced by them on his own mind. I have therefore had no doubt that this book ought to be written, and the decision to write it needs no excuse or apology.

Whether it should be published now, or reserved for a later time, is open to question.

War has stirred passion, enlisted sympathies, and aroused hatreds; many of the war generation have formed opinions that nothing will modify, and are dominated by predilections or prejudices that have become an inseparable part of their lives. With such people mental digestion ceases to be able to assimilate anything except what nourishes convictions already formed; all else is rejected or resented; and new material or reflections about the war are searched, not for the truth, but for fuel to feed the flame of pre-conceived opinion. Especially is this likely to be the case in the country into whose soul the iron of adversity and defeat has most deeply entered; and not till a new generation rules will books about the war be read, not to be refuted or acclaimed, but to be understood.

There is also another consideration that makes against immediate publication. When a writer has taken a prominent part in controversial affairs the reception of all that he says about the past is apt to be coloured by the desire of readers to encourage or to depress the part that he may yet take in present or future controversies. A book of this character, therefore, fails less in its influence if published after the life of the writer, when praise or censure can have no effect upon him.

On the other hand, there is a new generation now growing up whose opinions about the war are yet to be formed; and there are many even of the war generation who are dispassionately and increasingly anxious to discover truth. They ought to have the fullest material at their disposal now, and it is mainly for these that this book is written.

It must not, however, be supposed, because the writer was for so many years, and those the most critical, at the centre of affairs that his account is necessarily authoritative and complete. It is precisely the man at the centre who is often unable to see the wood for the trees. In addition to this it must be remembered that the scope of each individual mind is fragmentary. Try as he may, each one of us can grasp but one aspect of the truth; and this is all that he can convey to others. Probably some historian of the future, more remote than we are from the actual events, will reach an eminence of view about the war to which we cannot yet attain.

Two temptations that impair the value of their work inevitably beset public men who write memoirs. One is a tendency to reconstruct the past to suit the present views and feelings of the writer; the other is a natural desire to set his own part in affairs in a pleasing light. It is probably not given to any human being to be superior to

*Portrait by George Richmond, R.A.*

SIR GEORGE GREY
Grandfather of Viscount Grey of Fallodon.  Aged  about  60

these tendencies; even the effort to avoid them, on one side, may land him in error on another. Someone has said that there may be as much vanity in wearing fustian as smart clothes or uniform, and the writer who determines not to vaunt his own part in affairs may easily fall into the vanity of self-depreciation.

I have, however, made an attempt to avoid these pitfalls, and to describe events as they actually happened, and my own part in them and my feelings about them as these actually were at the time.

This book naturally presents the British view, or, at least, that portion of it which was, and is, my own; but in it an endeavour has been made to envisage also the international aspect of the war. Indeed, the main purpose and desire has not been to make vindication or condemnation of any country the final word. That would be a barren and unprofitable end. The endeavour has been made to present the facts in such a way as to discover, or help others to discover and draw, conclusions that may avoid another war of the same scope and character.

There is comparatively little mention of persons with whom the writer worked at the Foreign Office. This is not from lack of gratitude to men like Sir Charles Hardinge and Sir Arthur Nicolson who were in succession the Under-Secretaries and Heads of the Department, while I was Secretary of State, and to many others in the Foreign Office. It would require many pages to make adequate mention of them all, but I do pay an earnest and sincere tribute to their public spirit and able service to the State. It was a privilege as well as a pleasure to work with them.

It has been a great satisfaction, since I left office, to see great knowledge, ability, and unsurpassed devotion to the public service recognized in the promotion of Sir Eyre Crowe[1] to be head of the Foreign Office. To this I may add another pleasure: that of having seen Sir Eric Drummond, who had been closely associated with me during the war, selected, with the approval of high foreign opinion as well as of his own chiefs, to be Secretary-General of the League of Nations.

One other name must be specially mentioned: that of Sir William Tyrrell, who was for many years my chief Private Secretary. The public has little or no means of knowing how much it owes in public service to special gifts or qualities in individual civil servants in high positions in Departments of State. In each case, where such qualities exist, a man renders service, peculiarly his own, besides taking an able part in the conduct of business in the Department. Tyrrell's power of understanding the point of view of foreigners has been of the greatest value in making the British position both more intelligible and more acceptable to them. For nothing so predisposes men to understand as making them feel that they are understood. I had occasion, in office, to know the great value of Tyrrell's public service; but the thing that I prize is our friendship, that began in the Foreign Office, and has continued uninterrupted and intimate after official ties ceased.

This book has been written under one great disadvantage—the disability of impaired sight. This has made it impossible for me to search through masses of documents and to select for myself. It would not have been fair to ask that anyone in the Foreign Office should be

[1] Since these words were written the public service of the country has suffered an irreparable loss in the death of Sir Eyre Crowe.

diverted from public work to undertake this heavy task, for the book is entirely personal and unofficial.

Other personal notes of friendship or close association will be found in this book, and these are not entirely limited to British friends. The chapter on America will show how quickly the official relations of individuals may pass into something closer and more intimate; something that has a place in the affections as well as in the memory. The mention of Roosevelt, Page, and House will be an example.

I therefore asked Mr. J. A. Spender, a friend of many years, to undertake this for me, and the book has had the great advantage of his collaboration. His long experience as a writer on public affairs and his able impartiality of mind have made his help invaluable. From the masses of material at the Foreign Office he would select the documents that seemed to him to be the most salient and typical and to throw the clearest light on policy. These he would send to me with marked passages or comments, to direct attention to special points. From the selection so made I have chosen the documents to be quoted. I am sure that his trained ability and judgment have selected well, that the documents chosen do give a fair and not a tendencious or distorted impression of policy and transactions at the Foreign Office. Masses of other documents in the Foreign Office of course there are: many of them would perhaps be deemed of equal importance with those quoted in this book; but, according to my recollection, and to Mr. Spender's own opinion after much search, there are none that would put British policy in a different light or that would make any new revelation. My grateful thanks are due to the King for gracious permission to have access to documents among

His Majesty's papers; and to Lord Curzon,[1] who, as Secretary of State, gave the permission that I asked for Spender to consult all official records at the Foreign Office belonging to the years when I was there as Under-Secretary or Secretary of State. I am also very grateful to Mr. Gaselee, the librarian at the Foreign Office, and to his Department for the help given to Spender in searching for special documents. All my private papers, with two exceptions, were left at the Foreign Office for safe keeping, and are still there. These were placed by me at Spender's disposal, and from them he has made some selections. What has been said about the fairness of selections from official documents applies also to those made from private papers. But it would be very unfair to the Foreign Office to transact important matters through private channels. If the staff of an Office is to serve the State well they must know what is being done, and the record must be accessible to them in official documents. The private papers, therefore, have no State secrets to reveal. The two exceptions mentioned above, which were not with my papers at the Foreign Office, are a private letter from Lichnowsky and the "House" Memorandum and my covering note upon it; both these are printed in the places in this book to which they are appropriate.[2]

All care has been taken to ensure that nothing of real or great importance should be overlooked and that inac-

---

[1] The news of Lord Curzon's death came while these sheets were in the Press, and to the expression of gratitude must now be added that of great regret at the close of his brilliant life of public service.

[2] It may perhaps be convenient to explain to the reader who is unacquainted with diplomatic forms that the practice of the Foreign Secretary is to give his record of a conversation with a Foreign Ambassador the form of a despatch to the British Ambassador in the country concerned. Nearly all the conversations recorded in these volumes are in that form. For details of the practice of the Foreign Secretary in this and other matters see Vol. II, Chapter XXX.

curacies should not creep in; but in a book that extends over so many years and deals with so many complex affairs some mistakes or inaccuracies may occur. Memory may err in some detail, but the main outlines it has traced and the impressions recorded are true.

My sight, which still enables me to write, is not equal to the sustained reading of long tracts of manuscript or even of print. Revision and the correction of proofs have therefore been left in the main to better eyes than mine.

What political value the book has must be left to others to determine. It presents my own views, but its object is much more to stimulate thought than to press that these views should be accepted as conclusive. Those of us who grew to maturity in the nineteenth century acquired our sense of values and formed our first opinions in the latter part of the Victorian age. The general point of view in domestic affairs was already changing rapidly before 1914. The war may be regarded as the division between two epochs in foreign affairs as well. We, who were in foremost places in 1904, belonged to one epoch and have lived on into another. We are now confronted by problems that are new to us, our vision may be rendered unsteady by things that seem disquieting or alarming, because they are strange to us. Control of affairs has already passed in part and must soon pass entirely to younger and fresher minds, who may see further and more clearly, because much that preoccupies us with its strangeness will be to them familiar and intelligible. It is not for us to be confident that, because we know more of the past, we can therefore see more clearly than they into the future. What we can do is to record for them our experience, and our reflections upon it, in the hope that these may provide some suggestion and impetus to thought that in their fresh minds may be fruitful.

This book is not intended to be a biography, and therefore no account will be given of boyhood, of school or college, or of marriage and home life, except in so far as they had influence upon public life or were affected by it.

In early years public affairs had no interest for me: my recollection is most meagre and trivial.

I remember being asked by my father, at the outbreak of the Franco-Prussian War in 1870, on which side I was. My age was then about 8¼ years and I had little feeling in the matter; but, moved probably by what I had heard of Waterloo, and perhaps also by a liking for a game called "German" as distinct from ordinary dominoes, I replied that I was on the side of the Germans. My father [1] had been in the Rifle Brigade and had fought in alliance with the French in the Crimea. My answer did not please him; he reproved me for my preference, and I relapsed into the indifference from which, but for his question, I should never have emerged.

It must have been a few months later that I was called out on to the balcony at Fallodon on a winter evening to see a display of Aurora Borealis. A great part of the sky was not only irradiated with light, but suffused with pink. The recollection of the apparition has always been very positive and distinct to me; and I have never, in after-years, seen any display of Aurora Borealis that approached this. It may be, therefore, that imagination has enhanced the glory and beauty of it, but it remains in

[1] Capt. George Henry Grey (afterwards Lieut.-Col. of Northumberland Militia), Equerry to the Prince of Wales 1859-74. See *Life of Edward VII*, vol. i, p. 155.

memory as a wonderful vision. I remember my grandfather saying, as we stood on the balcony, that if Paris had not been so distant we might have thought that the Prussians were burning it and that this was causing the illumination of the sky.

In the late summer of 1873 I was taken on a visit to the Highlands. We were returning by train from Inverness. My grandfather and I were alone in the compartment. At one of the stations where the train stopped (Kingussie, probably) my grandfather looked out of the window and I heard a greeting from someone on the platform. A gentleman, who was a stranger to me, was welcomed into the compartment, and thence to Perth an incessant and animated conversation went on, of which I understood nothing and took no heed. At Perth the stranger parted from us, and when he had gone my grandfather told me it was Mr. Gladstone. The information meant nothing to me at the time, but years afterwards my grandfather asked me if I remembered the occasion, and told me what the subject of the talk had been. It was the technical but very embarrassing difficulty in which Mr. Gladstone, then Prime Minister, was placed by having taken a second office without vacating his seat and being re-elected. My grandfather, Sir George Grey,[1] though no longer in office, had been a colleague of Gladstone's in previous Cabinets; he had had very great experience as Home Secretary, and had been forty years in the House of Commons, of which he was still a member. He was an authority on parliamentary procedure, and no doubt

[1] Chancellor of the Duchy of Lancaster in Lord Melbourne's second Government (1841); Home Secretary in Lord John Russell's first Government, 1846-52; Colonial Secretary in Lord Aberdeen's Government, 1854-5; Home Secretary in Lord Palmerston's first Government, 1855-8; Chancellor of the Duchy of Lancaster, and subsequently Home Secretary in Lord Palmerston's second Government, 1859-66.

Gladstone welcomed the opportunity of discussing this particular point with him.

At the end of 1874 my father died. After his marriage he had still continued to live at Fallodon with his parents, and he and my mother had kept house there when my grandparents were absent for the Sessions of Parliament. After his death my mother and all of us remained at Fallodon, my grandfather now taking a father's place with his grandchildren.[1]

As for school-life, it is but necessary to say that I was fortunate in being sent in 1873 to Temple Grove, at East Sheen, a preparatory school conducted by O. C. Waterfield, an able man, who endeavoured, not without some measure of success, to teach boys, even at the age of 13, how to think as well as to learn.

In 1876 I was sent to Dr. Bowley's house at Winchester, under the Headmastership of Ridding; and thence in 1880 to Oxford, to Balliol College, of which Jowett was Master. I left both places with feelings of affection second only to those felt for home.

I do not remember taking any interest in public events till the news of the murder of Lord Frederick Cavendish in Dublin in 1882. I was then an undergraduate at Balliol, and I joined in the clamour for martial law. This I repeated to my grandfather, who met it with the critical comment, "Martial law is the suspension of all law."

A few months later my grandfather died, and I inherited the house and property at Fallodon. In 1884, after a long spell of what is generally called idleness, but

[1] There were seven of us, four boys and three girls. A *Memoir of Sir George Grey,* written by Dr. Creighton (Bishop of London), was published in 1901 by Longmans, Green & Co. It gives an account, written with intimate knowledge, of a singularly lovable as well as upright character. Whoever reads it will get some impression of how much happiness and benefit we owed to our grandfather's affection and influence. See Appendix A.

CAPTAIN GREY
Father of Viscount Grey of Fallodon

which was in my case very active and strenuous pursuit of pleasure in the form of sport and games, interest in all manner of serious things came suddenly. I began to read good literature, poetry excited me to enthusiasm, and I read everything serious, however prolix, with interest. I remember being absorbed in the *Life of George Eliot,* when it appeared. The same rush of interest applied itself to public affairs. I read political leading articles and magazines, but at the very outset of this awakening a thing happened that decided the course of life for me.

In 1884 Gladstone's Government proposed an extension of the franchise to the counties on similar terms to those on which a Conservative Government had given it to the boroughs in 1867. The House of Lords rejected the proposal; there was great indignation in the counties, and a franchise demonstration was arranged at Alnwick, the county town near Fallodon.

Nothing was known of my politics, but my family name was notably associated with the Reform Bill of 1832; my grandfather had sat from 1848 to 1852 for the district, and had in fact been the last Liberal representative for it. I was asked to take the chair at the demonstration at Alnwick. It seemed to me very unfair that men in the counties generally, and in Northumberland especially, should not have the franchise that had been given to the boroughs so many years before. I was country-bred, and a sense of fair play and strong local feeling enlisted all my sympathies with the demonstration. The invitation was accepted without hesitation; my speech was short and commonplace enough; it was my first attempt at a public speech or at any speech on politics, but I got through it, after much previous anxiety, more easily than I expected. The extension of the franchise was at this moment the dividing line between parties, and thus was decided the party to which I was to belong.

I was chosen as Liberal candidate for the new constituency of the Berwick-on-Tweed Division of Northumberland, which included Alnwick and all the neighbourhood of my home. The new electors, who had long resented their exclusion from the franchise to which they were now admitted, went to the poll in large numbers for the party that had given them the vote. I was thus elected to Parliament in November 1885.

In a very short time there came another turning-point. From 1880 to 1885 Gladstone's Government had been driven to coercive measures to govern Ireland. They had been in bitter conflict with the Irish Home Rule members led by Parnell, whom Gladstone had denounced as marching through rapine to the dismemberment of the Empire. This had not deterred the Conservative Government that succeeded on Gladstone's resignation in the summer of 1885 from entering into friendly relations with Parnell, with whom Lord Carnarvon, a member of the Conservative Cabinet and Lord-Lieutenant of Ireland, was known to have had an interview. It was clear that the Conservative Government had not gone so far as to promise a separate Parliament in Dublin, but they had spoken of the advantage of large Local Authorities. Home Rule was in the air. The Conservative Party avowedly received the Irish vote at the General Election held in the autumn of 1885. After that election the number of Irish Home Rule members was more than doubled; there were now eighty-five of them.

Early in 1886 it was known that Gladstone would advocate Home Rule. The opinion that he was right in the conclusion that the old system of governing Ireland had broken down, is now confirmed by after-events. But the curve was a very sharp one, and a very important section of Liberals who had supported him in opposing Irish Home Rulers, could not adjust their course to it. There was a split in the party. For me there was no curve, for I was new to public life and was only making a start. It was open to me, without inconsistency, to be either a Home Ruler or a Unionist.

I have no doubt, taking force of character, energy, and intellectual power combined, that Gladstone was the greatest man in whose presence I have ever been. I had, however, not sufficient experience for this feeling to be as strong on my entrance to public life as it became after-wards and remains now, and Gladstone's new departure in 1886 was not alone decisive for me.

There is, however, a difficulty that besets, and probably always has and will beset, men of independent mind in public life. It is that great men are difficult to follow consistently, while lesser men have not the capacity to lead. Great minds do not travel for long on the average line of thought; the man of average mind, therefore, finds great men difficult to follow.

That a man of Mr. Gladstone's importance should advocate Home Rule was a fact so arresting as to make me feel the necessity for thought: the suddenness of the change puzzled and made me doubt.

Then I came across the articles written by John Morley in the *Pall Mall Gazette* during the Irish coercion period of Gladstone's Government. When read in sequence they seemed irresistible in their argument that coercion was not, under modern conditions, possible as a permanent system of governing Ireland. The only alternative was

Home Rule. I was intellectually convinced: Morley seemed to be clear and consistent in his thought about Ireland.

Parliament met early in 1886; the Salisbury Government was turned out; Gladstone formed a Liberal Government with the avowed purpose of producing a Home Rule Bill. Morley was made Irish Secretary; on taking office he had to seek re-election in his constituency of Newcastle-on-Tyne. There was a contest; as member for a neighbouring consistency I was asked to help in it and did so whole-heartedly. Henceforward I was a Liberal Home Ruler.

Of the first six years spent in the House of Commons little need be said. I failed to deliver a maiden speech on the second reading of the Home Rule Bill in 1886. The press of members desiring to speak was so great, and there were so many new members with maiden speeches to make, that I was not called on, though for two days I rose more than once each day. At last I heard that the Speaker had intended to call me, but that the Government Whips had put in a strong plea for a member of the party senior to me, who had not yet succeeded in getting his chance. Probably this was fortunate: the occasion was too big for what I had to say or for my force of delivery as it was then; I was left with a feeling of relief at having been spared an ordeal, and not at all of disappointment at having missed an opportunity.

But the ordeal was one that had to be faced some time, and the next year I summoned courage to make another attempt, and succeeded in delivering a speech on the Irish question. The success of it did not approach that of Asquith's maiden speech in the same year, of which it was justly said that the House listened to it as to the speech of a leader. Nevertheless, mine had a modest success, and was immediately followed by an invitation to my wife and myself to dine with Sir William and Lady Harcourt.

In 1888 came the first sign of independence. The Conservative Government were promoting Irish Land Purchase, while opposing Home Rule. Land Purchase had been part of Gladstone's Home Rule policy of 1886, but the Liberal Party generally was not prepared to support it except as part of Home Rule. Some Unionists held that if the Irish land question could be settled by turning tenants into owners, the political agitation for Home Rule would disappear. I did not share this view, but was prepared to abide by the result of Land Purchase. If it did put an end to political agitation by all means let it do so; but, if it did not, we should then have the political question free from the complications of the land question. In any case, it would be a benefit to Britain and to Ireland to have the land question settled. In this Haldane and I found ourselves acting together, and an association and friendship thus began which endured and strengthened as years went on. We each spoke and voted against our party, but the recognized term "cave" was thought too dignified a word to apply to the independent action of only two very junior members of the party. Our effort was described as a "rabbit-hole." With this passing exception I spoke and voted whole-heartedly with the Liberal Home Rule Party. A sense of the unfairness and inequalities of life stirred me and led me to act with what was then the advanced section of the party, including those of whom John Morley spoke, in a cautionary speech, as young men who dreamt dreams. Thus six years passed during which interest was centred on the domestic side of politics. Then came the General Election of 1892, when I was returned to Parliament for the third time. The next chapter will begin the narrative, which it is the object of this book to tell.

# TWENTY-FIVE YEARS
## 1892–1916

# TWENTY-FIVE YEARS

## CHAPTER I

### (1892-1895)

### FIRST DAYS IN OFFICE

The 1892 Election—Mr. Gladstone's Last Government—Under-Secretary to Lord Rosebery—The Work of the Under-Secretary—Continuity of Policy—Great Britain and the Triple Alliance—Principles of British Foreign Policy—The Balance of Power.

IN July 1892 the result of the General Election gave to Liberals and Irish Nationalists combined a majority of forty in the House of Commons. The political alliance between Liberals and Irish was complete; the Unionist Government was displaced on the meeting of the new House of Commons in August, and Mr. Gladstone formed a Liberal Home Rule Cabinet, the Irish standing out of office, but giving assurances of solid and thorough support, for the introduction and passing of a Home Rule Bill were to be the first and main objects of the Government.

Lord Rosebery went to the Foreign Office, entering office, it was said, with some reluctance and not without some representation from outside purely Liberal quarters that his presence at the Foreign Office was essential in the public interest. He selected me as his Parliamentary Under-Secretary.

I had had no special training for Foreign Office work, nor had I till then paid special attention to foreign affairs.

But special knowledge is not a necessary qualification in a young man appointed to a Parliamentary Under-Secretaryship. His business is not to be an expert, but to be trained in capacity for public affairs. The theory and practice of parliamentary government is not that of government by experts, but by men of general experience and proved capacity presiding over experts who are the civil servants in our public affairs.

The Parliamentary Under-Secretary at the Foreign Office had, in the official routine, little share in directing policy. He had access at all times to his chief, the Secretary of State; he could express his views of what was being done by memoranda or orally; he could resign if he did not agree. He saw all important telegrams and despatches, but they came to him after they had been settled and despatched. His business was to make himself thoroughly acquainted with all that was done in the Office, to get up carefully any particular point on which information was sought by Members of the House of Commons, to make statements on foreign affairs that should be in entire accordance with the policy of the Cabinet, and to defend and explain that policy without giving offence to foreign countries. It was not for him to take upon himself the responsibility of indiscretions; he had to be discreet without being unnecessarily reserved. It was an admirable and interesting training, particularly when, as sometimes happened, there had been differences of opinion in the Cabinet resulting in a decision that was a compromise. On such occasions the Under-Secretary was informed by his chief of the decision reached and received general instructions from him. He had then to interpret and expound the policy to the House of Commons, sometimes at considerable length, in such a way as to satisfy one party in the Cabinet without saying a word that might seem to the other party to be disloyal to the compromise to which they had agreed. He had to do this without having been present at the Cabinet discussions at which the differences and shades of opinion had been manifested and at which the decision of policy had been reached. The statement had to be made in public, in face of an opposition alert and on the watch for an opening, and with Cabinet Ministers who were parties to the policy sitting on each side of him. A compromise is generally a dull conclusion of interesting, sometimes painfully interesting, discussions; it is anodyne and sedative, but it is not always the negation of two opposite policies and the adoption of a middle course between them. It seemed to the Under-Secretary that it sometimes consisted of one section getting its way as to what should be done, while the other section made conditions as to how the policy should be formulated and announced.

There were not, however, differences of opinion in the Cabinets of 1892-5 about grave matters of foreign policy; the main difference was as to whether British East Africa and Uganda should become definitely British possessions, and whether a railway to Uganda should be made. These questions were under the Foreign Office, but they were questions of Imperial Expansion not of foreign policy, and later on they were naturally transferred to the Colonial Office. They were made the subject of controversy and attack by the Unionist Opposition, whereas on matters of foreign policy that Opposition gave general support to the Liberal Government, both while Lord Rosebery was at the Foreign Office and when he was Prime Minister. I will, therefore, not dwell further on these matters that seemed so difficult and important at the

time, and will come to matters of foreign policy that
are the chief subject of this narrative.

Before and during the Election of 1892 r. Gladstone kept foreign affairs out of party politics; indeed,
he expressly said in one speech that he did not find fault
with the foreign policy of Lord Salisbury from 1886
to 1892, and thereby ruled it to be not a matter of controversy between parties.

Lord Rosebery, when he took the Foreign Office, informed the Ambassadors of the Triple Alliance that it
was his intention to continue Lord Salisbury's policy.
One of my first recollections is that of reading the record
of the conversations in which this was conveyed to these
three Ambassadors, and in which they expressed their cordial satisfaction at the intimation.

The traditional policy which the new Government
took up was that of a distinct friendship with the Triple
Alliance; there was no engagement, no promise, no definite agreement; it was a policy that could be changed at
any moment.   Great Britain had remained sufficiently
detached and free for Mr. Goschen, a member of Lord
Salisbury's Cabinet, speaking from the Treasury bench in
the House of Commons, to describe our position as one of
"splendid isolation." On the other hand, there was something that in practice manifested itself as a working arrangement; so manifest and well known was it that French
newspapers, when particularly provoked by friction with
Great Britain, would write wrathfully not of the Triple,
but of the Quadruple Alliance.  British Governments in
these years sided diplomatically with the Triple Alliance.
Those who affirm that England's policy has always been
that of the Balance of Power in Europe should consider

whether British policy in these years does entirely agree with this theory of it.

I have never, so far as I recollect, used the phrase "Balance of Power." I have often deliberately avoided the use of it, and I have never consciously set it before me as something to be pursued, attained, and preserved. I am not, therefore, qualified to explain or define what it is. I imagine it to mean that when one Power or group of Powers is the strongest "bloc" in Europe, our policy has been, or should be, that of creating, or siding with, some other combination of Powers, in order to make a counterpoise to the strongest Power or Group and so to preserve equilibrium in Europe. Now the Triple Alliance in 1886 and the following years, when Lord Salisbury and Lord Rosebery were Prime Ministers, was indisputably the strongest political combination, the most powerful thing in Europe. Nevertheless, the policy of friendship with it was followed by the British Government even before the Franco-Russian Alliance had come into existence as a counterpoise; and this policy was continued for many years, while the Triple Alliance continued, in spite of the Franco-Russian Alliance, to be the dominant factor in European diplomacy. During this period, therefore, Great Britain did not attempt to create any counterpoise to the strongest group; on the contrary, the British Government sided with that group. I do not affirm that this, when closely examined, disproves the theory that the tendency of British policy has been to preserve a balance of power; but there is sufficient apparent inconsistency with the theory to make it necessary to examine what may be called the Triple Alliance policy of the British Government from 1886 to the end of the century and to ask why it was followed.

I suppose that in this, as in most investigations of British foreign policy, the true reason is not to be found in far-sighted views or large conceptions or great schemes. A Minister beset with the administrative work of a great Office must often be astounded to read of the carefully laid plans, the deep, unrevealed motives that critics or admirers attribute to him. Onlookers free from responsibility have time to invent, and they attribute to Ministers many things that Ministers have no time to invent for themselves, even if they are clever enough to be able to do it. If all secrets were known it would probably be found that British Foreign Ministers have been guided by what seemed to them to be the immediate interest of this country without making elaborate calculations for the future. Their best qualities have been negative rather than positive. They would not execute sharp turns or quick changes of front; they were not disposed to make mischief or stir up strife amongst other nations, or to fish in troubled waters; for their instinct was that peace and stability in Europe were the conditions best suited to British trade; and they have generally shrunk from committing themselves for future contingencies, from creating expectations that they might not be able to fulfil, and from saying at any time more than they really meant. On the whole, the British Empire has been well served by these methods. It has, at any rate, been saved from capital and disastrous mistakes; such mistakes as are made by a great thinker, calculating far ahead, who thinks or calculates wrongly. It has also been saved from the disaster of seeing a policy that needs for success the continuous supervision of a great man break down and be wrecked when its great author has been succeeded by inferior men. Critics may find many mistakes and short-

comings in British foreign policy of the last hundred
years, and these may be legitimately exposed, or even de-
rided; but, when all has been said, let them ask, what
other nation in Europe can, after a review of the last
hundred years, say confidently of its own policy, "si monu-
mentum quaeris, circumspice?" The result, no doubt,
is due to qualities of character or industry inherent in
the race, to advantages of geographical position, to things
that were not to be placed to the special credit of Ministers for Foreign Affairs; but it is at least a tenable view
that the conduct of those affairs has been suited to the
development and needs of the Empire.

Whether the great European catastrophe of 1914 could
have been prevented by any British statesmanship and
other questions connected with that issue will be examined when the narrative reaches that point. I return
to consider the reasons that made British policy in 1886
and afterwards lean to the Triple Alliance. The most
obvious reason was that the British Empire had occasions
of acute friction with France or with Russia, friction
much more frequent and acute than the countries of the
Triple Alliance. We therefore sided with those with
whom we had least cause of quarrel. It was also necessary to have diplomatic support in Egypt. Lord Cromer's
work there was too important to be given up without loss
and prejudice to British interests; it was also too in-
trinsically good for Egypt, both financially and humanely,
for us to think of abandoning it without a sense of shame.
But it could not be carried on without diplomatic support
from the foreign representatives at Cairo, and, since we
were confronted there by French and Russian opposition,
the support of the Triple Alliance was essential to us.
These are obvious, and, some people will perhaps think,

sufficient reasons, but underlying and strengthening them, there was, I think, a belief that the power of the Triple Alliance made for stability and therefore peace in Europe; that France and Russia, though militarily the weaker, were the restless Powers, while the Triple Alliance was on the whole contented. The conclusion I would draw is that Great Britain has not in theory been adverse to the predominance of a strong group in Europe when it seemed to make for stability and peace. To support such a combination has generally been her first choice; it is only when the dominant Power becomes aggressive and she feels her own interests to be threatened that she, by an instinct of self-defence, if not by deliberate policy, gravitates to anything that can fairly be described as a Balance of Power.

# CHAPTER II

## (1892-1895)

### FRICTION WITH GERMANY AND FRANCE

An Incident at Cairo—The Rough Side of German Friendship—French Suspicions—A Siamese Crisis—A Timely Apology—Trouble in West Africa—The "Grey Declaration"—And Its Origin—Cabinet Objections—Great Britain and Japan—The Beginning of Friendship.

I SOON became aware that the policy of friendship with the Triple Alliance, however satisfactory it might be to the Governments of Germany, Austria, and Italy, was not altogether comfortable for ourselves. Lord Rosebery had not been long at the Foreign Office before he had an unpleasant experience.

Turkey was entertaining projects for making railways to develop Asia Minor. Concessions for railways, or anything else, were not then to be obtained from the Turkish Government without diplomatic effort. An applicant for a concession, however economically sound and attractive the terms he offered, had little prospect of success unless supported by his own Government. Where diplomatic pressure was the rule, commercial interests could not succeed without it. British firms were applying for railway concessions in Asia Minor, and the British Ambassador at Constantinople was, with the approval of the Foreign Office, giving them support. German firms were also applying, and the German Ambassador supporting them. Suddenly there came a sort of ultimatum from Berlin, requiring us to cease competition for railway concessions in Turkey for which Germans were ap-

9

plying, and stating that, unless we did so, the German Consul at Cairo would withdraw support from British Administration in Egypt. Instructions in this sense were actually sent without delay to the German Representative at Cairo, and the German ultimatum was followed— almost accompanied—by a despairing telegram from Lord Cromer pointing out that it would be impossible to carry on his work in Egypt without German support in face of French and Russian opposition.[1]

It was the abrupt and rough peremptoriness of the German action that gave me an unpleasant impression. In a humorous account of the description given by one woman of another with whom she had had an altercation in an omnibus, the phrase occurs "with her the word *is* the blow." This was the German method. It cannot be said that in substance the contention was absolutely unreasonable; the Germans were, at any rate, entitled to ask that, in return for German support in Egypt, we should not oppose some specified German interests elsewhere. Had this been suggested we could not fairly have refused to consider an arrangement, if one had been proposed, that on the face of it was reasonable. But the method adopted by Germany in this instance was not that of a friend. There was no choice for us but to give way, unless we were ready to face the opening up of the whole Egyptian question without a single Great Power on our side. Lord Rosebery withdrew competition for the railway concessions in Turkey; things in Egypt resumed

[1] For the relations of Great Britain and Germany in regard to Egypt see Fitzmaurice's *Life of Lord Granville,* vol i, chapters ix and xii: "Soon after the fall of the third Administration of Mr. Gladstone, Lord Salisbury, once more installed in power, recognized the necessity of an *entente* with Germany, and for many years to come the position of Great Britain in Egypt had to depend on the good-will of the Triple Alliance and of Germany in particular, which in that Alliance held the prerogative vote" (i. 453).

their normal course, and the incident was over.  But it left a sense of discomfort and a bad taste behind.  It exposed rudely the insidious weakness due to our position in Egypt.  It was open to Germany to repeat the squeeze, whenever she desired to exclude us from a commercial field in which she was interested.  As long as we assumed responsibility for the government of Egypt, the Capitulations were like a noose round our neck, which any Great Power, having rights under the Capitulations, could tighten at will.  In this case the noose had been roughly jerked by Germany.  The episode was an illustration of the hollowness of the phrase "splendid isolation."  It was not "isolation," and it was far from being "splendid." This particular incident passed without any conscious effect on our policy, but it gave rise to some reflections upon the weakness of our position, and it may be that similar experiences were an element in the policy of our successors, the Unionist Governments of Lord Salisbury and Mr. Balfour.

There were, however, other things incidental to British policy at this period which were much more serious and unpleasant than an occasional exhibition of the rough side of German friendship.  Among these was the constant friction, rising on the slightest provocation to quarrel and hostility, between Great Britain and France or Russia.  The ground-swell of ill-will never ceased.  British interests touched those of France and Russia in many parts of the world; and where interests touch, an atmosphere of ill-will is always dangerous.  The blackest suspicion thrives in it, like a noxious growth under dark skies in murky air.  The most simple and straightforward acts of one Government are attributed by the other to sinister motives; the agents of each Government on the spot prick and stir their Colonial Office at home with accounts of what the agents of the other Government are doing; the smallest incident may assume proportions that threaten the peace between great nations. So it was especially between Great Britain and France at this time. The controversy that arose about Siam in 1893 is an instance of how quickly and suddenly a catastrophe might have been caused by something that had little real importance. It is so good an illustration of this that it may be worth while to recall it in some detail.

France was laying claim, on behalf of her own possessions in Eastern Asia, to a frontier which the Siamese Government contended was an encroachment on Siamese territory. In Eastern Asia there are many points where territorial claims provide material for argument; they grade from the most solid substance to the faintest shadows. It is not necessary now to revive argument over the merits of the controversy between France and Siam. Strange names, the river Mekong with its "Great Bend," Battambang and Angkor, and others were for a time "familiar in our mouths as household words," though we were only indirectly concerned. We had commercial interests in Siam, and the independence and integrity of Siam were therefore of concern to us; Siam was a comparatively weak State, and we waxed chivalrous. One leading member of the Conservative Party even threatened the French from the front Opposition bench with the Siamese Fleet, which he described as a compact and serviceable little squadron. We made no doubt that the French were making excessive claims, but we avowedly limited our action to precautions for the protection of British subjects and property at Bangkok, the capital of Siam situated on the river Menam.

For this purpose certain ships of the British Navy were sent to Siamese waters. The cruisers lay outside the mouth of the Menam; one gunboat, the *Linnet,* was sent up the river to lie at Bangkok and be absolutely on the spot to protect British lives and property in case of disorder. The French had sent ships of the French Navy to put pressure on Siam to yield to their territorial claims on the frontier. For this purpose the French declared a "pacific blockade" of Siam, and their ships of war drew the line of blockade outside the mouth of the Menam.

The British view was that there is no such thing as a "pacific blockade" and that we could not recognize what had no existence in international law. We could only recognize a "blockade" if it were an act of war. Controversy at once arose on this point. Then came two incidents that, for twenty-four hours, were thought to make war between Great Britain and France inevitable.

A telegram was received saying that one of the French cruisers blockading the mouth of the Menam had turned its guns on a British cruiser at anchor, while steaming past it. This was a gross naval insult that would in naval etiquette have justified the captain of the British ship in firing on the French ship. The gesture of the French captain, though it was not replied to at the moment by opening fire, could not be ignored. An apology at least must be demanded, and, as the French act was apparently deliberate and intentional, it was presumed that an apology would not be forthcoming.

About the same time another telegram arrived saying that the French Admiral had ordered the *Linnet* to leave Bangkok. The *Linnet,* having been sent to Bangkok to protect British lives and property in case of disorder and the prospect of trouble being now more imminent than ever, we could not think of moving her. Nor, in any case, could she be ordered about by French naval officers. Lord Rosebery at once sent a telegram saying that the *Linnet* must stay at Bangkok. For some twenty-four hours it was supposed that the French had deliberately challenged us and that war was inevitable. It was reported in the Foreign Office that the telegrams had been shown to the German Emperor, was was then visiting Queen Victoria on his yacht at Cowes, and that he had expressed with evident satisfaction the opinion that there was no way out of the incident but war.[1] So for some hours the Foreign Office remained in a state of tense expectation. Presently came two more telegrams: one to say that the French Admiral had not ordered the *Linnet* to leave Bangkok, but had requested that, as he was establishing a line of blockade, the *Linnet* should either stay at Bangkok or come outside to avoid crossing the French line and thereby breaking the blockade. This put the *Linnet* incident in a very different light. We had not recognized the blockade, and might refuse to comply with the French Admiral's request; but, as we wanted the *Linnet* to remain at Bangkok, we had no present intention or need to use her to defy the French blockade.

Another telegram arrived saying that the French Admiral, without waiting for any demand from us, had sent the captain of the French cruiser to apologize to the British captain for the unprovoked breach of correct naval conduct. Before there was time for legal authorities to report fully on the question of "pacific blockade," or for the controversy thereon to be developed, the Siamese conceded the French demands, the "pacific block-

---

[1] It must not be assumed, however, that his attitude was unfriendly; on the contrary, if the current-reports were true, he seemed disposed to give German support to British action.

ade" disappeared, and the whole matter ceased to have any importance.

It seems incredible that two great European nations should have become nearly involved in war about anything so ephemeral. The incident remained in my mind as an illustration of the danger of a state of ill-will between nations. It provided also another point for reflection. There were some murmurs, as there always were, when such incidents occurred under a Liberal Government, that the British Government had not shown proper firmness and spirit. It was told me that one of the most influential men on the Unionist side had said that it was evident that war between ourselves and France must come, and that it would be better to have it at once. I remember at the time feeling strongly, but by instinct rather than reflection, that deliberately to precipitate the waste and suffering of war before it became clearly inevitable was not only unsound policy, but a crime; it was indeed an act likely to bring unforeseen retribution. Further experience and reflection upon the complexity and uncertainty of human affairs have made me question whether any human brain can so calculate the long chain of consequences as to render it safe for anyone to make unnecessary war. Bismarck may appear an exception; whether he was really or only apparently an exception may be considered when we come to the events of 1914. Far-seeing men may be able to calculate the direct consequences of a public act or policy; the indirect consequences are beyond human calculation; and it is the indirect consequences that in the long run are most important. A public man must have opinions and form decisions. He must act, and sometimes without delay; but when it comes to adopting unscrupulous means to be justified by the ends in view, some of the most brilliant public intellects have failed from not sufficiently remembering that they are fallible. What the indirect consequences would have been if Great Britain and France had gone to war in 1893 is a very interesting subject for speculation. Whole books might be written about it, but none of the conclusions would be convincing enough to anyone but their author to make the speculation profitable.

It was not only about Siam that we had friction with France. There were constant disputes and incidents in West Africa, besides a perpetual dispute about what we called the Treaty Shore and the French called the French Shore in Newfoundland. The national interests involved on the French side in Newfoundland were very slight, but the controversy was time-honoured—dating from the Treaty of Utrecht—and an incident might at any moment arise that would involve sovereign rights on one side and be made a point of honour on the other. The British occupation of Egypt was a perpetual exasperation to the French, and their attitude with regard to it a constant irritant to us.

It was in West Africa that incidents most frequently occurred. British officials explored the country and made treaties with native chiefs on which we based our rights. French officials would overlap ours in their explorations and treaties; hence claims and counter-claims and confusion. It was sometimes possible to argue that a treaty had been made with a native chief who was not independent but subordinate, and that the treaty was therefore valueless; it may even have happened that an independent chief was ready for a consideration to make a treaty both with a British and a French official provided one came after the other. At any rate, one morning

in March 1895 there came to the Foreign Office news of
what were regarded as very unwarranted and provocative
encroachments in West Africa. This sort of thing had
been going on for some time, and it was always possible
that someone in the House of Commons would question
me about it. Though the leaders of the Opposition gave
general support to the Liberal Government in foreign
policy, there were always free-lances who used any report
of foreign aggression to criticize a Liberal Government;
there were also enthusiasts for Imperial expansion, particularly in Africa, who were genuinely anxious about
French aggression or encroachment. The Foreign
Office vote was to be taken in the House of Commons
that afternoon and evening. I went to Lord Kimberley,
who had come to the Foreign Office when Lord Rosebery
became Prime Minister in 1894; I told Lord Kimberley
that the question of French proceedings in West Africa
might be raised, and asked for his instructions as to what I
should say in view of the latest and very provoking reports.

In conversation, or perhaps it would be more accurate
to say in talk, Lord Kimberley was the most copious of
men. He had a great store of knowledge of books and
experience of men and affairs, including affairs incidental
to the life of a country squire; he had much to say of all
these matters, and when the Under-Secretary went to
ask him to read and approve drafts of answers to questions that were to be asked in the House of Commons in a
quarter of an hour's time, it was sometimes embarrassing
that he would embark on an account of the ravages
wrought among trees by a great gale in Norfolk; though
the weather and the trees were topics not uncongenial to
the Under-Secretary himself. On paper, and when addressing himself to a point to be decided, Lord Kimberley

was admirable—concise, definite, and clear. As draft answers to questions were presented to him he would read each, consider it rapidly but thoroughly, and initial the draft either as it stood or with amendment in firm, distinct handwriting. He was devoted to the work of his office, absolutely free from all egotism in transacting it, a chief who would trust and never throw over or let down a subordinate. On this occasion, after settling the draft answers to questions on the order paper for the day in the House of Commons, he considered the hypothetical point I had put to him. What was I to say if the question of French encroachments in West Africa was raised in the House of Commons? "You must do the best you can," he said, "but I think you should use pretty firm language." West Africa was not mentioned in the debate that evening, but I was pressed on the question of the Nile Valley and French designs thereon. The Soudan was still in the hands of the Khalifa. The claim of Egypt to it, however, had never been abandoned, though, since the overthrow of Egyptian rule by the Mahdi in 1886, it was clear that the Soudan would never be reconquered by Egypt again without British assistance, nor would the Soudanese again tolerate the purely Egyptian rule against which they had revolted. It was, at any rate, evident that no other Power except Egypt or someone acting on behalf of Egypt had any claim whatever to the Soudan and the Nile Valley.

There were vague rumours that a French expedition was on its way to that region, and it was on this that I was pressed. We felt sure no French expedition was on the way to the Nile, in which belief we were quite justified, for the Marchand expedition, as was ascertained later on, did not start while we were in office. There was, therefore, time to give France full warning of our view without putting her in a position of having to retreat or to abandon anything that she had yet done; it was impossible to provide an incident on the spot, for there were neither French nor British in the Soudan. Some such thoughts as these worked in my mind on the Treasury bench as I considered what I should say. The French would really be going far out of their way if they came right across Africa to the Upper Nile, and I felt some heat at the suggestion thrown out in the course of debate that the French might come into the Nile Valley. Whatever language I had thought of using about West Africa, where there were conflicting claims and action, and where both British and French officials were active, was not suitable to the question of the Nile Valley. I therefore transferred to the subject of the Nile the firmness I had been authorized to show about competing claims in West Africa, and throughout, as carefully as the brief time and the obligation to give at any rate one ear to the speeches of others would allow, the words that I should use. Then I got up and did the best I could, being very careful to associate Egypt with Great Britain in any claim to the Soudan.[1]

The next day there was a row in Paris, and (so I understood) in Downing Street. Some members of the Cabinet, opposed to any expansion whatever in Africa and regarding even the occupation of Egypt as a regrettable commitment, disapproved of my speech; others, including, I gathered, Lord Rosebery, the Prime Minister, and

[1] House of Commons, March 28, 1895: "The advance of a French Expedition under secret instructions right from the other side of Africa into a territory over which our claims have been known for so long would be not merely an inconsistent and unexpected act, but it must be perfectly well known to the French Government that it would be an unfriendly act and would be so viewed by England."

Lord Kimberley, maintained that what I had said was defensible and salutary. Fortunately, for the purpose of composing this difference of opinion, the word "Egypt," which I had so carefully associated with Great Britain, had accidentally been omitted in the report of my speech. On this omission I gather that those who disapproved of the speech fastened. The way was then open to compromise. Those who thought that the speech should be approved agreed that the word "Egypt" should be inserted, and on this condition the others gave their consent to the speech being allowed to stand. The question of political rights and titles in the Soudan is now the subject of acute controversy with Egypt. Amid all political and juridical arguments, one fact stands out hard and solid, which is that without British military organization, British effort and firm diplomacy, Egypt would have no hand in the Soudan at all to-day.

The decision reached me by special messenger at my cottage at Hampshire, where I had gone to prune my roses at the week-end. I readily agreed to the insertion of a word that I had been careful to use; but the incident had its personal inconvenience for me. I find in the little journal that I kept of visits at the cottage an entry for March 30 and 31, 1895: "Pruning Sunday. Disturbed by work, and have to go up on Sunday evening." A few years later, when Lord Kitchener had taken Khartoum and come upon the Marchand expedition and the French flag, I saw my speech appear like a State Paper in the documents published in the controversy that arose. As things turned out, the speech must have proved very useful, when I was out of office, to the Government that succeeded Lord Rosebery; but, looking back, I ask myself whether it may not have provoked the Marchand expedition; whether, if nothing had been said here, the French would ever have sent that expedition at all. If so, the speech would have been better left unspoken. If the Marchand expedition had already been determined upon in Paris, then the speech was not only defensible but valuable, and almost essential for defining in advance a position that the British Government would, if challenged, insist on maintaining at all costs. It is necessary to have a clear opinion at the time as to what is right, and to act upon it, but when an affair is over and one's own part is done, it is more interesting to put what is past to question in one's own mind and to review it, than simply to defend it without question, as if one were no wiser after the event than before.

On another matter that caused trouble with France at the time I will not dwell at length. King Leopold had occupied a claimed territory in the Upper Nile region that we held did not belong to the Congo State. We made an agreement to regularize his occupation, but to secure to us the reversion of this non-Congo territory later on. The agreement also gave us a wayleave for a railway passing behind German East Africa to connect railways from South Africa with Uganda and thus to make a Cape-to-Cairo Railway practicable.

The Germans at once protested that this was contrary to a previous agreement between our Government and theirs, safeguarding them against a railway in this region that might prejudice railways in German territory. Investigation in the Foreign Office showed that this German protest was well founded: there was such an agreement, and it had been overlooked. This part, therefore, of the arrangement with King Leopold was at once withdrawn.

The French, claiming an interest in the Congo under a Franco-Belgian or Congo agreement giving France a contingent right of pre-emption to the Congo State declared our agreement "nulle et non avenue" as far as they were concerned. This contention we did not admit, as we held that the territory in the Nile region with which the agreement dealt did not belong to the Congo State at all. The agreement was certainly not fortunate at its birth, but it worked, and after the death of King Leopold it settled these troublesome matters without friction with Belgium and with France, with whom the Entente of 1904 had smoothed away all these causes of dispute.

Two other transactions towards the end of this period must be recalled, which must have had their effect on future policy.

We made an agreement with Japan by which we gave up all those rights of jurisdiction over our British subjects in Japan that were still retained by European and American Governments over their own subjects in Oriental countries. It has sometimes been represented that in this negotiation Japan got the better of us and exacted from us more than we intended to concede. This was not so: we had made up our minds that the time had come when dealings with Japan must be put on the same equal terms as exist between nations of European origin; only so would cordial political and successful commercial relations be preserved. We were the first country to negotiate such an agreement with Japan, and we were prepared to make it complete and to put our relations with Japan on the same footing as those with other nations.

Another step was also taken towards friendly relations with Japan, though it was one that arose out of circumstances not of our making, and was not foreseen or planned by us.

Japan had a short and successful war with China; no

other Power took part or interfered while hostilities were in progress; but after they were over France, Germany, and Russia invited us to join in an intimation to Japan that she would not be allowed to take all the fruits of victory that she claimed. Lord Kimberley refused to join in putting pressure on Japan; the three other Powers acted without us and Japan had to give way to diplomatic *force majeure.*

I do not believe that Lord Kimberley had any ulterior motive in the decision he took not to interfere. We did not consider that British interests required us to join in this interference with Japan's claims; the threat to her by the European Powers appeared harsh and uncalled for, and it was repugnant to us to join in it. This decided us to stand aside; there was certainly no thought in our minds then of a future alliance with Japan. We were moved simply by the feeling of the moment to stand aside from action that seemed to us disagreeably harsh and in which British interests did not require us to participate. Japan no doubt resented the interference of the European Powers, and resented it still more when Russia, not long afterwards, occupied Port Arthur herself and Germany exacted the concession of Shantung as compensation for the murder of a missionary. The very Powers who had upheld against Japan the principle of the integrity of China proceeded to violate it themselves. The proceedings could not have been made more pleasant to Japan when the British Government, to counteract the presence of Russia at Port Arthur, secured from China the port of Wei-Hai-Wei, though, so far as I am aware, the concession of Wei-Hai-Wei was made willingly by China and deemed by her to be in her own interest after the Russian occupation of Port Arthur. Japan was now thus confronted with the establishment of three new European bases opposite her own shores, after having been forcibly prevented from taking one for herself. The integrity of China was to be a principle sacred against Japan, but not against European Powers, who had proclaimed it after Japan's victory over China.

The action of Great Britain in refusing to join in the coercion of Japan was naturally much appreciated by the Japanese. The direct consequence of the coercive action of France, Germany, and Russia upon Japan after the Japanese war with China was that Japan retired without the fruits of victory, which she much wished for: the indirect consequences were the Russian occupation of Port Arthur, followed by the Anglo-Japanese Alliance and the war between Russia and Japan. What the further indirect consequences were of that war and that alliance may be left to those who have sufficient imagination to divine. It would be interesting to know how much the statesmen at Berlin, Paris and St. Petersburg saw of the future consequences of their action, when in 1895 they decided on joint action to restrain Japan. I am sure that British Ministers at the time did not look beyond the moment. Probably it is seldom that public men see much beyond direct consequences. Even in looking back with full knowledge of the event it is impossible to trace the indirect consequences of a past act beyond the earlier stages: after that they are merged in the great movement of consequences of other acts; and the mind, in endeavouring to trace them, loses itself as it does in the attempt to conceive infinity. Even historians with knowledge of the event, and with the materials before them on which to form a judgment, see but a little way into the causes and consequences of the great events of history.

# CHAPTER III

## (1892-1895)

## FREEDOM FROM RESPONSIBILITY

Training in Office—Life in London—Town Life and Country Life—
The Fishing Cottage and Its Uses—An Early Flitting—Rest and
Recreation—True Luxury—A Depressing Contrast—Methods of
Work and Public Speaking—Leaving the Foreign Office—An
Unfulfilled Intention.

I HAVE now dealt with the episodes of work in the
Foreign Office during the two years and ten months
from August 1892 to June 1895 during which I was
Under-Secretary. The first years of office are necessarily
very important in the life of a young man. He undergoes
steady training in industry and despatch; he learns how
to brace his mind to plough through the stiffest and least
attractive material, to break up the most intractable clod;
his memory is practised in storing things in an orderly
way in his head so that each is out of the way when not
wanted, and yet can be found at once when required. The
habit of quickly arriving at facile conclusions is checked;
for he is brought in contact with limitations and difficulties, which are encountered inside a public office and were
not apparent when he was outside; he finds the use of his
own qualities, he is made aware of the inconvenience, perhaps the danger, of his defects. The whole experience
of office life is new to him and has its effects not only on
his public but on his private life. It may not be out of
place here to say something of this.

I had been elected to Parliament in 1885. My wife and I took a small furnished house in London for the Session of 1886. We had neither of us yet made much trial of town life, and the first spring did not pass without our becoming aware that it was intensely distasteful to us. The advantages, intellectual and social, of town life are obvious. To many people the very external circumstances and surroundings of this life become not only agreeable, but essential. Someone has told me the story of the town-lover, who, after a short trial of a quiet country retreat, left it because he could not endure the "tingling silence." To the lover of the country, its sights and sounds, its quiet and its pursuits, become as essential, as much part of his being as the advantages and circumstances of town life are to the lover of the town. It is as if there were two different atmospheres; some, perhaps most people, are so constituted that they can enjoy or tolerate either; there are some who feel they can breathe in the one and not in the other. If to an incompatibility of habit and temperament with town life, there be added exile from the home, not only of manhood but of boyhood, with all its familiar rooms and furniture and surroundings and interests, it is inevitable that town life must be very uncongenial. This I knew well enough by 1892, and, realizing that the ties of office must intensify the exile, I entered it without any elation; indeed with depression. It would be untrue to imply that the new position brought no interest or excitement; it brought both, but without cancelling the drawback.

A permanent house in London was now necessary, and the salary as Under-Secretary was sufficient to enable us to take on lease a house in Grosvenor Road which we

could furnish and where we could have furniture of our
own choosing, while still keeping the country home available for such times as I could get there.   But Northumberland was too far for week-end journeys, and already in
1890 we had put up a small bungalow in Hampshire,
which could be shut up in the week and opened at week-
ends.   There I had one rod on a fishing on the Itchen,
and the bungalow, or cottage, as we called it, was originally designed as a fishing cottage only.   In the stress
of office it became a sanctuary.   The Session of 1893 was
a strenuous one, Parliament met as usual early in the
year; there were, I think, five days' holiday only at Easter,
including Good Friday, Easter Sunday, and Monday;
the House of Commons did not adjourn till well on in
September; it met again in October, and the Session lasted
over Christmas and the New Year into January 1894.
The Government majority was at most only forty, including over eighty Irish Nationalists; it was incumbent on
all supporters of the Government to attend assiduously;
the Irish did their part with that discipline and thorough-
ness with which the party always carried out any policy
or arrangement upon which they had entered in the House
of Commons, and they did it equally well, whether it
was Irish Home Rule or an English measure like the
Parish Councils Bill, in which they had no interest, that
was under discussion.   Liberal M.P.'s had to do equally
well, and Under-Secretaries attended during the whole
of every sitting, seldom or never venturing to leave the
House for dinner.   They had rooms in the lower regions;
my own room had quite sufficient accommodation, and
was comfortable enough, but it was like living in a cellar.
The stream of Foreign Office boxes gave me compara-

tively little time to listen to debates. In these days the House of Commons had its short sitting on Wednesday; there was the normal late sitting on Friday evening, and no leaving London till Saturday.

The spring and summer of 1893 were unusually warm and fine. Every Saturday morning we left Grosvenor Road about half-past five in the early morning. We had no baggage, and at that hour there were no hansom cabs, so we walked across Lambeth Bridge, the river and houses presenting the same aspect of calm and quiet that inspired Wordsworth's "sonnet on Westminster Bridge." Thence our way went past St. Thomas's Hospital and along the street that then led to the entrance to Waterloo. This street we called Wood Street; at that early hour it was deserted, the houses shut, the only sound in it was the vigorous song of a thrush in a cage that hung outside one of the houses. The thrush was always singing at that hour, and the lines

> "At the corner of Wood Street, when daylight appears,
>   Hangs a thrush that sings loud,"

being familiar to us, we always spoke of the street as Wood Street, though that was not its real name. From this street the way led through the most unsavoury tunnel to the old Waterloo Station, and so we got away by the 6 o'clock train from Waterloo and to the Hampshire cottage soon after 8 o'clock, in time for breakfast.

The start from London each Saturday morning was one of rapture of anticipated pleasure:

> "Bliss was it in that dawn to be alive,
>   But to be young was very heaven,"

and week after week the Saturday and Sunday fulfilled anticipations.  On Saturday, in hot summer weather, I would fish till about two o'clock, and again from seven to nine o'clock in the evening.  Sunday was not a fishing day then on that part of the Itchen, and we spent it reading great or refreshing books, going long walks in some of the most beautiful country in all the south of England, watching birds, much in the spirit of Keats's Sonnet, "To one who had been long in city pent," except that there was no fatigue.  The cottage, which had sprung into existence for the sake of the fishing, became much more than a fishing cottage and more even than a week-end retreat from London.

It revealed a peculiarly happy way of life.  For twenty-five years it was tended with faithful and devoted care by one woman, and after her death in 1915 by her sister. They lived together in a cottage some few hundred yards away.  There they had their own surroundings, garden and friends.  Service for us did not mean absence from home for them; when we were at the cottage we wanted rest, books, the enjoyment of the beauty of the country, and opportunity to watch outdoor life.  For this we wanted to be alone, and to have only the food and attendance that were really required for comfort.  Work, duties, social intercourse, were for London.  Life at the cottage suggested a definition of luxury—that of having everything that we did want and nothing that we did not want.  It seemed to us that the omission of the second part of this definition made the failure of so much that is thought to be luxurious: by accident we had come upon true and exquisite luxury.  The difficulty was to enjoy it in moderation: when I was in office the compulsion of official work enforced moderation; when we were free we had to determine how many days we could from time to time spend with a good conscience at the cottage.[1] Some Foreign Office papers there might be to read, but the Foreign Office work went on irrespective of whether the Parliamentary Under-Secretary was there or not, and there was no burden of responsibility on me. Then, every Monday morning, we went back to London, I to spend the morning at the Foreign Office and the rest of the day after luncheon in the cellar-room under the House of Commons, in which I could hear the unpleasant sounds, when the obstruction in the House was very rampant and demonstrative, as it frequently was then, or when, as sometimes happened, there was open disorder in the House. Party feeling ran high in those days. We on the Liberal side felt we were right, that Unionist Government in Ireland had failed, and would continue to fail, that till there was Home Rule there would be no peace, and Ireland would be a source of perpetual weakness to us and a misery to herself. We had a parliamentary majority, which made any other policy than Home Rule impossible, and we considered ourselves entitled to pursue it. The Unionist Opposition disbelieved in Home Rule and hated it, and probably thought that we were straining the Constitution in attempting to pass so large a measure with so small a parliamentary majority, indeed without a British majority at all.

In time the contrast between the life that I loved and the life that I led for five days every week affected my spirits.

I did the work of Parliamentary Under-Secretary to the best of my ability. I got up thoroughly every subject

---

[1] The cottage was accidentally burnt, in January 1923, and after 1918 the failure of sight had interfered with much of the enjoyment of reading and outdoor pursuits.

of which I had notice that I was to be questioned or that it was to be raised in the House; and I read all that went on in the Foreign Office so carefully that I could deal with matters that might be brought up without notice on the Foreign Office vote. In fact, whenever foreign affairs were to come up in the House I went there much better equipped to pass an examination than I had ever been at school or university. But there was no pleasure to me in the House of Commons work. I could express clearly to others what I had previously made clear to my own mind, but beyond that there was no natural gift for speaking. I never had a peroration; I could neither compose one nor repeat it by heart, if I had been able to compose it; and yet I had not the art of stopping effectively without a peroration, as Samuel Butler says Handel does in his music. "When Handel means stopping he stops as a horse stops, with little, if any, peroration" (I quote from memory). Early in 1894 Mr. Gladstone retired; I was personally devoted to Lord Rosebery, who succeeded him, and was particularly in agreement with him on Imperial matters, and his succession as Prime Minister had my warm support and placed me under a special obligation to work for his Government. By extraordinary ill fortune Lord Rosebery had a severe and most depressing attack of influenza in the short time he was Prime Minister, and I became increasingly aware that, with the great figure of Mr. Gladstone retired, with the unifying influence of his authority and prestige removed, the Liberal Party, with its differing shades of opinion, personal and political, was for the present no instrument fit for achieving great things. A sense of the futility of it all now added to the depression caused by party bitterness and by town life and exile from home.

In June 1895 the Government of Lord Rosebery was defeated in a division on the War Office vote in the House of Commons and resigned. I was set free, and left office with the expectation and the intention of never returning to it.

Inside the Foreign Office I had found the personnel pleasant, and I left it with a grateful sense of their kindness and of the experience gained there. I had from the first·taken the view that we must take over British East Africa and Uganda, and the Cabinet had eventually come to the same conclusion. For the rest, I had been content to follow and to understand without attempting to influence policy. The general impression left of our position in the world was not comfortable; we relied on German support in Egypt, and received it; but we never could be sure when some price for that support might not be exacted. At any moment we were liable to have a serious difference with France or Russia, and it was evident that these differences were not unwelcome at Berlin and to German diplomacy. But I certainly had no idea of a change of policy, and I do not think that my chiefs contemplated anything of the kind.

In the light of after-events, the whole policy of these years from 1886 to 1904 may be criticized as having played into the hands of Germany. I am not concerned to examine that criticism here. The Liberal tenure of the Foreign Office from August 1892 to June 1895 was but a short period of the time. Mr. Gladstone's Government continued the policy of Lord Salisbury as they found it; when Lord Salisbury returned to the Foreign Office in 1895 he saw no more reason to change that policy than Lord Rosebery or Lord Kimberley had done; he continued it. Indeed, as will presently appear, his Govern-

*Portrait by Sandys*

SIR EDWARD GREY, 1892

ment went farther on the road of complaisance and advance to Germany than before. The time to review this policy will be when the period—nine years later—is reached in which the Government of which Lord Lansdowne was Foreign Secretary made at last a new departure.

# CHAPTER IV

## (1895-1905)

## OUT OF OFFICE

Two Tendencies of these Years—The Strain with France—Increasing Difficulties with Germany—A New Situation in the Far East— The Russians at Port Arthur—Chamberlain's "Long Spoon" Speech—The Fashoda Incident—Lieut. Marchand's Gallantry— Chamberlain's Overture to Germany—A German Opportunity and its Rejection—A Secret Agreement—The South African War— Continental Hostility—Beginning of the German Big Fleet—The Anglo-Japanese Alliance—The Anglo-French Agreement—Reasons for Welcoming it—German Suspicions—Lord Rosebery's View— The Dogger Bank Incident—The Hard Case of Russia—The Pleasures of Opposition—Railway Work—The Chairmanship of the North-Eastern Railway.

TEN years and a half were now to pass before I entered the Foreign Office again. After I returned to it I heard incidentally in conversation with officials in the office, some interesting comments and information upon some of the episodes in foreign politics, that happened in this period. I was, however, when Secretary of State, much too hard pressed by current work to have leisure to look up old papers and read the records in the Foreign Office of what had been done while I was in Opposition; and, since I was not responsible during these years, I have purposely refrained, in preparing this book, from asking for documents relating to them. I can therefore write of the events of this period only as anyone may do who did not participate in them and knew them only by the Press and other public sources of information. We all know what happened and what was done; we do not know, or know only in part, how things happened and why they were done by those who did them. Those who are outside see the result; the real motive and the full thought can be told only by those who decide and execute policy.

It is, however, necessary to give some account of the events in foreign affairs of this period, for during it the foreign policy of Great Britain slowly took another direction; bent thither, I judge, rather by the persistent pressure of circumstances than by any definite plan or initiative of Lord Salisbury. It was not till after his retirement in 1902 that any change of direction was apparent; indeed, in November 1899 there was an attempt, manifested by a speech of Mr. Chamberlain's, to which reference will be made presently, to push British policy in the direction of closer relations with Germany, which was not the direction subsequently taken.

What, then, do we see in the course of events after June 1895? In the main we see two tendencies. One is that the strain of our relations with France and Russia is intensified. The Russian occupation of Port Arthur, the Anglo-Japanese Alliance, the Russo-Japanese War and the incidents consequent upon it illustrate what I mean as regards Russia. Lord Kitchener's advance into the Soudan, his discovery there of the French expedition of Lieutenant Marchand at Fashoda, and the controversy thereon with France illustrate what is meant with regard to France. Things were constantly happening that brought us nearer to an open breach with France or with Russia.

The other tendency was for Anglo-German relations

to become stiffer. What I have called the rough side of German friendship became more rough. A brief account of leading events will show these two tendencies at work.

In the first months of Lord Salisbury's Government, in which Mr. Chamberlain took the Colonial Office, there occurred the Jameson Raid upon the Transvaal. When all the facts were known many people at home felt indignant that an act of gross aggression should have been perpetrated by any British persons or organized on British territory; they were disgusted by the hollow pretext, put forward by those who defended it as necessary to protect women and children in Johannesburg: to everybody the collapse of the Raid showed that it was an act of folly. We could not, therefore, be surprised that the raid was condemned by foreign opinion, nor could we justly resent that condemnation. But why should the German Emperor make it his business, and his alone, to appear as the friend and even the champion of President Krüger? The German Emperor's telegram to President Krüger did undoubtedly cause both surprise and resentment in Britain. It passed, however, without incident, for the raid had put Britain clearly in the wrong and President Krüger in the right, and our business was to clear up the mess as best we could by legal prosecution of the chief actors in the Raid and by parliamentary enquiry into the responsibility for it. It is not necessary to pursue the matter further, but the German Emperor's telegram, though it made no diplomatic "incident," had its effect on British minds. Suspicion grew, later on, that Germany was encouraging President Krüger in order to make trouble for Britain in South Africa, and, though the dramatic demonstration of the German Emperor's telegram may not have initiated this suspicion, the recollection of the telegram strengthened it in later and more dangerous years.

Another event, already glanced at, that had much more immediate impact and repercussion on foreign policy was the Russian occupation of Port Arthur. This caused a serious potential alteration of the naval position in the Far East. Russia, it is true, had already a port at Vladivostok, but it was frozen in winter. Port Arthur, more sheltered and farther to the south, was a port open all the year and presumably capable of being made a permanent and formidable naval base. The Russian occupation of it was therefore a matter of serious concern in its relation to the British naval position in the Far East. The British Government negotiated with the Chinese to lease Wei-Hai-Wei as a counterpoise to the Russian move, the object no doubt being to have a base in the north of China, where a British naval force could be stationed to control any naval force that Russia might base upon Port Arthur. Even so, however, the relative naval position in the Far East was felt to be altered to our disadvantage, and there was much criticism of Lord Salisbury's Government, to which some members of that Government were no doubt sensitive. The Russian method of procedure had also caused resentment. British ships had been on a visit to Port Arthur; the Russian Government had, in a friendly manner, pointed out that the presence of British ships of war in that region was a source of uneasiness. Lord Salisbury, in a friendly spirit, had let the British vessels depart. The Russians then went to Port Arthur themselves, not on a visit, but on a long lease.

This result was very provoking; criticism at home was sharp, the Russian methods were exasperating. The feeling aroused found its strongest expression in a speech of

Mr. Chamberlain's. This was not the first time that Mr. Chamberlain had occasion to put a foot down about Russia. In a speech that I heard at the Eighty Club early in 1885 he had referred to the Penjdeh incident. He was then the leader of what were considered extreme Radicals, and the speech was devoted to domestic affairs; he was supposed by his Conservative opponents to be a Little Englander, in favour of a weak and retiring policy abroad. There was at the time sharp friction with Russia over the Penjdeh incident on the Afghan frontier and Mr. Chamberlain spoke of it in a very firm manner, though that was not then the rôle expected of him. Not more than ten years later he was not only a leading member of a Unionist Government, but looked up to as the great Imperialist in British politics. There was no question, when he spoke, of going to war about Port Arthur; the Russian occupation was an accomplished fact, but Mr. Chamberlain expressed the resentment felt by the comment that "he who sups with the devil must have a long spoon." A notable milestone, indeed, on the road to war with Russia.

British relations with France were once more heated to the point of danger by the Fashoda affair. Soon after the Unionist Government came into power it was decided to reconquer the Soudan. The operation was completely successful, and Khartoum was occupied in September 1898. In advancing farther up the Nile, Lord Kitchener came upon a French expedition that had crossed Africa from the west, and, after a very bold and adventurous journey, had established itself and the French flag at Fashoda. The situation was at once acute. The leader of the French expedition, Lieutenant Marchand, with his gallant but small party, was in no position to offer serious resistance to Lord Kitchener's army; he was far away from any touch or communication with French territory. Indeed, till Lord Kitchener opened up the Soudan by his advance it is doubtful whether the French Government knew what had become of the Marchand expedition or where it was. But, being there with the flag, Lieutenant Marchand could not yield except to force. If Lord Kitchener used force there was an act of war between Britain and France. The facts were disclosed to the world, and the men on the spot waited for their respective Governments to decide what should be done. The diplomatic contest began, and public opinion and the Press on both sides were excited. It was impossible for Britain to admit any foreign claim to the Nile Valley, and the Government could say only one thing, viz. that the French expedition must withdraw.

We had given ample warning of our claims (here my speech of 1895 was quoted), and the French expedition was a wanton challenge to them, for France had really no interest of her own to protect in the Nile Valley. On the other hand, France did not admit our claim, and French honour was involved. The situation did not admit of compromise; it could not be settled on paper; one side or other had to give way. For a time there was an angry diplomatic impasse. Happily, there were aspects of the situation that were soothing and some which irresistibly suggested an under-sense of humour. There are situations in which two people are very earnest and serious and yet in which each knows that, if he were not so deadly serious, he would be laughing. The soothing side of the Fashoda discovery was that Lieutenant Marchand had really performed a remarkably bold and skilful feat of African travel and thereby, by common consent, con-

Army was the German. The Fleet and the Army could not fight each other; let there be an alliance between them, and they could maintain their own interests and keep Europe in order. The speech was a public invitation to Germany and a public recommendation of policy to Britain and the British Empire. It made a great and critical moment, fraught with the greatest possibilities. How far Mr. Chamberlain was authorized to speak for Lord Salisbury and his colleagues, or how far he had consulted them, I cannot say. On this point I heard nothing, then or afterwards; but I was told in the Foreign Office in after years that the speech was made after Mr. Chamberlain had met the German Emperor and Count (afterwards Prince) Bülow, then German Secretary for Foreign Affairs, who were on a visit to England. The Foreign Office information to me was very definite that Mr. Chamberlain's speech was not made without reason to expect that it would meet with response from the German Government.[1] In short, the belief in the Foreign Office was that the German Emperor or Count Bülow, one or both, had encouraged the idea of a public pronouncement in England in favour of an Anglo-German Alliance. The Foreign Office account to me of the matter was, that the suggestion for an alliance with us was coldly received in Germany, and that at Paris and St. Petersburg German diplomacy turned it to account, representing it as an offer that Germany might have accepted and had declined. If so, it was very short-sighted of the agents of the German Government. There is nothing more futile than a momentary diplomatic score off a Foreign Minister or his country. It is worse than futile; it has later on to be paid for, and it wrecks that confidence

[1] See, on this subject, Asquith's *Genesis of the War*, p. 22.

which is as essential in permanent relations between Governments as it is between great commercial houses.   It is sometimes suggested that it was British Imperialism that brought us into conflict with Germany.   Let those who think so, either in this country or outside it, take note of the fact that the policy of alliance and co-operation with Germany was, up to the time of Mr. Chamberlain's speech, desired and advocated by the two most convinced, energetic, and influential exponents and promoters of British Imperialism.   Mr. Chamberlain's speech and Mr. Cecil Rhodes's will are striking evidence of this.

At this moment Germany had the opportunity of a British Alliance, based on the fact that one had a fleet and the other an army; that the fleet and the army could not be rivals, but could give invincible support to each other.

In the light of after-events ought we to wish that the alliance had been made?   And what would have been the probable course of history if it had been made?   It will be better to discuss the answers to those questions when the after-events have been reviewed.   Germany let the suggestion of an alliance drop; the opportunity passed; Lord Salisbury made no change in policy; Germany presently embarked on the policy of a great fleet, and other events happened that prevented the suggestion of an Anglo-German Alliance from being renewed.

For some time British foreign policy went on much as before.   There was the same dependence on German support in Egypt; the same concession from time to time to some German demand.   The instance I have in mind is the Secret Agreement with Germany about the Portuguese Colonies in Africa.   It is still officially "Secret," but, as the German Government made it public to the world during the war, there was no secrecy about it.   I had to deal with the question when I was at the Foreign Office, and when I come to that part of the narrative a full account of the final stage will be given. I had occasion then to look at the old papers in the Foreign Office to see what agreement was made. It seemed to me clear, from what I saw in them, that the Agreement had been made very reluctantly so far as Lord Salisbury was concerned, and only in deference to German insistence—pressure would hardly be too strong a word. Crudely put, the German insistence was this: "You [Britain] are on bad terms with Russia and on bad terms with France. You cannot afford to be on bad terms with us." Years afterwards, when I was at the Foreign Office, the Marquis de Soveral gave me an entertaining account of how the Agreement came to be signed. He was Portuguese Minister in London at the time; he had known all about the negotiation and the signature of the "Secret" Agreement, and had made no secret to Lord Salisbury of his knowledge of it. This transaction must have given further cause for serious reflection at the Foreign Office.

In 1899 came the South African War. There was much division of opinion at home about it. Many people thought that President Krüger's policy had the larger share of responsibility. Some Liberals, of whom I was one, as well as the supporters of the Government, took this view.

Others who admitted, as Mr. (afterwards Lord) Bryce had said in his book about South Africa, that President Krüger's policy had been a cause of trouble, yet held that the war was unjustifiable. This view, as I understand it, was that President Krüger was an old man; that the defects of his policy were recognized by the younger men with broader outlook, who would succeed him; and that the British Government, by the exercise of a reasonable amount of patience, could have in no very long time secured British interests and put peace on a firm foundation of good-will in South Africa without any war at all.

There were others who, with less study of the question, regarded the war as an attack upon a small country by aggressive British Imperialism.

It is unnecessary to discuss now which of these three views was right at the time, or what degree of justice there was in any of them. It is well not to revive old unhappy things, or reopen wounds that time and true statesmanship on both sides have done so much to heal, though the scars may still be in the memory of those who suffered.

It was the last of these three views that prevailed on the Continent. The war was regarded as aggression upon a small State; and sympathy with the Boers and dislike of Britain found free and even vehement expression. In Germany this feeling was as pronounced as in other countries—if anything, it was even stronger. This was particularly resented in Britain, and I have heard a German complain that we should have resented so strongly in the case of Germany, a manifestation of feeling that was generally shared and expressed in other countries. The reasons for public sentiment are often more unconscious than conscious, and are not always easy to analyse; but in this instance it was suspected, if not entirely known, that President Krüger had for some time received German encouragement in a policy unfriendly to us. Support was given to this view by recollection of the German Emperor's telegram to President Krüger at the time of the Jameson Raid and by the fact that, when President Krüger came to Europe, it was the German Emperor that he asked to see. It is true that, when it came to the point, the Emperor declined to see him, but the evidence of previous communications, combined with the hostility of the German Press, prevented this from being regarded as an act of friendship. The friction with Germany found expression in an open passage of arms between Count Bülow, the German Chancellor, and Mr. Chamberlain. In this Mr. Chamberlain stood his ground, and British opinion supported him. All this had its effect on British opinion, and if in Government circles more was known than the public knew there must again have been serious cause for reflection on the discomfort, if not the actual insecurity, of Britain's position.

By the year 1900 Germany had made it manifest that she was adopting a new naval policy—that of a big fleet. Hitherto British naval ship-building had been based on a two-Power standard. The French and Russian fleets had been regarded as the only potential enemies. The South African War had shown that we were completely isolated, that every fleet was a possible enemy. Would it not be positively dangerous for the British Government to let matters drift as they had been doing in foreign policy for so many years? Could we afford to let probable causes of conflict remain without any attempt to remove them? Some such questions, I suppose, must have become urgent in the thought of British Ministers of the day. Two steps, at any rate, they took that were more definite and positive acts of policy than anything that British Governments had done for a long time. The first was the Anglo-Japanese Alliance, made in 1902; the other was the Agreement with France in 1904. It is interesting to observe that these two steps were apparently not parts of one settled policy. Each was like a first step in a different policy.

France and Russia were allies. Protection against their
joint fleets was our standard. There were two alternative
policies or ways by which we might endeavour to guard
against causes of conflict—one was to make an alliance
with another Power for protection against France or
Russia, the other was by friendly negotiation with these
Powers to smooth away and remove possible causes of conflict. The Anglo-Japanese alliance was a step in the
direction of the first policy; the Anglo-French Agreement
was a step in the direction of the second.

The explanation of the Anglo-Japanese Alliance is
simple enough. The fact and circumstances of the Russian occupation of Port Arthur had made it appear that
the most probable cause of conflict with Russia was in the
Far East. In the seventies of the last century the danger-
point had seemed to be Constantinople and the Near
East. Russia had dropped the policy of pushing against
Turkey, and Turkey was now fortified by German friendship and the increasing commercial stake that Germany
was acquiring in Turkey.

Then, in the eighties, there had continued the excursions
and alarums about Russian advances towards the Indian
frontier. These had died down or evaporated on the
great altitudes or in the deserts of Asia. It was in the
Far East that Russia seemed now to be concentrating.
This was a menace more serious to Japan than to us; the
recollection of the diplomatic coercion of Japan in 1895
by Russia, Germany, and France, and of British refusal to
join in that coercion, made the Anglo-Japanese Alliance
an easy, almost an obvious, transaction.

It was, however, with France that the most vital points
of dispute were likely to occur: it was between Britain
and France that a storm might most suddenly arise and

be so violent as to sweep the two countries into war with
each other. The counterpart to the Anglo-Japanese Alliance, the application of the same policy to France would
have been an alliance with Germany. But the opportunity
for that had passed, when Mr. Chamberlain made his
overture. It is interesting to observe how inevitably one
comes, in this period, to quote Mr. Chamberlain to illustrate tendencies in foreign policy. It was he who spoke
the strong word about the Russian occupation of Port
Arthur; it was he who advocated a German Alliance;
it was in his passage of arms with the German Chancellor
that friction with Germany over the South African War
found expression. It is as if he had been the most sensitive
barometer by which to read tendencies in foreign policy.
The time when it had pointed to "set fair" in Anglo-
German relations had gone by. The Government of Mr.
Balfour, who had succeeded Lord Salisbury as Prime
Minister, adopted with France the policy of an understanding that should remove causes of dispute by mutual
good will and agreement.

Lord Lansdowne and M. Delcassé were the Secretaries
for Foreign Affairs in London and Paris respectively, and
I imagine that the ground must have been prepared by
long and patient work in which M. Cambon, the French
Ambassador in London, no doubt took great part. Egypt
was the perpetual sore point: French objection to British
occupation of Egypt had for long been a cardinal point
of French policy and opinion. It could not be easy to
make an agreement on this point that would be acceptable
to France. In countries like Egypt, where foreign nations have extra-territorial rights, it is not enough that
they should cease to object to our presence; active support
is required for some essential problems of Government,

such as taxation and the administration of justice. To make our position satisfactory we were bound to have French support, not merely the assurance that there would be no French obstruction. Otherwise causes of friction would continue, and we should remain as dependent as before upon the Triple Alliance, that is, upon German support. Eventually an agreement was made of which the salient point was that France would give diplomatic support to us in Egypt, and we would give the same to her in Morocco.

On the face of the Agreement with France there was nothing more than a desire to remove causes of dispute between the two nations, to make up old quarrels, to become friends. It was all made public, except a clause or two of no importance, which were not published at the time, owing to regard, as I suppose, for the susceptibilities of the Sultan of Morocco: even these were published a few years later. Was it in the minds of those who made the simple, straightforward Agreement for settling present differences that it would develop into something more, into what was called the Entente Cordiale—a general *diplomatic* alliance with no new obligations, but with preparations for the contingency of a German attack on France? Was this in the minds of the men in London and Paris when they were making the Agreement? Or was it brought about solely by the efforts of Germany to shake or break the Agreement after it was made?

I cannot say. There is in great affairs so much more, as a rule, in the minds of the events (if such an expression may be used) than in the minds of the chief actors. I remember very well what my own feeling was when I read the Agreement. It was a feeling of simple pleasure and relief. I saw all that had been most disagreeable in my experience at the Foreign Office from 1892-5 swept away. We should no longer be dependent on German support in Egypt, with all the discomfort that this dependence had entailed. I had no desire to thwart German interests, but we should now be able to negotiate with Germany without the handicap of the Egyptian noose round our necks. That was a welcome relief; but that appeared to me an incidental and not the main advantage of the Agreement—a by-product and not the chief matter.

The real cause for satisfaction was that the exasperating friction with France was to end, and that the menace of war with France had disappeared. The gloomy clouds were gone, the sky was clear, and the sun shone warmly. Ill-will, dislike, hate, whether the object of them be a person or a nation, are a perpetual discomfort; they come between us and all that is beautiful and happy. They put out the sun. If the object be a nation with whom our interests are in contact they poison the atmosphere of international affairs. This had been so between Britain and France. The writing of the Press on each side of the Channel had been a constant source of annoyance and wrath. That was all to be changed; it was to become positively pleasant. To see what is pleasant, where we have seen before only what was repellent; to understand and to be understood where before there had been misrepresentation and misconstruction; to be friends instead of enemies—this, when it happens, is one of the great pleasures of life. That was enough for me at the time; I felt as if there were some benign influence abroad, and in that spirit I spoke in welcome of the Agreement in the House of Commons.[1]

It was indeed obvious that Germany would not like

[1] See Appendix B., Vol. ii., p. 293.

the Agreement. She had profited by the constant dissensions between Britain and France. Was it not said that after 1870 Bismarck had deliberately encouraged French expansion in Africa, foreseeing that this would keep Britain and France occupied with each other? But really good relations with Germany could not be founded on bad relations with France; I saw no reason why we should be hostile to German interests, where Germany was expanding, and, if we were not, why should the Agreement with France mean bad relations with Germany? In British minds, certainly in my own, the Anglo-French Agreement was not regarded as more than I have described it. It was the subsequent attempts of Germany to shake or break it that turned it into an Entente. These attempts were not long in coming. The German Emperor made a visit that was like a demonstration at Tangier, and in 1905 the German Government forced the French, by what was practically a challenge, to dismiss M. Delcassé (their Minister for Foreign Affairs who had made the Franco-British Agreement) and to agree to an international conference about Morocco.

One man there was, of great position in public life, who was an exception to the general approval of the Anglo-French Agreement. I do not know that he ever expressed his views in public, but he made no secret to me that he thought it a mistake and that he disagreed with my support of it. The German Army, he remarked, was the strongest in the world. When M. Delcassé was sacrificed he said to me, "Your friends the French are trembling like an aspen." The time cannot have been comfortable for Lord Lansdowne and for the British Government. The French were being humiliated because of an Agreement that we had made with them. The Agreement bound us

only to *diplomatic* support, but the German attitude
threatened more than diplomatic action.  If Germany
used force, and France were in serious trouble, what was
our position to be?  We had no obligation, none whatever,
to which France could appeal, to go beyond diplomatic
support; but could we stand aside complacently and see
her suffer for something in which we were her partner?

Such was the prospective situation with which Mr.
Balfour's Government were confronted in 1905.  Of what
they did, or how they regarded it, I knew nothing at the
time and I had no expectation then of ever having to deal
with it myself.  The French tided over the crisis in 1905
by letting M. Delcassé go from the Foreign Office, the
German Emperor emphasized the occasion by making
Count Bülow a Prince.  The personal triumph over M.
Delcassé was complete, and by the French agreement to
a Conference the question of Morocco was postponed.
The crisis had passed for the moment, to be faced again
later on when the Conference should meet.  Before that
time came there had been a change of Government at
home.  I had gone to the Foreign Office, and from that
point this narrative will resume the account with full
knowledge and in detail.

One other outstanding event at the end of this period
must be noticed.  The Anglo-Japanese Alliance had put
Japan in a position to avenge the slight and retrieve the
loss inflicted upon her by the combination of European
Powers in 1895.  She could now try conclusions with
Russia alone.  If any other European Power were to help
Russia, then Britain would be bound to come to the assist-
ance of Japan; and the British and Japanese fleets to-
gether would be amply strong enough to prevent any
European combination against Japan.  The Russo-

Japanese War came in due course. It was not without incident for us. The Russian fleet, on its way out to the Far East, fired on British fishing vessels in the North Sea. The act was due to a high state of suspicion and nervous tension on the part of the Russian fleet. It was not credible that the Russians knew they were firing on unarmed peaceful fishing vessels, though it was difficult to believe that they really thought it possible for Japanese torpedo-boats to be in the North Sea, as they said. It was therefore not easy to understand what the Russians did think they were firing at, and why their guns went off at all. There was a moment of great and natural excitement in public opinion, but the British Government kept the affair under control, and it was settled without further consequences.

The Russian fleet pursued its journey. In Madagascar it received facilities and hospitality from the French beyond what the rules of international law were generally understood to allow to belligerent ships in neutral ports. It seemed to me at the time that Japan might have urged that the action of France had gone beyond the limits of neutrality; that Japan could have appealed to the Anglo-Japanese Treaty and have requested us to take some counter-action. So far as I knew, Japan did not raise the question, being confident, no doubt, of her ability to deal with the Russian fleet when it arrived, and not desiring to invoke the letter of the Anglo-Japanese Treaty for help that she did not need. The Russian fleet, without further incident, went to its fate at the battle of Tsushimi. Japan won the war, and peace was made by the representatives of Russia and Japan meeting on American soil under the auspices of President Roosevelt. One of the conditions of peace was the cession of Port Arthur by

Russia to Japan. The method by which Russia had acquired Port Arthur made the cession of it to Japan seem to be an act of mere justice. Japan had been ordered away in 1895 by Russia, France, and Germany, after a successful war with China, on the ground that the integrity of Chinese territory was a sacred principle that must not be violated. Russia had then occupied the place herself on a long lease extorted from China, without regard to the principle of integrity of Chinese territory, so lately proclaimed sacred against Japan. If Port Arthur was not to remain Chinese, Japan clearly had a better right to it than Russia, after all that had passed.

On the other hand, I could not but reflect that, apart from the merits of the Port Arthur affair, the case of Russia was hard. This mighty Empire needed and was ever seeking an outlet to a sea that did not freeze. By far the greater part of the world's commerce is sea-borne; the oceans are the great highways of commerce. With few exceptions, every nation, small or great, had its own ports on this great thoroughfare. Russia, with the most extensive territory and a huge population, had no outlet under her own control; not one where she could keep a fleet that would not be frozen up in winter. In the Near East access to the Mediterranean had been barred to her, notably by Britain under Lord Beaconsfield. Lord Lansdowne, the British Minister for Foreign Affairs, had lately made a declaration that was a warning not to touch the Persian Gulf. That barred the Middle East outlet to a warm sea. And now the British Alliance with Japan had deprived Russia of the outlet of Port Arthur in the Far East. Was it possible ever to have peace and quiet, or indeed to have anything but recurrent friction with Russia on such terms? The question of Port Arthur might be settled on terms of justice as between Russia and Japan, but the problem of British relations with Russia remained.   Our most important points of contact with Russia were not in the Far East, and it was in the Far East only that the Anglo-Japanese Alliance made us secure.   It did not apply elsewhere.   Something, at any rate, of this I remember to have been in my mind at the time.

After the war Japan was extremely popular.   The smaller nation had beaten the giant; British sporting instincts were gratified; we admired the efficiency to which the Japanese had attained and the rapidity with which they had learnt what we had to teach of naval construction and equipment, and the handling of things so complicated as modern ships of war.   This feeling seemed to us natural, reasonable, and right.   Not long afterwards I was told a story that put it in another light.   The story ran that a Japanese in England, finding himself and his nation to be objects of admiration, reflected thus upon the course of events: "Yes," he said, "we used to be a nation of artists; our art was really very good; you called us barbarians then.   Now our art is not so good as it was, but we have learned how to kill, and you say we are civilized."

The story was familiar to me long before the Great War; whether it is a true story I never knew, but there was a truth in it that gave a feeling of discomfort, of question. What was the answer to such an observation?   Was there something very wrong about our civilization and the virtues of which we felt so sure?   The Great War has given a terrible answer.

For me personally these years of opposition were a time of happy detachment.   I could take as much or as little share in public life as I felt moved to do.   I could express individual views, and did so, sometimes differing from the majority of the Liberal Party. If this was resented in the Liberal Party my reply was that I had no desire for office, and that, if my constituents did not approve my views, I was ready and should even be pleased to stand aside. The leaders of the Liberal Party themselves were not all in harmony, and the leadership changed three times in these ten years. By 1902, however, the things on which I had differed from many Liberals had ceased to be present and active causes of difference. The South African War was over; the reconquest of the Soudan was accomplished and the occupation was proving a success and an indisputable boon to that country and its people. In 1902 I found myself in full and active agreement with the Liberal attitude to the Conservative Elementary Education Bill. Then, in 1903, came the Fiscal Controversy, on which I felt stirred to take an earnest part against what seemed to me the fallacies and dangers of Protection. This brought me thoroughly into line with the Liberal Party, and it was impossible to have clear views on a question so vital as the Fiscal Controversy without being drawn to take a more sustained and active part in politics than I had intended or wished. For in this period there had opened the prospect of another sort of life, much more congenial to my wife and to me than politics and London.

In 1898 I had been elected to the Board of the North-Eastern Railway Company. In mileage and gross receipts and in financial strength combined the North-Eastern ranked amongst the four greatest British railways. The work was interesting; the conditions under which it was done were exceedingly pleasant and congenial. The full Board consisted of twenty members; twice a month

Photograph by J. Candlish Ruddock

THE OLD HOUSE, FALLODON

they assembled, generally at York, on a Thursday, and remained till after the Board meeting on Friday, working in Committees on Thursday and spending the evening together. In this way they got to know each other well, and for all the time they were at York they were in the atmosphere of the business of the railway. The Board included some of the ablest and most experienced and soundest men of business in the country; the meetings were always interesting, as well as pleasant. The railway was a great separate organization, playing a great part and spending large capital in the development of the prosperous industrial area of the North-East of England from the Humber to the Tweed, on which our whole interest and attention were concentrated.

Only twice in the year did the railway business take me to London; the other meetings were all at York or Newcastle. The North-Eastern Railway no longer exists as a separate institution, and many things have changed since those easier and simpler days. In 1898 Sir Matthew Ridley was Home Secretary, and yet retained a seat on the Board and attended our meetings, and his doing so was taken as a matter of course; he himself was the last person to do anything that bordered on inconvenience or impropriety. But it would be out of the question for a Home Secretary to sit on a Railway Board to-day. In 1902, not long after his retirement from the Government, Lord Ridley (as he had then been made) became Chairman of the North-Eastern Railway. He died suddenly in 1904— a great loss to our district, for he was a man of ability, whom everyone trusted. I was chosen to succeed him. The year 1905 was one of the happiest of my life; the work of Chairman of the Railway was agreeable and interesting, but it left in those days plenty of leisure. There were many days spent at home, in the Itchen Valley or in Scotland. If only I could be free altogether from politics, there was the prospect of permanent and interesting work with income sufficient for all we needed, and a more constant home and country life than we had yet enjoyed. Life, which had been very pleasant since 1895, promised to become more pleasant and settled still. It was not to be.

# CHAPTER V

## (1905)

## BACK TO THE FOREIGN OFFICE

Balfour's Resignation—Campbell-Bannerman's Government—Difficulties in joining it—An Interview with the Prime Minister—Reasons for Coming in—Back to the Foreign Office—The Importance of Free Trade—Campbell-Bannerman's Characteristics—The Qualities of a Good Colleague.

IN December 1905 the Unionist Government resigned. The party that supported it was really a Unionist Party in those days, its object being to maintain the Act of Union that united Great Britain and Ireland. By the irony of things that Union was destroyed by a Government of which the majority belonged to the Unionist Party, and the name has now become an anachronism. The party in 1905 was still united on the subject of Ireland, but the energy of Mr. Joseph Chamberlain had made Tariff Reform the dominant issue before the country. He had resigned from the Government in 1903 to head a Tariff Reform crusade in which it was understood that he would have the support and sympathy of Mr. Balfour and the Government, which had been purged of its Free Trade Members.

By December 1905 there was every reason for taking the opinion of the electors. For ten years there had been no General Election except that of 1900, which had been taken in the middle of the South African War, and was therefore no opportunity for the expression of popular opinion on anything else except the war. Tariff Reform was a new issue: it had now been debated before the country for over two years. It was therefore altogether reasonable, right, and proper that there should now be a dissolution and a General Election. But there was no apparent reason why Mr. Balfour's Government should have resigned: they had a good majority in Parliament; it was more than two years since the Free Trade Members of the Government had resigned; the shock of that had not broken up the Government then and could not be the cause of its resignation now. The only conceivable reason was that the Government was exhausted and tired —not a good recommendation for giving them support at the polls. There is no doubt that this resignation was a great tactical disadvantage to them.

Campbell-Bannerman was, as leader of the Opposition, invited by the King to form a Government. The Liberal and Irish parties together were in a minority in Parliament; it was clearly impossible for a Liberal Government to meet the House of Commons as it then was, and Campbell-Bannerman undertook to form a Government on condition that there was an immediate dissolution of Parliament.

He had no difficulty in forming a Government, but I made difficulty for some days about joining it. I was closely associated with Asquith and Haldane in House of Commons work, and our view was that, with Campbell-Bannerman as Prime Minister, the leadership in the Commons should be in Asquith's hands. There had not been differences about foreign policy, but there had been about Imperial affairs such as the South African War and the Soudan, and my view was that Asquith would be the more robust and stronger leader in policy and debate in the Commons. I explained this with some frankness to

Campbell-Bannerman; I had no feeling but one of liking for him personally, and I wanted him to know just where I stood, and to feel that I was not suppressing in his presence things that I had said about him elsewhere. Perhaps it was some understanding of this that made him take all I said in good part. Asquith had from the first been prepared to take office. Arthur Acland, who had retired from public life, but with whom I had worked closely and intimately in past years, had a long talk with me. Haldane decided to go into office; there were no substantial reasons for standing out alone, and, as Campbell-Bannerman still offered it, I went to the Foreign Office.

It will be understood from what has been said in the last chapter that the decision brought no joy either to my wife or myself; it meant exile again from home, life in London, and a number of those social functions which Sir George Cornewall Lewis probably had in mind when he said that "life would be tolerable if it were not for its amusements." Probably my wife's comment had much to do with the decision. "If we had refused office," she said, "we could not have justified the decision to the constituents." It was the constituency that had kept us in public life. They had returned me to Parliament at the age of twenty-three, a young and untried man; for twenty years they had continued their confidence, giving me generously freedom to indulge individual views even when these differed from those of the majority of the party. I had not been in a position to spend much money on organization or propaganda; I had indeed paid an agent's fee with other election expenses, but in the years between elections I had, up to 1906, had no paid agent. All the necessary work had been done with the very slender resources of the local association and by voluntary work. As in most country constituencies, the majority of those who had wealth or large property were on the Conservative side. The Liberal strength lay in the number of devoted men scattered throughout the constituency to whom Liberal politics were a matter of conviction, and to work for the return of a Liberal Member was a matter of conscience. They had done it with the minimum of help from me. Time after time my wife and I had watched the counting of the votes with the feeling that, if I were beaten, our greatest regret would be for the disappointment of those who had worked so hard for a Liberal success: we, too, should have been sorry no doubt on public grounds, but I felt, almost with a sense of guilt, that the relief of being set free from Parliament would be an irresistible joy.

It was for the constituents that we should have minded defeat. My wife had done much to found and encourage Liberal Associations, not so much for party purposes as from a belief that such Associations were good for women. She thought that to take an intelligent interest and an organized part in public affairs broadened outlook and enlarged life. Her views had met with response and cooperation, and she had made many friends. Thus we were conscious of responsibility to a number of earnest people, who had a right to expect me to do my best in Parliament. It may be added that the home associations of all my life were in the district: this gave a touch of sentiment and intimacy. Ties of sentiment and moral obligation there must be between every member and a constituency that has returned him for twenty years, and in my case these were exceptionally strong and compelling. Now suddenly I was asked to take one of the highest offices in public life, and when my wife said that refusal could not be justified to the constituents, I felt that this was indeed the truest and decisive judgment on the matter.

The other considerations that then seemed important were based upon a mistaken sense of values. I had a notion that the public interest required that every member of the Liberal Party who counted for anything should contribute his help to the Liberal Government. The Tariff Reform issue was a great crisis. I believed that Protection would undermine our Trade; but the weight of the Press was against us. The arguments for Protection are more easily made attractive than those for Free Trade; the issue of the contest seemed doubtful. It was a time when every Free Trader, who might be counted for strength to Campbell-Bannerman's Government, should join it. Such reflections were a consolation after the disagreeable choice of office was made. The result of the Election, with its enormous and unprecedented Liberal majority, showed what a delusion it had been to suppose that it mattered anything to the cause of Free Trade whether I joined the Government or not: the country had made up its mind that it was tired of the Conservative Government and that it would not have Tariff Reform, and it did not make any difference whether people like myself joined the Government or not.

I had made difficulties, as I now think unnecessarily, about going into office, but when in it I made none. Campbell-Bannerman's leadership in the Commons was accepted, and there was complete loyalty to him. Experience showed that it had been quite unnecessary to raise any question of his leaving the House of Commons. Things went well enough as they were, and the differences and divisions of opinion that had existed when the party was in opposition never reappeared. Campbell-Bannerman's own personality contributed greatly to this result. He provoked no rivalry or ambition in others. It is true that, once installed as leader of the party, he showed a dogged determination to stay there and not to be dislodged from it, but everyone knew that he had never worked to get the leadership or desired it for himself. He had been loyal to previous leaders, and had not been concerned in the intrigues either for himself or against others. He was a strong party man, but it was for the success of the party, not for his own prestige as its leader, that he cared.

From the moment his Cabinet was formed he made no distinction in personal relations, in intimacy and sympathy between those who had helped him and those who had made difficulties for him when the party was in opposition. He was said to have regarded Haldane as one of those who had worked most actively against his leadership. Haldane was now at the War Office. Campbell-Bannerman's previous experience and knowledge enabled him to give special help to anyone who held that very difficult post, and he gave it unsparingly and wholeheartedly to Haldane. In return, he expected equal loyalty from everyone, and he received it. His personality has been given, more fully and better than I could do it, in Spender's Life of him, but one quality may be mentioned here that he possessed in a peculiar degree. He had an unusually just as well as keen perception of the weaknesses of other men, and it was extraordinarily detached. No personal devotion to himself blunted or dulled the edge of his discerning eye. He was not more conscious of the weak points of his critics than he was of the weak points of his admirers. If he had taken the trouble to do it, he could probably have given the best and most just criticism of himself. He seemed to have no favourites, not even himself for one. Whether he had an equally keen and just appreciation of excellence is more doubtful; he seemed rather to appreciate freedom from weaknesses that he despised or disliked than to admire positive qualities. He was always ready, however, to give credit for good or successful work done by colleagues without thought of himself. For the two years of his Premiership the Cabinet was peculiarly and happily free from personal differences and restlessness.

Asquith was the only man who could then aspire to succeed to the post of Prime Minister, and Asquith was not only free from all self-seeking, but ready, as later experience showed, to carry loyalty to colleagues to the point of generosity and chivalry, if need be. The ambitions of younger men were for the present satisfied by being in a Cabinet for the first time. All of us who had big offices were absorbed in getting to know the work of our Departments and in transacting it.

Reflection has suggested some regret for the personal difficulties made in taking office: on the other hand, it brings the thought that, when in office, I was entitled to the character of a good colleague in respect of two things, at any rate, that go to qualify a man for that character.

One of these is to put his mind into the common stock; to work sincerely in matters of difference of opinion and difficulty for a Cabinet decision. This does not mean that what is regarded by a Minister as vital to the public interest should be compromised. A Minister should resign rather than agree to that. It means that a Minister should not press his personal views unduly about what is not essential, that he should contend for substance not for form, that he should consider without *amour-propre* how his own opinion can be reconciled with that of others. Subject to the one qualification of not sacrificing what he regards as vital to the public interest, he should not contend for victory, but work for agreement in the Cabinet.

The other qualification is that of accepting full personal responsibility for Cabinet decisions, when once agreed to. Perhaps a third qualification might be mentioned, that of never threatening resignation or talking about it, except in the last resort on a matter of vital importance, and then only when resignation is really intended.

# CHAPTER VI

## (1906)

## THE FIRST CRISIS (ALGECIRAS) AND THE MILITARY CONVERSATIONS

The Algeciras Conference—French Apprehensions—Testing the Anglo-French Agreement—A Question for the New Government—The Impossibility of Answering It—Interviews with M. Cambon—Military Conversations and Their Limitations—An Interview with Metternich—Campbell-Bannerman's View—Ought There to Have Been a Cabinet?—Preparations and Precautions—Armaments and War—A Later Transaction—The Grey-Cambon Letters of 1912 —Endorsement by the Cabinet.

ONE duty of a Cabinet Minister is to make the work of the Department assigned to him the first charge upon his time. The Foreign Office leaves the Secretary of State, who is in charge of it, no choice but to fulfil this duty. The work besets and besieges him. If he gets into arrears he cannot overtake them and also deal with the current work of every day. He is like a man in deep water, who must keep on swimming or be submerged.

On the afternoon of Monday, December 11, 1905, the Liberal Ministers received the seals of office from the King. There was on that afternoon one of the very worst of London fogs: I do not remember whether any sarcastic or ominous comments were made on the coincidence. I drove to Buckingham Palace in a brougham hired for the occasion, and John Morley, Henry Fowler, and I drove away in it together after receiving our seals. We had got but a little way from the gates when the brougham came to a stand, completely lost in the fog. Thinking I could do better on my feet, I left the brougham; in a few steps I had lost my way and sense of direction. I walked into the head of a horse, and felt my way along its side, till I found a hansom-cab attached to it. The driver, when asked if he could find his way to Bird-cage Walk, said he had just come from it and would try; he succeeded after some time, and it was then easy to follow the kerb at a foot's pace to the Foreign Office, where I then took over the work.

The Election was already upon us; the polls were to be held in January; the campaign of speeches was beginning. I devoted the time before Christmas to the work of the Foreign Office. We spent Sunday the 24th and Christmas with Rosebery at the Durdans. He had often made it clear, after his retirement from leadership of the party in 1900, that the formation of the next Government would be no concern of his: it was therefore the general assumption that he would continue to stand aside, and there had been no surprise at his doing so. But the separation made a great blank, not only to me, but to my wife. She had always felt that he gave distinction and interest to politics and lifted them out of the drab and commonplace. I was oppressed by the stress of work at the Foreign Office, making myself acquainted with so much that was new or unfamiliar after an absence of ten and a half years; and before me was the prospect of combining this work with the effort of an election campaign.

The constituency was a large rural area, including the towns of Berwick and Alnwick, and many villages large and small. There was a Conservative opponent addressing meetings, and I had to do the best I could. Relying on the forbearance of constituents and trusting them to make allowance for the strain of Foreign Office work, I arranged to spend three days a week at the Foreign Office. Every Wednesday night I left London, getting home in good time for breakfast; the last three days of the week were given to election speeches, the paper work of the Foreign Office that followed me being done each morning. Each Sunday night I returned to London and gave the first three days entirely to the Foreign Office. Other Cabinet Ministers were in the same position. It was of course impossible to hold any Cabinets. It was under these conditions that the first critical occasion in foreign policy came upon us.

I have already mentioned how, a few months before, Germany had forced upon France the dismissal of M. Delcassé, the French Minister who had made the Anglo-French Agreement with Lord Lansdowne in 1904. France, under this pressure, had agreed to an international Conference about Morocco, to be held at Algeciras. Germany had intended thus to shake or to test the strength of the Anglo-French Agreement while the Conservative Government, that had made the Agreement, was in office; she was not likely to be less resolute in that intention now that a Liberal Government had succeeded, which had not been directly responsible for the Agreement.

Campbell-Bannerman, after becoming Prime Minister, had publicly stated his agreement with the main lines of policy followed by Lord Lansdowne; but his Government was not likely to be more stiff or positive than their predecessors. It was therefore certain that the change of Government in Britain could not have dissipated the cloud that was gathering, and that might burst in storm at Algeciras. The date fixed for the meeting of the Conference was not so very far off. French apprehensions were naturally great; it was vital to them to know, before the Conference met, how they stood with regard to British support.

On Wednesday, January 10, M. Paul Cambon, the French Ambassador, who had returned from Paris with instructions from his Government, put the critical question to me. My record of the conversation is printed in Spender's *Life of Campbell-Bannerman,* but it must have its place also here:

*Sir Edward Grey to Sir F. Bertie*

FOREIGN OFFICE,

*January* 10, 1906.

SIR,—After informing me this afternoon of the nature of the instructions which M. Rouvier was addressing to the French Plenipotentiary at the Conference about to meet at Algeciras on Moorish affairs (as recorded in my immediately preceding despatch), the French Ambassador went on to say that he had spoken to M. Rouvier on the importance of arriving at an understanding as to the course which would be taken by France and Great Britain in the event of the discussions terminating in a rupture between France and Germany. M. Cambon said that he did not believe that the German Emperor desired war, but that His Majesty was pursuing a very dangerous policy. He had succeeded in inciting public opinion and military opinion in Germany, and there was a risk that matters might be brought to a point in which a pacific issue would be difficult. During the previous discussions on the subject of Morocco, Lord Lansdowne had expressed his opinion that the British and French Governments should frankly discuss any eventualities that might seem possible, and by his instructions your Excellency had communicated a Memorandum to M. Declassé to the same effect. It had not been considered necessary at the time to discuss the eventuality of war, but it now seemed desirable that this eventuality should also be considered.

M. Cambon said that he had spoken to this effect to M. Rouvier, who agreed in his view. It was not necessary, nor, indeed, expedient that there should be any formal alliance; but it was of great importance that the French Government should know beforehand whether, in the event of aggression against France by Germany, Great Britain would be prepared to render to France armed assistance.

I replied that at the present moment the Prime Minister was out of town, and that the Cabinet were all dispersed seeing after the elections; that we were not as yet aware of the sentiments of the country as they would be expressed at the polls; and that it was impossible therefore for me, in the circumstances, to give a reply to his Excellency's question. I could only state as my personal opinion that, if France were to be attacked by Germany in consequence of a question arising out of the Agreement which our predecessors had recently concluded with the French Government, public opinion in England would be strongly moved in favour of France.

M. Cambon said that he understood this, and that he would repeat his question after the elections.

I said that what Great Britain earnestly desired was that the Conference should have a pacific issue favourable to France.

His Excellency replied that nothing would have a more pacific influence on the Emperor of Germany than the conviction that, if Germany attacked France, she would find England allied against her.

I said that I thought the German Emperor did believe this, but that it was one thing that his opinion should be held in Germany and another that we should give a positive assurance to France on the subject. There could be no greater mistake than that a Minister should give such an assurance unless he were perfectly certain that it would be fulfilled. I did not believe that any Minister could, in present circumstances, say more than I had done, and, however strong the sympathy of Great Britain might be with France in the case of a rupture with Germany, the expression which might be given to it and the action which might follow must depend largely upon the circumstances in which the rupture took place.

M. Cambon said that he spoke of aggression on the part of Germany, possibly in consequence of some necessary action on the part of France for the protection of her Algerian frontier, or on some other grounds which justified such action.

I said that, as far as a definite promise went, I was not in a position to pledge the country to more than neutrality—a benevolent neutrality, if such a thing existed. M. Cambon said that a promise of neutrality did not, of course, satisfy him, and repeated that he would bring the question to me again at the conclusion of the elections.

In the meantime, he thought it advisable that unofficial communications between our Admiralty and War Office and the French Naval and Military Attachés should take place as to what action might advantageously be taken in case the two countries found themselves in alliance in such a war.  Some communications had, he believed, already passed, and might, he thought, be continued.  They did not pledge either Government.

I did not dissent from this view.—I am, etc.,

EDWARD GREY.

It was inevitable that the French should ask the question; it was impossible that we should answer it.

I sent the record of the conversation to Campbell-Bannerman and also to Lord Ripon.  The latter led the party in the House of Lords.  He was a Minister of great experience—he had indeed been a colleague with my grandfather, Sir George Grey, in the last Cabinet of Lord Palmerston in the early sixties of the last century.  Soon after we went into office he told me that he knew there were always some Foreign Office papers that were sent to the Prime Minister, and not circulated to the Cabinet, at any rate in the first instance; he asked that these should also be sent to him, as he would have to speak on foreign affairs in the House of Lords.  To this I readily agreed, and it was regularly done.

It was not till some time after I entered office that I discovered that, under the threat of German pressure upon France in 1905, steps had been taken to concert military plans, in the event of war being forced upon France.  It had been done without incurring any obligation beyond what was contained in the published Anglo-French Agreement—that is to say, there was no obligation to go beyond diplomatic support.  I was quite clear that no Cabinet could undertake any obligation to go to war, but the Anglo-French Agreement was popular in Britain.

It was certain that if Germany forced a quarrel on France upon the very matter of that Agreement, the pro-French feeling in Britain would be very strong, so strong probably as to justify a British Government in intervening on the side of France or even to insist on its doing so. We must, therefore, be free to go to the help of France as well as free to stand aside. But modern war may be an affair of days. If there were no military plans made beforehand we should be unable to come to the assistance of France in time, however strongly public opinion in Britain might desire it. We should in effect not have preserved our freedom to help France, but have cut ourselves off from the possibility of doing so, unless we had allowed the British and French staffs to concert plans for common action.

My recollection is that M. Cambon put some such considerations before me; they were at any rate present to my mind, and the force of them is obvious. Therefore, besides sending the record of the conversation to Campbell-Bannerman and Lord Ripon, I spoke to Haldane, now Secretary of State for War; he, like myself, was fighting for his seat in the country constituency of East Lothian. We met on one of my election platforms at Berwick, and I took the occasion to tell him of the request for military conversations between British and French military authorities. This despatch to Lord Bertie records the result:

*Sir Edward Grey to Sir F. Bertie*
FOREIGN OFFICE,
*January* 15, 1906.

SIR,—I told M. Cambon to-day that I had communicated to the Prime Minister my account of his conversation with me on the 10th instant. I had heard from the Prime Minister that he could not be in London before January 25, and it would therefore not be possible for me to discuss things with him before then, and the Members of the Government would not assemble in London before the 29th; I could therefore give no further answer to-day on the question he had addressed to me.  He had spoken to me on the 10th of communications passing between the French Naval Attaché and the Admiralty.  I understood that these communications had been with Sir John Fisher.  If that was so, it was not necessary for me to do any more; but, with regard to the communications between the French Military Attaché and the War Office, I understood from him that these had taken place through an intermediary.  I had therefore taken the opportunity of speaking to Mr. Haldane, the Secretary of State for War, who had been taking part in my election contest in Northumberland on Friday, and he had authorized me to say that these communications might proceed between the French Military Attaché and General Grierson direct; but it must be understood that these communications did not commit either Government.  M. Cambon said that the intermediary in question had been a retired Colonel, the military correspondent of the *Times,* who, he understood, had been sent from the War Office.—I am, etc.,

EDWARD GREY.

Plans for naval and military co-operation had, I found, begun to be made under Lord Lansdowne in 1905, when the German pressure was menacing.  The naval conversations had already been direct; the military conversations had hitherto been through an intermediary: they, too, were henceforth to be direct.  But it was to be clearly understood that these conversations or plans between military or naval staffs did not commit either Government, and involved no promise of support in war.  The question that pre-occupied me most anxiously was how to answer M. Cambon's request for a promise of military or naval support if Germany forced war upon France.  I knew we could not give it, but what would be the effect of the refusal on France?  Would France say that the promise of diplomatic support contained in the Anglo-

French Agreement was worth nothing now without a promise to give help in war? Would the French Government go even further, and say that the net result of the Anglo-French Agreement had been to make things worse for France than before, to expose her to a menace from Germany, in face of which diplomatic support alone was useless, and then to leave her in the lurch?

My own opinion—perhaps it would be more accurate to call it an instinctive feeling rather than considered opinion—was, that if Germany forced war on France in order to destroy the Anglo-French Agreement, we ought to go to the help of France. We should be isolated and discredited if we stood aside; hated by those whom we had refused to help, and despised by others. I thought, too, that when the time came, if it ever did come, when Germany attacked France, public opinion here would be so moved that Britain would intervene on the side of France. But I was sure that much would depend upon how the war came about. If France appeared to be aggressive Britain would not help her—of that I felt sure—and also that the Cabinet and Parliament would not bind themselves by a promise in advance. Therefore I considered it would be both useless to expect and unreasonable for me to ask the Cabinet to authorize me to give any promise. When M. Cambon repeated his question the answer must be that we could give no promise; nothing must be said by me that would entitle the French Government to say that they thought they might count on anything more than diplomatic support. On the other hand, to say that under no circumstances must France even hope for our armed intervention would not be in accordance with British feeling or with the facts. This was the situation that would have to be handled in conversation when M. Cambon repeated his "question" after the Elections were over.

Meanwhile the Election went on. My own poll was declared on Thursday, January 25, the next day my wife and I went to London; thence on Saturday till Monday to Windsor Castle; on Tuesday my wife went to Fallodon, and on Thursday, January 31, the critical conversation with M. Cambon took place. It is recorded in a despatch to Lord Bertie as follows:

*Sir Edward Grey to Sir F. Bertie*

FOREIGN OFFICE,

*January 31, 1906.*

SIR,—The French Ambassador asked me again to-day whether France would be able to count upon the assistance of England in the event of an attack upon her by Germany.

I said that I had spoken on the subject to the Prime Minister and discussed it with him, and that I had three observations to submit.

In the first place, since the Ambassador had spoken to me a good deal of progress has been made. Our military and naval authorities had been in communication with the French, and I assumed that all preparations were ready, so that, if a crisis arose, no time would have been lost for want of a formal engagement.

In the second place, a week or more before Monsieur Cambon had spoken to me, I had taken an opportunity of expressing to Count Metternich my personal opinion, which I understood Lord Lansdowne had also expressed to him as a personal opinion, that, in the event of an attack upon France by Germany arising out of our Morocco Agreement, public feeling in England would be so strong that no British Government could remain neutral. I urged upon Monsieur Cambon that this, which I had reason to know had been correctly reported at Berlin, had produced there the moral effect which Monsieur Cambon had urged upon me as being one of the great securities of peace and the main reason for a formal engagement between England and France with regard to armed co-operation.

In the third place, I pointed out to Monsieur Cambon that at present French policy in Morocco, within the four corners of the

Declaration exchanged between us, was absolutely free, that we did not question it, that we suggested no concessions and no alterations in it, that we left France a free hand and gave unreservedly our diplomatic support on which she could count; but that, should our promise extend beyond diplomatic support, and should we make an engagement which might involve us in a war, I was sure my colleagues would say that we must from that time be consulted with regard to French policy in Morocco, and, if need be, be free to press upon the French Governments concessions or alterations of their policy which might seem to us desirable to avoid a war.

I asked Monsieur Cambon to weigh these considerations in his mind, and to consider whether the present situation as regards ourselves and France was not so satisfactory that it was unnecessary to alter it by a formal declaration as he desired.

Monsieur Cambon said that in Morocco, if the Conference broke up without favourable result, Germany might place herself behind the Sultan and acquire more and more influence, that trouble might be stirred up on the Algerian frontier, that France might be obliged to take measures to deal with it as she had done before, and that Germany might announce to France, as she had already once done, that an aggression on Morocco would be an attack upon her, and would be replied to accordingly. In such an event war might arise so suddenly that the need for action would be a question not of days, but of minutes, and that, if it was necessary for the British Government to consult, and to wait for manifestations of English public opinion, it might be too late to be of use. He eventually repeated his request for some form of assurance which might be given in conversation. I said that an assurance of that kind could be nothing short of a solemn undertaking. It was one which I could not give without submitting it to the Cabinet and getting their authority, and that were I to submit the question to the Cabinet I was sure that they would say that this was too serious a matter to be dealt with by a verbal engagement but must be put in writing. As far as their good disposition towards France was concerned, I should have no hesitation in submitting such a question to the present Cabinet. Some of those in the Cabinet who were most attached to peace were those also who were the best friends of France; but, though I had no doubt about the good disposition of the Cabinet, I did think there would be difficulties in putting such an undertaking in writing. It could not be given unconditionally, and it would be difficult to describe the conditions. It amounted, in fact, to this; that, if any change was made, it must be to change the "Entente" into a defensive alliance. That was a great and formal change, and I again submitted to Monsieur Cambon as to whether the force of circumstances bringing England and France together was not stronger than any assurance in words which could be given at this moment. I said that it might be that the pressure of circumstances—the activity of Germany, for instance—might eventually transform the "Entente" into a defensive alliance between ourselves and France, but I did not think that the pressure of circumstances was so great as to demonstrate the necessity of such a change yet. I told him also that, should such a defensive alliance be formed, it was too serious a matter to be kept secret from Parliament. The Government could conclude it without the assent of Parliament, but it would have to be published afterwards. No British Government could commit the country to such a serious thing and keep the engagement secret.

Monsieur Cambon, in summing up what I had said, dwelt upon the fact that I had expressed my personal opinion that, in the event of an attack by Germany upon France, no British Government could remain neutral. I said that I had used this expression to Count Metternich first, and not to him, because, supposing it appeared that I had overestimated the strength of feeling of my countrymen, there could be no disappointment in Germany; but I could not express so decidedly my personal opinion to France, because a personal opinion was not a thing upon which, in so serious a matter, a policy could be founded. In speaking to him, therefore, I must keep well within the mark. Much would depend as to the manner in which the war broke out between Germany and France. I did not think people in England would be prepared to fight in order to put France in possession of Morocco. They would say that France should wait for opportunities and be content to take time, and that it was unreasonable to hurry matters to the point of war. But if, on the other hand, it appeared that the war was forced upon France by Germany to break up the Anglo-French "Entente," public opinion would undoubtedly be very strong on the side of France. At the same time, Monsieur Cambon must remember that England at the present moment would be most reluctant to find herself engaged in a great war, and I hesitated to express a decided opinion as to whether the strong feeling of the Press and of public opinion on the side of France would be strong enough to overcome the great reluctance which existed amongst us now to find ourselves involved in war. I asked Monsieur Cambon, however, to bear in mind that, if the French Government desired it, it would be possible at any time to re-open the conversation. Events might change, but, as things were at present, I did not think it was necessary to press the question of a defensive alliance.

Monsieur Cambon said the question was very grave and serious, because the German Emperor had given the French Government to understand that they could not rely upon us, and it was very important to them to feel that they could.—I am, with great truth and respect, sir, Your Excellency's most obedient, humble servant,

E. GREY.

It seems to me now, as it did then, that the line taken in this conversation was the only one that it was possible for a British Minister to take at that time. No one could then have pledged this country in advance to go to war on behalf of France; on the other hand, to say that under no circumstances should we do so would have been untrue and therefore wantonly impolitic. Whether the line taken might have been better expressed or the situation more skilfully handled, is a subsidiary question that may be left to others to judge. I was not confident about that. My own feeling about it at the time is expressed in a letter that I wrote to my wife the next day. Here is the extract that refers to this conversation: "I had tremendously difficult talk and work yesterday, and very important. I do not know that I did well, but I did honestly." It has been necessary to dwell on this conversation at length, because it defines the position that was maintained up to the very outbreak of war. From time to time the same question was raised, but never did we go a hair's-breadth beyond the position taken in the conversation with M. Cambon on January 31, 1906. In April 1914, at the request of the French, it was agreed to let conversations take place between British and Russian naval authorities, as will be told later on, but it was on the same explicit understanding (recorded by that time in writing in letters exchanged between the French Ambassador and myself in 1912) that no obligation was involved.

The record of the following conversation with the German Ambassador shows what was said to him at this critical time. It contains a statement of what I believed to be the state of British feeling at this period. In this it agrees with what was said to the French Ambassador as to the prospect of our siding with France in the event of war:

*Sir Edward Grey to Sir Frank Lascelles*
FOREIGN OFFICE,
*January* 9, 1906.

SIR,—I told the German Ambassador on the 3rd instant that, since we last had a conversation on the subject, I had been giving further attention to the question of Morocco, and that I felt uneasy as to the situation. I had noticed that a little time ago Prince Bülow had described the question as *très mauvaise*. I had also heard that Lord Lansdowne had said to Count Metternich that, in the event of war between Germany and France, public feeling in England would be such that, in his opinion, it would be impossible for England to remain neutral. Count Metternich said that Lord Lansdowne said that it would be so in the event of an unprovoked attack by Germany on France, and that of course the question of what was unprovoked was one of interpretation.

I said that we did not intend to make trouble at the Morocco Conference. We wanted to avoid trouble between Germany and France, because I really thought that, if there was trouble, we should be involved in it. Public feeling here would be exceedingly strong, not from hostility to Germany, but rather because it had been a great relief and satisfaction to the English public to find themselves on good terms with France, and if France got into difficulties arising out of the very document which had been the foundation of the good feeling

*Photograph by Lafayette, Ltd.*

M. PAUL CAMBON
French Ambassador in London, 1898-1921

between us and France, sympathy with the French would be exceedingly strong.

Count Metternich restated again emphatically the German point of view, which was that we and the French had no right to dispose of the interests of a third party in Morocco, however we might deal with our own. I said that we had undertaken distinct engagements to give diplomatic support to France for the purposes of the Agreement—the engagements which were published in Article IX. Count Metternich observed that all we had promised was diplomatic support, and that what Germany resented was that public opinion in England spoke as if armed support had been promised. I said that I could only speak on such a matter as a private individual, my opinion being worth no more than that of Lord Lansdowne speaking in the same way, but the opinion was the same. It was not a question of the policy of the Government; what made a nation most likely to take part in war was not policy or interest, but sentiment, and, if the circumstances arose, public feeling in England would be so strong that it would be impossible to be neutral.

Count Metternich said that Germany felt herself too strong a nation and in too strong a position to be overawed by a combination even of two other Great Powers. I said I understood that, but I was speaking frankly now because such a contingency had not arisen, and therefore it was possible now to talk frankly, whereas at a later date, if things became very difficult, he might be much less willing to listen and I might be unable to speak freely. "But," I said, "if things go well at the Morocco Conference, you may be sure of this, that the Anglo-French 'Entente' will not be used afterwards to prejudice the general interests or the policy of Germany. We desire to see France on good terms with Germany. This is the one thing necessary to complete the comfort of our own friendship with France, and we shall certainly not 'egg on' France at the Conference further than she wishes herself to go." I said this because Count Metternich had told me the other day that he considered that the British Government had been "more French than the French." He said he entirely believed now that we were not more French than the French, and that what I had said represented our real attitude. I said that it really was so, and that our diplomacy was perfectly open and frank. We had gone to a certain point in our engagements with France, from which we could not think of receding. We must keep those engagements, but if the keeping of those engagements proved, at the Conference, to be compatible with Germany's view of her own interests, there would be a sensible amelioration immediately in English public opinion.

We spoke of the tone of the Press both in England and in Germany. Count Metternich complained of a recrudescence of a bad tone in our Press, and its mis-statements. I said that we could not control our Press and that we were not inspiring it, and if I were to say anything in public now to promote a better tone I should at once be told by the Press that this was all very well, but that they must wait till the Morocco Conference took place before they could accept my view. On the other hand, if things went well at the Conference, it would be possible afterwards for anyone in my position to speak in a friendly tone with effect.

We had some conversation on the details of the Conference. Count Metternich said that Germany could not content herself simply with guarantees for her economic interests, because such guarantees would be worthless if France really had the control of affairs in Morocco. German commerce would then suffer, as foreign commerce had suffered in Tunis and in Madagascar. I said that there were guarantees for the open door in Morocco which did not exist in the cases of Tunis and Madagascar. Count Metternich said that that would not be enough. If French influence was supreme in Morocco, concessions and so forth would be entirely in French hands. I said I understood that there was to be a State Bank for Morocco, and that the French had already agreed to German participation in the Bank, and surely that in itself was a certain guarantee.

Beyond general statements that Germany could not allow France a special position in Morocco, Count Metternich gave me no idea of what the proposals of Germany were likely to be or of her attitude at the Conference.—I am, with great truth and respect, sir, Your Excellency's most obedient, humble servant,

E. GREY.

My object in these interviews was to make the Germans understand that the situation was serious, and let the French feel that we were sympathetic, while carefully avoiding anything that might raise expectations in their minds which this country might not fulfil. To do this it was necessary to avoid bluff in the one case and promises in the other.

Campbell-Bannerman was apprehensive lest the military conversation should create an obligation or at least an "honourable understanding." His view is expressed in a letter to Lord Ripon printed in *The Life of Sir Henry Campbell-Bannerman,* vol. ii, p. 257. With more experience I might have shared that apprehension at the time. But the honourable understanding between myself and M. Cambon was very clear, and it was that nothing that passed between French and British military authorities was to entail or imply any obligation whatever on either Government. It was an understanding that was honourably kept, even in the week of anxiety and distress before the outbreak of war in 1914. In that week the most pressing appeals were made to us to promise help, but not once in all the arguments used to me did either the French or Russian Government or their Ambassadors in London say or imply that we were under any obligation of any kind. The appeal was made to our interest; it was never suggested that our honour or good faith were involved.

There has been much criticism of the line we took. It has been urged that we ought to have given France a definite promise of support, if not in 1906, at any rate at some time before the war came; that we ought to have made greater preparation for war. Others contend that even the non-committal preparation that we did make was improper and impolitic. These criticisms will all be discussed in later chapters. My chief concern at this point is to state the facts, to make clear what was the position actually taken by us.

Another criticism, not of policy, but of procedure, must

be dealt with here. Ought there not to have been a Cabinet, with the whole situation put to it, before my conversation with Cambon on January 31? Campbell-Bannerman, writing to me on January 21, when the Election was in progress, had asked: "When would you like to have a Cabinet? Would 30th, 31st, or 1st do? Would you like the answer to the French to be confirmed by a Cabinet before it is given?" I have no recollection, and no record is found, of my answer to this question. My answer now would be that I ought to have asked for a Cabinet; in after-years, and with more experience, I think there should have been a Cabinet, and I can only say by surmise now why there was not. The answer to be given to Cambon was to commit us to no obligation beyond the diplomatic support to which the Anglo-French Agreement publicly committed us. The earliest date suggested was January 30; probably no earlier date was possible, as the declaration of my poll on January 25 was by no means the last of the country constituencies. The French had been kept waiting long enough for a reply. It must be noted too that neither Campbell-Bannerman nor Ripon, the two men with most experience of Cabinets, suggested, after they had the full record of conversation with Cambon before them, that a Cabinet should be held. The rest of us, with the exception of Asquith, had never been in a Cabinet before. That Campbell-Bannerman and Ripon considered the record of the conversation with Cambon is evident from the letter of the former to Ripon, dated February 2, already referred to. The question whether the matter should have been put before the Cabinet *after* the answer had been given will be dealt with later in relating the discussion that did take place at the Cabinet in 1912, when the matter of military conversations was before it.

What was the effect of the answer on the French? I had been very anxious as to that, when giving it, but as will be explained presently, I was summoned home on February 1 and did not see Cambon again for some time. Campbell-Bannerman saw my private secretary, then Louis Mallet, in my absence, and in the same letter of February 2 to Ripon writes: "The Secretary says that Cambon appears satisfied." I recollect very distinctly the impression that Cambon's manner gave me of his personal opinion in the conversation both of January 10 and January 31. It was that he himself knew that we could not give the promise for which he was instructed to ask; that he had prepared the French Government for a negative answer, but that they had insisted on his putting the question; that he himself considered that the utmost to be expected was that we should agree to the continuance of the naval and military conversations that had been going on, when Lord Lansdowne was at the Foreign Office, with the difference that the military conversations should be direct between the two Staffs, as the naval conversations already were with Sir John Fisher, instead of being carried on through an intermediary. Probably, therefore, Cambon was satisfied. That the French Government was satisfied is not so probable; but more was impossible, and no doubt their Ambassador told them so. The prospects of the Algeciras Conference became less menacing, and the request for more than diplomatic support was not pressed again for some time.

During this critical period a change took place in the Foreign Office. Lord Sanderson, who had been Permanent Under-Secretary for several years, retired, and was succeeded by Sir Charles Hardinge, British Ambassador at St. Petersburg. Sanderson had become Under-Secretary while I was at the Foreign Office from 1892 to 1895. He welcomed me back in 1905 with a kindness that had a touch of the paternal. Patronizing he never was—he was too modest a man to patronize anyone; but his long experience and great knowledge gave his opinion weight. He was devoted to the work of the Foreign Office, and lived for it and in it; he was not prompt to initiate policy, but he was wise in counsel and in advice, and indefatigable in carrying it out, an admirable draftsman of an important despatch, and an altogether most valuable public servant.

At one of the important conversations with Cambon—I suppose the first one, that of January 10—I had asked Sanderson to be present to help me out, if need were, with French. He and I sat side by side on the leather sofa in the room of the Secretary of State: Cambon in an arm-chair opposite to us. The recollection of the whole scene is vivid to me. Cambon proceeded to develop the views of his Government and to put the question asking for a promise of armed help in the event of German aggression. Sanderson felt all the awkwardness of the situation; he knew the unsettling consequences of not answering the question favourably; he knew that it was impossible for me to answer it; one hand was resting on his knee, and, as Cambon pressed the French view, the hand kept uneasily and restlessly beating up and down upon the knee, a movement of which Sanderson no doubt was quite unconscious, but which was eloquent of the entanglement of the moment.

My inability to speak French was happily no drawback in conversation with Cambon. I could read French easily, but had no practice, and therefore no power of expressing myself in it. Cambon's position respecting English was exactly the same. He understood, but could not speak it. He spoke his own language so distinctly and with such clear pronunciation that every word could be visualized when listening to him. To listen to him was like reading French. Each of us, therefore, spoke his own language, and each understood perfectly. To make sure that we did understand we each exchanged the record that we had made separately and afterwards of one of these early conversations. The comparison of our records left no doubt that each of us had followed every word spoken. From that time we trusted each other completely, and it was never again necessary to compare records or to have a third party in the room. All the other Ambassadors of the Great Powers spoke English, and spoke it well; so that the drawback of my deficiency in French was less than I had feared it would be.

In reviewing the French anxiety for military arrangements between the British and French Staffs, and our own consent to this, it must be borne in mind that Germany was not inactive on her side. Before my conversations with Cambon there were reports of German activity, and on January 31, the same day as the important conversation with Cambon, I had a conversation with Count Metternich, reported to Lascelles, our Ambassador at Berlin, as follows:

*Sir Edward Grey to Sir F. Lascelles*
FOREIGN OFFICE,
*January* 31, 1906.

SIR,—The German Ambassador spoke to me a week ago about an interview with Sir Frederick Maurice which had been published in the French papers. I told His Excellency to-day that I had, in consequence of his reference to it, read the interview and very much disapproved of it, but no doubt he had now got the explanation which had been published in *The Times*. I said it had occurred to me that some of the information which constantly reached me here in connection with the German Army, their unusual purchases of material for war, and so forth, might account for the way in which Sir Frederick Maurice and others discussed the eventuality of war; but I said that I regarded all information of this kind as indicating on the part of Germany not preparations for war, but precautions, which, in view of the state of feeling which existed six months ago, it was quite natural that Germany should take, and which were not the least inconsistent with the pacific intentions which Count Metternich had assured me were hers. "Preparations," I used in the sense of an intention to attack; "precautions," on the other hand, indicated only the intention to defend.

Count Metternich said that France also, according to the statements which Sir Charles Dilke and others had made, had been strengthening her position very much. I said I had no doubt it was true, and that also, in view of the state of feeling which had existed a few months ago, was a perfectly natural precaution for her to take; but I could assure him as long as I remained at the Foreign Office, or indeed as long as the present Government remained in office, whatever we countenanced would be purely precautions in the sense in which I had used the word, and not aggressive preparations.—I am, etc.

EDWARD GREY.

This conversation is worth a little reflection. The distinction between preparations made with the intention of going to war and precautions against attack is a true distinction, clear and definite in the mind of those who build up armaments. But it is a distinction that is not obvious or certain to others. Bismarck is reported to have said, in his years of retirement, that he *made* three wars—the wars being, of course, those against Denmark in 1862, Austria in 1866, and France in 1870. The world knows, from the revelations about the Ems despatch, that the war with France was intended by the German militarists; the German armaments were then a preparation for making war with France, and not simply a precaution against attack by France. Ever since the Bismarckian revelations other countries have been entitled to regard German armaments with special apprehension. It would also follow that Germany would be specially prone to regard the intention of other countries in perfecting armaments as suspect, for we are all disposed to attribute to others motives and views that we have entertained ourselves. Each Government, therefore, while resenting any suggestion that its own measures are anything more than precaution for defence, regards similar measures of another Government as preparation to attack.

The moral is obvious: it is that great armaments lead inevitably to war. If there are armaments on one side there must be armaments on other sides. While one nation arms, other nations cannot tempt it to aggression by remaining defenceless. Armaments must have equipment; armies cannot be of use without strategic railways. Each measure taken by one nation is noted and leads to counter-measures by others.

The increase of armaments, that is intended in each nation to produce consciousness of strength, and a sense of security, does not produce these effects. On the contrary, it produces a consciousness of the strength of other nations and a sense of fear. Fear begets suspicion and distrust and evil imaginings of all sorts, till each Government feels it would be criminal and a betrayal of its own country not to take every precaution, while every Government regards every precaution of every other Government as evidence of hostile intent. At the date of the conversation with Metternich this reflection upon the situation would have seemed to me a counsel of despair, an unwarranted and culpable pessimism, calculated to precipitate a catastrophe that was not inevitable.

I shall suggest and examine, later on, what more effort could have been made by us to avert war in 1914; I shall explain how it seemed at the time, and still seems true to me, that the military power in Germany chose the time and precipitated the war; and that, had there been a real will for peace in Germany, there would have been no great European War arising out of the Austro-Serbian dispute. But, though all this be true, it is not in my opinion the real and final account of the origin of the Great War. The enormous growth of armaments in Europe, the sense of insecurity and fear caused by them —it was these that made war inevitable. This, it seems to me, is the truest reading of history, and the lesson that the present should be learning from the past in the interest of future peace, the warning to be handed on to those who come after us.

An illustration of the effect of armaments and precautions on each side of a frontier is to be found in an outburst of the German Emperor to Captain Allenby on January 16, 1906. Here is an extract from Captain Allenby's report of the conversation, giving the words used by the Emperor:—

"Here France has spent 200,000,000 francs in the last six months in putting her frontier in order, replenishing her ammunition, and repairing the fortresses in preparation for the anticipated incursion of my troops, while I have not moved a single ammunition-wagon."

It was in the preceding months in 1905 that France had consented, under German pressure, to the humiliation of dismissing M. Delcassé. She had felt compelled to consent because the German armaments were so much more ready for war than her own. The German pressure left her no option but to bring her own forces and equipment up to date. Yet the effect of her doing so on the mind of the Emperor in 1906 is as obvious and unfavourable as the effect of the German armaments had been on the French mind.

Though it anticipates my narrative, let me conclude the story of the military conversations by briefly relating what took place in subsequent years.

The Algeciras Conference crisis passed; the fact of the military conversations was not at that time made known to the Cabinet generally, but must subsequently have become known to those Ministers who attended the Committee of Imperial Defence. Nothing more respecting it appears in my papers till 1911. In January of that year there seems to have been a Cabinet Committee on Foreign Affairs. It consisted of Asquith, Morley, Lloyd George, Crewe, Haldane, and myself, but I have no recollection of whether this matter of the military conversations came before it.

On April 6, 1911, however, I directed attention to the subject in the following letter to Asquith. The despatch from Bertie to which the letter refers should be in the official archives of the Foreign Office, but search there has not been able to identify it. The letter is taken from a copy found in my private papers.

*April* 16, 1911.

MY DEAR ASQUITH,—Please look at Bertie's despatch of April 13. I have marked it for you, Morley, or Haldane, and I would suggest that, as soon as Haldane returns, that you and Morley should have a talk with him.

Early in 1906 the French said to us, "Will you help us if there is war with Germany?"

We said, "We can't promise, our hands must be free."

The French then urged that the military authorities should be allowed to exchange views, ours to say what they could do, the French to say how they would like it done, if we did side with France. Otherwise, as the French urged, even if we decided to support France, on the outbreak of war we shouldn't be able to do it effectively. We agreed to this. Up to this point C.-B., R. B. H., and I were cognizant of what took place—the rest of you were scattered in the Election.

The military experts then conversed. What they settled I never knew—the position being that the Government was quite free, but that the military people knew what to do, if the word was given.

Unless French war plans have changed, there should be no need of anything further, but it is clear we are going to be asked something.

Yours sincerely,

E. G.

In the summer of the same year came the Agadir Crisis. There was apprehension lest it should lead to war between France and Germany; there was anxiety in France to know whether, in that event, Britain would give France earnest support. The situation was precisely the same as at the time of the Algeciras Conference; we could give no pledge. But the military conversations [1] must naturally have been active, and in September Asquith wrote to me as follows:

ARCHERFIELD,
*September* 5, 1911.

MY DEAR GREY,—Conversations such as that between Gen. Joffre and Col. Fairholme seem to me rather dangerous; especially the part which refers to possible British assistance. The French ought not to be encouraged, in present circumstances, to make their plans on any assumptions of this kind.          Yours always,

H. H. A.

To this I replied:

[1] These conversations referred to the question whether the Germans would come through Belgium, and to the co-operation of the British Expeditionary Force.

FOREIGN OFFICE,
*September* 8, 1911.

MY DEAR ASQUITH,—It would create consternation if we forbade our military experts to converse with the French. No doubt these conversations and our speeches have given an expectation of support. I do not see how that can be helped.

The news to-day is that the Germans are proceeding leisurely with the negotiations, and are shifting the ground from Congo to economic concessions in Morocco. Cambon has just been to see me, and on the whole thinks well of the prospect.

To me it looks as if the negotiations were going to enter upon exceedingly tedious but not dangerous ground.

Yours sincerely,
E. GREY.

It will be observed that these letters relate, not to a *general* expectation on the part of France that military support would be forthcoming, but to an expectation concerned only with the Agadir Crisis, and founded partly on the speeches we had made in public with reference to that crisis.

The Agadir affair had thus brought the military conversations into prominence. They must have been familiar to several members of the Cabinet in discussion at the Imperial Committee of Defence, and in 1912 the fact of their taking place became known to other members of the Cabinet. Those Ministers who had not been directly informed of them were entitled to know exactly how we stood with the French. There was no reluctance to have the whole matter discussed at the Cabinet. The only difficulty arose from the thing having gone on so long without the Cabinet generally being informed. Ministers who now heard of these military conversations for the first time suspected that there was something to conceal. If the conversations really did not commit the country, as I stated, why should the knowledge of them have been withheld? There was a demand that the fact of the military conversations being non-committal should be put into writing. I had the impression that some Ministers, who had not been members of the Committee of Defence, expected some demur to this, and were suspiciously surprised at the immediate assent to the proposal given by myself and Asquith. I had made it so plain to Cambon that the Government must remain absolutely free and uncommitted, that I anticipated no difficulty whatever in getting a satisfactory exchange of notes with him on behalf of ourselves and the French Government. I knew he understood and accepted the position, and would make no difficulty; and, if there had been any doubt raised, I was prepared to contend that the military conversations must stop and not be resumed till the condition of them was made clear. I therefore agreed, readily and at once, to the proposal that this condition should be put in writing.

We proceeded to draft the letter in the Cabinet, and again I thought I was conscious of a little surprise that words unqualified and explicit were agreed to. The letter, as approved by the Cabinet, was signed and given by me to Cambon, and I received one in similar terms from him in exchange. From that time onwards every Minister knew how we stood, and the letters became familiar to the public in 1914, but they may be repeated here:

*Sir Edward Grey to M. Cambon, French Ambassador in London*

FOREIGN OFFICE,
*November* 22, 1912.

MY DEAR AMBASSADOR,—From time to time in recent years the French and British naval and military experts have consulted together.

It has always been understood that such consultation does not restrict the freedom of either Government to decide at any future time whether or not to assist the other by armed force. We have agreed that consultation between experts is not, and ought not to be, regarded as an engagement that commits either Government to action in a contingency that has not arisen and may never arise. The disposition, for instance, of the French and British fleets respectively at the present moment is not based upon an engagement to co-operate in war.

You have, however, pointed out that if either Government had grave reason to expect an unprovoked attack by a third Power it might become essential to know whether it could in that event, depend upon the armed assistance of the other.

I agree that, if either Government had grave reason to expect an unprovoked attack by a third Power, or something that threatened the general peace, it should immediately discuss with the other whether both Governments should act together to prevent aggression and to preserve peace, and, if so, what measures they would be prepared to take in common. If these measures involved action, the plans of the general staffs would at once be taken into consideration, and the Governments would then decide what effect should be given to them.

Yours, etc.,

E. GREY.

*M. Cambon to Sir Edward Grey*
*(Translation)*
FRENCH EMBASSY, LONDON,
*November* 23, 1912.

DEAR SIR EDWARD,—You reminded me in your letter of yesterday, November 22, that during the last few years the military and naval authorities of France and Great Britain had consulted with each other from time to time; that it had always been understood that these consultations should not restrict the liberty of either Government to decide in the future whether they should lend each other the support of their armed forces; that, on either side, these consultations between experts were not, and should not be, considered as engagements binding our Governments to take action in certain eventualities; that, however, I had remarked to you that, if one or other of the two Governments had grave reason to fear an unprovoked attack on the part of a third Power, it would become essential to know whether it could count on the armed support of the other.

Your letter answers that point, and I am authorized to state that, in the event of one of our two Governments having grave reason to fear either an act of aggression from a third Power, or some event threatening the general peace, that Government would immediately examine with the other the question whether both Governments should act together in order to prevent the act of aggression or preserve peace. If so, the two Governments would deliberate as to the measures which they would be prepared to take in common; if those measures involved action, the two Governments would take into immediate consideration the plans of their General Staffs and would then decide as to the effect to be given to those plans.

Yours, etc.,<br>PAUL CAMBON.

So far as I remember, there was no other matter of importance in foreign affairs that was not within the cognizance of the Cabinet.

I have always regretted, however, that the military conversations were not brought before the Cabinet at once: this would have avoided unnecessary suspicion. But it has also been a great satisfaction to me that they did come before the Cabinet some two years before we were called upon to face the outbreak of war. The Cabinet were wise in having the understanding put into writing. Cambon and the French Government, with their own record of diplomatic conversations before them, would never have disputed the point; but to have it in writing and signed on both sides made it quite clear for public opinion in Britain and in the outside world, when the crisis came in 1914.

# CHAPTER VII

## (1906)

### THE ATMOSPHERE OF SUSPICION

Death of Lady Grey—The Algeciras Conference—British Diplomatic Obligations—Mistrust in France—The Testing Case of Casablanca —German Operations in Paris—And at St. Petersburg—Reassuring France—The Strengthening of the Entente—A Letter to Campbell-Bannerman—The German Place in the Sun.

THOUGH this narrative is in form autobiographical, it will in substance be confined to what is directly or indirectly relevant to politics, and more especially to foreign policy. Much that would be proper or even essential to autobiography is not touched upon or mentioned at all. I come now to a break in my life too intimate even for autobiography, and yet with such effect on my public work that it must have a place here.

On the afternoon of Thursday, February 1, the day after the critical conversation with Cambon, a telegram was brought to me while I was at the Committee of Imperial Defence; it told that my wife had been thrown from a carriage while driving near Fallodon and was lying unconscious in the village schoolmaster's cottage, close to the place of the accident. I got there that night; she never recovered consciousness, and died in the early hours of Sunday, February 4.

It is not possible, in reviewing my work afterwards, to look back and say, "Here, if she had lived, I should have taken another decision," or "There I should have thought or spoken differently." But the effect on my work, though it cannot be defined and weighed, must needs have been very great.

For twenty years I had had the upholding support, inestimable in its value especially to a man in public life, of constant companionship at home with one to whom nothing small or mean was tolerable. I now lived alone; this, in itself, was a change so great that, though it was in private life, it was bound to affect character and public work. To this must be added a further reflection.

Through all our married life I had been in the habit of discussing public affairs and sharing all thoughts with my wife; and she had been interested in discussing these with me. Her interests and outlook on life were wide, and her opinion on what came before her and on all that we talked of was always fresh and independent, sometimes so original as to penetrate to new aspects and throw new light on the subject; never was it commonplace or second-hand, never the outcome of conventional or party or class thought. All this was now withdrawn from me. We had acquired knowledge and shared thought together, and developed tastes and pursuits in common. For some time, to the one left alone, the past seemed more real than the present. Thought was arrested and work was crippled. The letter already quoted, written to her about my conversation with Cambon, reached Fallodon too late to be read by her. If she had lived, the substance of it would have been discussed between us.

I wrote to Campbell-Bannerman saying I was very much shaken, and suggesting that I should resign. He encouraged me to go on, and after a week the Foreign Office work was sent to me at Fallodon. The mechanism of the brain began to digest work as that of the body digests food; that is how life continues in such an ordeal for a time, but personality seems stunned and work is done mechanically. It does not, however, appear, nor do I remember, that any important decision was taken or required in the interval before I returned to London at the opening of Parliament and again took my place at the Foreign Office and in the Cabinet.

In reviewing the transactions that preceded the Algeciras Conference, I have already given some account of the apprehensions aroused, and of the precautions taken. The apprehension of a man so versed in great public affairs as Lord Ripon are expressed in a letter to Lord Fitzmaurice quoted in the *Life of Lord Ripon,* pages 292-3. The following extract with reference to the coming Conference gives one aspect of it that was present to our minds: "That a European War should come out of the matter seems almost impossible, but when one has to deal with a potentate like the German Emperor one can feel no real security. One of his principal objects, I imagine, is to break down the Entente Cordiale, and separate us from France, and I have some fear that he may succeed in doing that."

Lord Ripon goes on to express the opinion that he would decline to go further than the full diplomatic support to which we were publicly engaged, and he foresees that if the Conference broke down and serious trouble arose the French people would be disappointed with our attitude.

My own mind was preoccupied by the first stage of the Conference; whether more than diplomatic support would be required, and if so whether we should give it, was a further hypothetical stage that we had not yet reached, and with which it was useless to concern myself further at the moment. No pledge whatever of armed support could, in my opinion, be given; the General Staff was not in a position to be ready to give it; but Parliament and public opinion alone could decide, when the time came, whether it should be given. About this there was nothing more to be done or thought yet.

But the performance of our obligation to give diplomatic support to France was not hypothetical but actual. The moment was at hand when that obligation must be fulfilled. If it were not fufilled, then the Entente with France would disappear; all that had been gained by the Anglo-French Agreement would be lost. We should be back where we had been in 1892-5, constantly on the brink of war with France or Russia or both, and dependent for our diplomatic position in the world on German good-will. My recollection of the discomforts and dangers of that position, when I was inside the Foreign Office in those years, was vivid and disagreeable; the relief felt at the conclusion of the Anglo-French Agreement was very present to my mind. I was determined not to slip back into the old quaking bog, but to keep on what seemed then the sounder and more wholesome ground. There was no thought, in this, of using our better relations with France or with Russia against Germany; it was hoped that relations with Germany would improve. Indeed, the experience of present years led some minds in the Foreign Office to consider that our relations with Germany would now be better than they had been, when German diplomacy was thriving, or at any rate looking with satisfaction, on the quarrels of Britain with France and Russia, and exploiting the situation created thereby. From 1886 up to the making of the Anglo-French Agreement in 1904 we had been through a very disagreeable experience; our diplomatic position had been one of increasing weakness and discomfort, and we were determined not to revert to that position again. So it was that attacks upon the Entente, as the Anglo-French Agreement had now come to be called, tended to confirm rather than to weaken it. It was a matter of interest to preserve it as well as a point of honour to act up to the diplomatic obligations contained in it.

I was not, however, immediately alive to the delicate nature of the situation; I did not realize the efforts that might be made to induce France to suppose that we should not act up to our obligations, nor how sensitive the French might be on this point and how easily confidence might be shaken. I was soon to be enlightened as to the difficulty of avoiding distrust in France. In diplomacy confidence has very shallow roots, and the Entente with France was still young and untried. The critical moment came very suddenly.

The French contention at the Conference was that the Moroccan ports should be policed with a force under Franco-Spanish auspices; the Germans used Austria to put forward a proposal that one port, that of Casablanca, should be an exception to this arrangement. France saw in this proposal a project for injecting other potential influences than that of France and Spain into Morocco: she assumed that Casablanca would become a centre of German political influence—a German port. If this was not the plan, why should Germany be so insistent in making Casablanca an exception to what was good enough for the other Moroccan ports?

The French considered the matter vital, and were firm in resistance; the German delegate at Algeciras was equally firm in insistence. Our diplomatic support was pledged to France, and was being given. At this crucial moment, when the tension was at the height, there suddenly was circulated a report that we were going to abandon the French point of view. One version was that Nicolson, the British delegate at Algeciras, had told his German colleague there that France ought to give way. At Algeciras, in Paris, in St. Petersburg, everywhere, we were confronted with this report and with belief in it. The thing came with the suddenness of an air-raid, though that simile was not then available. The first bomb fell on me in the form of a telegram from Bertie that reached me one evening in my room at the House of Commons. It was to the effect that M. Etienne, a member of the French Cabinet, had said to him, "So you are going to abandon us."

The assumption that we should throw over our obligation under the Anglo-French Agreement stirred me, and I wrote an indignant telegram to Bertie in reply, saying that we had given support to France throughout the Conference at Algeciras and in every capital of Europe, when requisite, and that we would continue to do so as long as the French Government desired it and would ¬lace reliance on us.

The proportions that the affair attained in Paris will be seen from the following despatch from Bertie.

*Sir F. Bertie to Sir Edward Grey*
(Received March 21)

PARIS,
*March* 17, 1906.

SIR,—By my despatch No. 104, Confidential, of the 11th instant, I had the honour to report to you the conversation which I had had on the previous day with the Minister for Foreign Affairs on the Austrian scheme for the policing of the ports of Morocco.

In the course of my interview with M. Rouvier, he read to me a letter from the French Ambassador in London which represented you to concur in his idea that the compromise to be offered to Germany should be an Inspector-General from one of the minor States for the police of all the ports, including Casablanca, which would be policed, like the other seven ports, by a force under French or Spanish instructors.

From the condition of public opinion in France in regard to the differences with Germany in the Algeciras Conferences, it was obvious that if His Majesty's Government pressed the French Government to give way to the demands of Germany as to Casablanca a very unfortunate impression would be caused in this country.

On the 13th instant I telegraphed to you some extracts from the *Temps* newspaper stated to be the instructions to the French Delegate confirmed by M. Rouvier before quitting office. As to the police, those instructions were stated to be to accept an Inspectorate, provided the police were Franco-Spanish, but on no account to admit that such Inspectorate should become a co-operation, and to refuse categorically to agree that the Inspectors should have the direct command at a port.

On the afternoon of the 14th instant I had the honour to receive your telegram No. 40, stating that, in view of those published instructions, you gathered that the French Government thought it impossible to make the concession as to the Casablanca police required by Germany, and, if so, His Majesty's Government would, of course, support them, that I was to so inform the French Government, and that you would make a communication to that effect to M. Cambon.

I went at once to the Quai d'Orsay and saw M. Louis, the Political Director. He told me that the writer of the article in the *Temps* had access to good information, and that the extracts to which I had drawn his attention gave the general sense but not the text of the instructions to the French delegate. Those instructions had not, he said, been altered in any way since they were communicated to you a few days ago.

The Government of M. Sarrien, which had just been formed, had in the Ministerial declaration made to Parliament that (14th) afternoon, confirmed the general foreign policy of M. Rouvier's Government, but had not yet sufficient time to study the details of it as regarded Morocco, and M. Bourgeois, who had that very day taken over from M. Rouvier the Ministry for Foreign Affairs, would probably require some twenty-four or forty-eight hours' time before coming to a decision as to what further instructions, if any, should be sent to the French delegate at Algeciras. He would be very grateful for the message from you which I had just read, and which would be communicated without loss of time to M. Bourgeois.

At a party at the German Embassy that (14th) evening I met the Minister of War. He told me that matters were going badly at Algeciras, as it appeared that England was not going to continue her support to France.

I replied that if the French Government were resolved not to accept the Austrian proposal about Casablanca His Majesty's Government would continue to support French views in the Conference as heretofore.

M. Étienne observed that he was glad to hear it, for he had been given to understand that such was not the case. To this I answered that, by your direction, I had given such an assurance to the Ministry for Foreign Affairs.

In the middle of the day of the 15th instant M. Crozier, French Minister at Copenhagen, who is an intimate friend of M. Bourgeois, came to see Mr. Lister, whom he knew at Copenhagen. M. Crozier said that he had had a long interview with M. Bourgeois on the 14th instant, and, from what I gathered from the Minister for Foreign Affairs the next evening (15th), he had commissioned M. Crozier to see Mr. Lister. The purport of what M. Crozier said was that several influential and competent members of the French Parliament had, when the Government was being constituted, endeavoured to persuade M. Bourgeois that the policy of England under the Government of His Majesty's present advisers, in view of the change of Government in France, would be to withdraw from any active part in continental politics and to adopt a policy of isolation. They maintained that the advice given to the French Delegate at Algeciras by Sir A. Nicolson as to the Austrian police scheme was a first indication of their intention to withdraw as soon as possible from supporting French policy.

M. Crozier stated that M. Bourgeois, not being acquainted with the details of recent events, was in a very anxious state, and could not make up his mind whether to believe or to discredit the representations which had been made to him. When M. Bourgeois commissioned M. Crozier to make this communication to Mr. Lister he had not received your message of the 14th, for which, as I informed you by telegram

No. 27 of the 15th instant, he requested me, when I met him that evening at the Élysée, to thank you most cordially, and to say that it had arrived at a critical moment, was most opportune, and had been made use of with excellent effect. I suppose, from what M. Clemenceau, the new Minister of the Interior, had said to me, which I am about to relate, that M. Bourgeois had in mind some doubting colleagues. M. Clemenceau, with whom I have been acquainted for some time, had paid me a visit late in the afternoon. He professes Anglophil tendencies, and has in his paper, the *Aurore,* been a strong advocate of a policy of intimate relations between France and England.

M. Clemenceau, who was accompanied by the Under-Secretary of the Ministry of the Interior, said that at the Cabinet Council on the 14th instant doubts had been raised as to the fidelity of England to France. She had been suspected of making some arrangement with Germany behind France's back, and Sir A. Nicolson's advice to the French delegate about Casablanca had been quoted as a proof of it. M. Clemenceau had, he asserted, been the only one at first to combat the supposition. He had said that he was sure that the advice as to Casablanca had been given under a misapprehension. He was glad to find from your message, which had reached M. Bourgeois after the Ministerial Council, that his conviction that England was not going to desert France had been proved to be true.

On the receipt of your telegram of the 16th instant, I called on M. Bourgeois, M. Clemenceau, and M. Étienne. I told them that you had authorized me to say that cordial co-operation with France in all parts of the world is a cardinal point of British policy, and that there had never been any question on the part of His Majesty's Government of discontinuing their support of France in the questions under discussion at Algeciras. That support had been given throughout the Conference and in every capital of Europe where requisite, and the same course would be continued, if the French Government desired it, and would place reliance in His Majesty's Government.

Sir Arthur Nicolson had given advice freely to M. Revoil in the confident expectation that his French colleague would well understand that the British delegate would continue to support him in the Conference; that in the observations made by you in conversation with the French Ambassador you had spoken in the same expectation, and you had no doubt that M. Cambon so understood and reported them.

M. Bourgeois, M. Clemenceau, and M. Étienne said that they were quite reassured.

M. Bourgeois told me, in the strictest confidence, that the Austro-Hungarian Ambassador had called on him on the 15th instant and asked him unofficially, but no doubt under instructions from his Government, sent with the concurrence of the German Government, whether some means might not be devised to get out of the impasse about Casablanca.

M. Bourgeois had, he said, told Count Khevenhuller that France could not accept the Austrian scheme on that point.

The Ambassador had then enquired whether some compromise might not be come to by which Germany would be compensated for a concession in regard to the Casablanca police question by some stipulation in regard to the bank.

M. Bourgeois had, he stated, replied that if the Austro-Hungarian Government would suggest at the Conference a scheme for a compromise the French Government would be happy to consider it, and M. Bourgeois is hopeful that some proposal will be made by the Austro-Hungarian Government which may be found acceptable by the French Government.

I have good reason to know that what alarmed the new French Cabinet was that when M. Revoil telegraphed the opinion of Sir Arthur Nicolson in regard to Casablanca he said that he supposed that it represented the views of His Majesty's Government, and denoted a change of policy on their part. The reports from the French Ambassador in London were also considered as indicating a tendency on the part of His Majesty's Government to regard the Austro-German proposals as being great concessions on the part of the German Government, and as such ought to be accepted by the French Government rather than allow the Conference to close without a settlement.

At the same time reports were being spread in Parliamentary circles here that England was likely to come to some arrangement with Germany, or perhaps had already done so. I know that some members of the new Government were disposed to think that there might be truth in this insinuation, and for the following reason: On April 25 last I had, by direction of the Secretary of State, spoken to M. Delcassé on the subject of a desire attributed to Germany to obtain a port on the coast of Morocco (see my despatch No. 156, Confidential, of April

25), and I had said that if the German Government asked for a port His Majesty's Government would be prepared to join the French Government in offering strong opposition to such a proposal ("Pour s'opposer fortement à une telle proposition"), and then begged that if the question were raised M. Delcassé would give full opportunity to His Majesty's Government to concert with the French Government as to the measures which might be taken to meet it ("les mesures qui pourraient être prises pour aller à l'encontre de cette demande").

The advice given to the French Government that they should in the last resort accept the Austro-German proposal for the police of Casablanca rather than break up the Conference was regarded as inconsistent with the communication to M. Delcassé, which I have quoted, for it is thought here that Casablanca might be converted into a useful port, and in German hands would be a danger to France, and the establishment at that port of a police force under a Swiss Inspector and Swiss instructors would be a step towards its occupation in some form by Germany at the first convenient opportunity, and that it is with such a view that the German Government have persisted in the stipulation that it should not be policed by a force under French or Spanish instructors.

It is unfortunate that Frenchmen of education and position should be found ready to believe imputations against England of bad faith, but the hereditary distrust of our country, which has for so long been a characteristic of the French race, has been ably worked on by persons acting in the interests of Germany in order to create discord between France and England.—I have, etc.,

FRANCIS BERTIE.

There was the same scene at St. Petersburg, and the following letter from Cecil Spring-Rice to the Russian Foreign Minister shows the trouble we had there:

*Mr. Spring-Rice to Count Lamsdorff*
(Personnelle et Confidentielle)
SAINT-PÉTERSBURG,

*le* 4 (17) *Mars,* 1906.

Mᴇ ʟᴇ Cᴏᴍᴛᴇ, Je tiens à faire part à votre Excellence des faits suivants:

L'Ambassadeur d'Allemagne à Londres, en appuyant auprès de Sir

Edward Grey la dernière proposition Allemande au sujet du Maroc, avait dit que même Sir A. Nicolson, en conversation avec son collègue Allemand avait exprimé l'opinion que la France devrait céder. Sir Edward Grey a tout de suit télégraphié cette information à Sir A. Nicolson, qui a répondu: "Je na'ai dit au Délégué Allemand ni directement ni indirectement que la France devrait céder sur quelque point que ce soit des questions encore en discussion."

En me faisant part de la réponse de Sir A. Nicolson, Sir Edward Grey a ajouté textuellement: "Le Gouvernement de Sa Majesté Britannique continuera certainement à appuyer la France à la Conférence du Maroc."

J'espère qu'il n'y a pas besoin d'ajouter que l'Angleterre, comme la Russie, fera tout son possible, dans les limites indiquées pour faciliter une solution.

J'ai cru utile de communiquer à votre Excellence, à titre privé, le télégramme de Sir Edward Grey, en vue des bruits qui seraient en cours ici au sujet de l'attitude de Sir A. Nicolson à la Conférence, qui ressemblent beaucoup à l'assertion ci-dessus mentionnée.

These reports were attributed to German sources. This did not surprise me, and left me cold. The Germans did not fear our Entente with France, or seriously think it a menace to them, but they disliked it: it had suited them that we should be on bad terms with France; it did not suit them that there should be an Entente. It was their game to sow distrust, if they could. A poor game, judged by ideal standards, but one that they were to be expected to play. To be surprised that a foreign Government did not raise its foreign policy to an ideal plane was to shut one's eyes to patent facts and practice; to be indignant about it was to beat the air. The German manœuvres therefore roused in me neither surprise nor indignation. But, if it were the German game to sow distrust between France and ourselves, it was equally clear that our game was to be loyal to each other, and I did resent the levity and ease with which France assumed that we should not play the game. It was diplomatic support only that was in question now, and the very frankness with which we had explained why we could not promise in advance armed support, to which we were not pledged, might have been taken by the French as evidence that we should give the diplomatic support to which we were pledged. How could any good take root in such shifting sands of suspicion and distrust?

However, the crisis passed; the Germans gave way about Casablanca, the Algeciras Conference came to a peaceable end, and the Anglo-French Entente survived all the perils of it. The net result of all the German effort, first in 1905, when Lansdowne, the author of the Entente, was still in office, and then in 1906, when a Liberal Government had succeeded, was to make the Entente stronger. We had been forced to contemplate the contingency that the Entente might have to fight for its life; we had, without making any alliance or new obligation, concerted measures to meet that contingency, if it were suddenly thrust upon us; and diplomatically the French trusted us more, and not less, after the Algeciras Conference than they had done before it.

As one looks about, and sees all the perils that there were, how little belief nations have in each other, how prone they are to disbelieve and to suspect it, it seems almost a miracle that the Entente survived. One false step, one indiscreet or incautious word, one necessary word delayed or unspoken at the critical moment, and the result might have been fatal. I was at any rate more alive to the delicacy of the situation at the end of the Conference than I had been at the beginning.

There was more delicate ground to be passed over before this year ended.

The wind of armed German pressure, though it had swept M. Delcassé out of the Foreign Office in 1905, had in the long run only caused France to draw the cloak of the Entente with Britain more closely about her. The sun of German cordiality was now to try what it could do. The sun shone, however, not on Paris, but on London. Friendly visits from German pressmen and from German burgomasters came, and were all well received. This was well enough, but not without anxiety. There was always the risk that these friendly demonstrations, desirable if made without *arrière pensée,* might be represented and used at Paris to create distrust. My own relations with Count Metternich, the German Ambassador, were frank and cordial, and after the Algeciras Conference was over there was little to cause friction or difficulty in our dealings with the German Government. If the Germans would only let well alone, what was now well would continue and get still better. Unfortunately, the German Government would try to improve the occasion in ways that made it difficult for us. The following despatch to Paris shows how this was done:

*Sir Edward Grey to Sir F. Bertie*
FOREIGN OFFICE,
*July* 9, 1906.

SIR,—The French Minister told me to-day that Prince Radolin had been to see M. Bourgeois, and had said to him that an entente was proceeding between Germany and England. Prince Radolin wished the French Government to know that this *entente* was in no way intended to impair the relations between France and England, and he hoped, therefore, it would not be disagreeable to France. M. Bourgeois had asked whether Prince Radolin had been instructed by the German Government to make this communication, and had been answered in the affirmative.

The French Minister showed me a note of the conversation which M. Bourgeois had sent him, in which it appeared that Prince Radolin had not actually spoken of an *entente,* but only of a *rapprochement.*

M. Bourgeois had replied that, as regards relations between England and Germany, that it was something with which it was not for the French Government to interfere, and that, on the general question of understandings which were intended to make for peace, M. Bourgeois was of course a friend of peace, and favourably disposed to anything which would promote it.

M. Bourgeois had, however, been surprised at receiving a communication of this kind in such a formal way, and had instructed the French Minister to tell me about it.

I said I was equally surprised that such a communication should have been made by the German Ambassador at Paris on the instructions of the German Government. As a matter of fact, there was nothing in the nature of an *entente* between the two countries, nor was there anything out of which an *entente* might be made. At present, there was nothing to discuss between the two Governments, except the trouble on the German South-West African frontier, an insignificant boundary question in some other part of Africa, and the German Concession in Madeira, as to which I had some time ago explained to the German Ambassador why we opposed it. In fact, I regarded the relations between England and Germany as being now normal, and I saw no reason for saying anything about them.

It would, I thought, be inconvenient for France that we should be on bad terms with Germany, just as it would be inconvenient for us that France should be on bad terms with Germany; for if we were called on to take sides, we must take sides with France, as at Algeciras. As long, however, as Germany kept quiet, there was no reason for trouble and things would go on quietly.

The French Minister asked me whether I thought Prince Radolin's communication was connected with the visit of the King to Germany.

I said the King was going to pass through Germany on his way to Marienbad, and, as the German Emperor was a near relation, the King could not go through the Emperor's country every year without seeing him. But I did not think this could have been the reason for Prince Radolin's communication. All I could suggest was that a great deal of attention had been paid to us from Germany of late. We had received visits from German burgomasters, German artists, and, lastly, German editors. Many people had attended meetings at which the visitors had been received, and they made very friendly speeches. But, as Germany seemed to be forcing the pace so much, some things had been said in conversation during the German editors' visit to the effect that, if Germany wished any good to come of her being civil to us, she must show some corresponding civility in Paris. I also called the French Minister's attention to what I had said in Parliament to the effect that our good relations with France must not be impaired, and any developments in our foreign policy must be such as not to prejudice them. I did not meet the German editors when they were here. But it was very likely that things of this kind had been said by others who had met them. These things had probably been reported to the German Embassy here, and thence to Berlin, and Prince Radolin's communication might be an outcome of them. Otherwise, I could throw no light whatever on this communication.

The only thing of which the Germans had complained for some time past had been the tone of the English Press. We had always answered this complaint by pointing out that the German Press was at least as bad. There had lately been a tendency on the part of the Press of both countries to write in a better tone about each other, or to leave each other alone, and that was the only thing that had so far happened in the form of a *rapprochement*.

There was nothing new proceeding between the two Governments.

I think it desirable that you should explain this in conversation to M. Bourgeois, and should assure him that we have said nothing hitherto to him about our relations with Germany because there is nothing to tell, and my statement in Parliament was intended to convey that civilities and hospitality, which are promoted here by independent persons in no way connected with the Government, do not imply any present or future change of policy.—I am, etc.,

EDWARD GREY.

The effect of such a step taken by the German Government at Paris was obvious. My desire was that things should go well in relations with Germany, but, to avoid distrust, it was necessary to keep French Ministers informed so that they might know certainly that nothing was being done by us that meant a change of policy or a double policy. The effect of the German communication at Paris must inevitably be to make the French Government suspect that something was going on behind their backs, in which we were concerned, and which I was keeping from them.

Later in the summer King Edward went to Marienbad, and on his journey very naturally saw the German Emperor. Haldane, our Minister for War, was also on the Continent, and was invited and went to Berlin. On such occasions it was explained to the French that they must not suppose that these friendly visits had any new political significance. We should enter into no engagements that were inconsistent with the Entente, and France must realize that, as long as this condition was observed, it was to her interest that our relations with Germany should be good. One difficult moment there was when it was discovered that the invitation to Haldane was for a date that coincided with the anniversary of the battle of Sedan and would entail his presence at the commemoration of that event. This incidental fact had not been mentioned by the Germans when the invitation was given; when it was discovered, arrangements were made to avoid any appearance of an anti-French character in the visit, and it took place without any of the untoward results that had been apprehended in the Foreign Office. This was not the last of delicate incidents of the kind. One by one, they had to be negotiated and adjusted as they arose. When one looks back on them, they produce a sense of distaste and weariness.

How much and how little I then understood of this whole situation appears in the following letter written to Campbell-Bannerman on January 9:

*Sir Edward Grey to Sir Henry Campbell-Bannerman*

FOREIGN OFFICE,
*January* 9, 1906.

MY DEAR SIR HENRY,—It is unfortunate that the Election clashes with the approach and meeting of the Morocco Conference, for I should like to have been in more frequent communication with you. But this cannot be helped. All that was passed has been sent to you, but I may sum it up as follows:

With the French, matters stand as Lord Lansdowne left them. I have promised diplomatic support in accordance with Article IX, and have let it be known at Madrid and Rome that we shall give this. I have not said a word of anything more, and the French have asked no inconvenient questions.

To the German Ambassador here I have given it as a personal opinion that feeling in England and sympathy for France, if she got into trouble over the document which originated our friendship with her, would be so strong that it would be impossible for any Government to remain neutral. In margin ("Lansdowne, I find, had also said as much").

But on behalf of the Government I have said that we shall not use the Anglo-French Entente against German policy or interests; that though at the Conference we must keep our public engagement to France, we shall not egg on France against Germany; and that if things go smoothly at the Conference it will be possible to use our influence with effect to ameliorate the tone of the Press and public opinion here respecting Germany. Also that we wish to improve relations between France and Germany.

In more than one part of the world I find signs that Germany is feeling after a coaling station or a port. Everywhere we block this. I am not an expert in naval strategy, but I doubt whether it is important to us to prevent Germany getting ports at a distance from her base; and the moment may come when a timely admission that it is not a cardinal object of British policy to prevent her having such a port may have a great pacific effect. It may, for instance, turn out that a port for Germany on the west Atlantic coast of Morocco would solve all the difficulties of the Morocco Conference and be regarded by the French as a means of obtaining the recognition which they want in Morocco without prejudicing their interests in the long run. I cannot yet say that this is likely to be so, but in view of possibilities I should like to know what is the real opinion of the Admiralty or Defence Committee on such a point. The concession of a port to Germany is a card which might any day take a valuable trick in diplomacy, and the S. of S. for Foreign Affairs ought to know whether it is a card which it is not inconsistent with British interests for him to play. Hitherto it has been assumed that all the efforts of British diplomacy must be used to prevent Germany getting a port anywhere.

Indications keep trickling in that Germany is preparing for war in the spring; France is very apprehensive. I do not think there will be war: I believe the steps taken imply precautions, but not intentions. But the War Office ought, it seems to me, to be ready to answer the question, what could they do if we had to take part against Germany, if, for instance, the neutrality of Belgium was violated. Fisher, of course, is prepared to answer the question for the Admiralty at any moment, but that only means driving the German fleet to anchor in Kiel and stay there.

At present I am in no difficulty as to what to say or do, but I am apprehensive of what may happen at the Conference when I may have to ask for a decision at a critical moment.

Yours sincerely,

E. GREY.

In the press of after-events this letter had passed entirely from my mind, till it was found in searching among private papers left at the Foreign Office for documents relating to this period. That the possibility of ceding a port to Germany on the west coast of Morocco should ever have been mentioned is evidence of how little I was aware of the pitfalls and quaking grounds about me; and also of what was real and actual. I was unaware, when writing the letter, that Lord Lansdowne had in the previous year, when the French were giving way temporarily under German pressure, urged them on no account to concede a port in Morocco to Germany. Lansdowne presumably was acting on strong naval opinion. This was before the development of submarine warfare and mines laid by submarines, and I thought the view tenable that ports and other possessions scattered over the world were at the mercy of the Power that had command of the sea. We were that Power, and German ports and colonies abroad were hostages for us to take. In any event, the idea of a port for Germany would not have been mooted till it had first been discussed at the Committee of Imperial Defence, and there it would have been vetoed and died. It would, therefore, never have been mentioned by me to the French; but what I evidently did not realize, when this letter was written, was that to mention it to the French would have been fatal to the Entente. The mere suggestion of yielding to Germany a port in Morocco would have shaken their confidence in our diplomatic support, and that confidence would never have revived.

To discuss anything, however delicate and tentative, with a Prime Minister is natural and proper. There are two persons with whom a Minister ought to be able to toss his thoughts of policy, however tentatively; one is his chief private secretary, and the other is the Prime Minister. If he feels that he cannot safely do that he cannot be comfortable while being served by the one or serving under the other.

I refer to this letter, however, not merely for its bearing on the immediate question of a port in Morocco, but for the general line of policy sketched in it.

Just as the conversation with Cambon of January 31 lays down the lines of our relations with France, so this letter to Campbell-Bannerman explains the parallel lines of our relations to Germay. It will be observed that I told Metternich that, in the event of France getting into trouble because of the Entente, public feeling would be so strong in sympathy for France that the British Government could not remain neutral. I could give this only as a personal opinion; but it was stated again and again, notably in the Agadir Crisis in 1911. It was a warning given in a way that could not be offensive, but was very serious.

The next point to be noted is that the Entente with France was not to be used against German policy or interests. This attitude, too, endured to the end. France was fully aware that no aggression on Germany would receive any countenance from us; in 1911, in the Agadir Crisis, while supporting France diplomatically, as we were bound to do about Morocco, we let it be understood that we regarded with good-will the negotiations on which France entered to give Germany some satisfaction elsewhere.

The third point of interest is the discomfort in my mind of finding us somehow engaged in blocking Germany's projects in other parts of the world. We were bound to oppose her plans, where they were inimical or dangerous to British interests, but was it necessary to assume that everything everywhere that Germany wanted was dangerous to us? On these lines my thoughts continued to run, but in effect there were only two matters of real importance to Germany that it lay with us to facilitate. One was Walfisch Bay, the only possible harbour for German South-West Africa. About this we could do nothing; it belonged to South Africa, and, though it was surrounded by German territory, the Government of South Africa would never dream of parting with it. The other, and chief matter of importance to Germany, was the Bagdad Railway; and about that we did eventually come to an agreement, as will be explained at the proper time.

There was much vague talk in Germany about "a place in the sun," and some equally vague sympathy in England with that aspiration of Germany. But if by a place in the sun tropical Africa was meant, Germany already had her place in South-West Africa, East Africa, and Cameroons and Togoland. A place in the sun was not what Germany wanted. The tropics do not provide an outlet for a white race. What Germany really wanted was a place in a temperate climate and a fertile land, which could be peopled by her white population and be German, part of the German Empire and under the German flag. We had no such place to offer; South Africa, Australia, New Zealand, North and South America, all the temperate lands of the world not populated or over-populated by yellow races, were taken up by and belonged to white races, who were in possession of them. Germans could go there and did go, notably to the United States; but they had to become one with the other white inhabitants and accept the separate Government of those countries, if they wished to share in the possession of them. These were the inexorable facts of the situation, and if the talk about a "place in the sun" was translated into terms of practical application and of fact, it became two things—Walfisch Bay and the Bagdad Railway.

## NOTE TO CHAPTER VII

In 1910, four years after the Algeciras Conference, I had a long talk in England, on various matters of interest, with Theodore Roosevelt. In the course of our talk he introduced the subject of the Algeciras Conference, and told me that he believed his own action had had great if not decisive influence in making Germany give way about the port of Casablanca. What he told me of his communications with the German Emperor supported this view. I do not know what record he kept of those communications, or even whether they still exist, and I shall not therefore say more about them. The fact, however, that Roosevelt believed, and from what he told me had reason to believe, that the part he took influenced a peaceful solution should be on record and is of interest.

# CHAPTER VIII

## (1906)

### AKABA AND DENSHAWAI

The Sultan and the Sinai Peninsula—His Claim to the Gulf of Akaba —Inviting an Ultimatum—Cromer and the Oriental Mind—The Disturbance of "Beech Sunday"—The Situation in Constantinople —Predominance of German Influence and How Obtained—A Cynical Policy—The Denshawai Incident—A Difficult Decision —Lord Cromer's Opinion—Life in London and the Country.

SOME other subjects must be mentioned, though they are not landmarks in the course of British policy, and though they do not directly affect the progress of the main issue.

Early in 1906 the Sultan, Abdul Hamid, demanded that Egyptian troops should be withdrawn from certain places in the Sinai Peninsula, and Turkish troops occupied certain posts in that peninsula. The Turks also demanded that Egyptian troops should be withdrawn from the island of Tiran, the only good anchorage in the Gulf of Akaba.

The question of right to these places depended on long usage, confirmed by a telegram from the Grand Vizier at Constantinople on April 8, 1892. This was understood to give the Khedive the right to administer the Sinai Peninsula in the same manner as his father and grandfather had done before him. The Turkish action was a gratuitous disturbance of this longstanding arrangement.

On the question of substance and importance this extract from a Foreign Office summary gives Lord Cromer's view:

Lord Cromer pointed out the danger underlying the Turkish demands. The construction of a railway down to the bank of the Suez Canal could not but be regarded as a menace to the liberty of Egypt and to freedom of transit through the Canal. The proposed line cutting the Suez Peninsula in half would also have the effect of rendering the Gulf of Akaba more available for torpedo-boats, which would lie on the flank of the route to India and within easy striking distance of that route: the Turkish frontier would also be brought within 100 miles of the Suez Canal and close to the town of Nekl, a place of much strategical importance; and a number of Arab tribes hitherto from time immemorial under the Egyptian Government would be handed over to the Turkish Authorities.

It is not worth while now to explain the geographical details of the Turkish demand to which Lord Cromer referred; the extract given will show that substantial importance attached to them both in the interest of Britain and of Egypt. A Joint Commission for delimiting the frontier was proposed to the Sultan, but he would have none of it.

The Khedive suggested that the telegram of April 8, 1892, should be taken as the basis of settlement, and that the line of frontier should run from Rafeh to a point on the coast three miles west of Fort Akaba.

The reply of the Grand Vizier is described in the following extract from the Foreign Office summary at the time; it was to this effect:

(1) That the Gulf of Akaba and the Sinai Peninsula were outside the territory defined in the Imperial Firman.

(2) That the telegram of April 8, 1892, only referred to the western side of the Sinai Peninsula.

(3) That the interpretation of that telegram was a matter which only concerned the Imperial Government.

And so on. Finally the hope was expressed that no occasion would be afforded for interference.

The summary already quoted continues as follows:

> The form of the Turkish reply was unusual, both on account of the uncompromising tone and the omission of the usual terms of courtesy.
>
> Lord Cromer said that the Khedive did not propose to send any reply. Two points were, he added, clear from this telegram. One was that the Sultan considered himself entirely free to interpret the telegram of April 8, 1892, in whatever manner he wished. The other was that he, at the least, laid claim to the whole of the western shore of the Gulf of Akaba and to a large portion of the Sinai Peninsula. The question, therefore, was not merely whether there should be any minor rectification of frontier, but whether the Turks should be put in a position which would enable them to be a standing menace both to the freedom of the Suez Canal and to the liberties of Egypt.

It was evident that Abdul Hamid wanted an ultimatum; why he had raised the question at all I could not imagine, unless it were from the Turkish passion for reopening questions for the sake of the manœuvring that ensues. Unless Abdul Hamid intended a serious encroachment on Egypt it was not worth his while to trouble the Sinai Peninsula at all; if he did intend serious encroachment, he must have known that we should take it seriously, and that he would have to give way.

I once heard Lord Cromer describe the impossibility of understanding the Turkish oriental mind. I am not sure that I recall quite accurately what he said, but it was to this effect.

If it is important to you to know what an Oriental is going to do you must ask yourself three questions: (1) What would you yourself do under the same conditions? (2) What do you think the wisest man you know would do? (3) What do you think the Oriental will do?

When you have answered these questions you will know three things that the Oriental certainly will not do. Nearer to his intention than that you cannot get.

Why Abdul Hamid should have desired an ultimatum was beyond the reach of speculation, but, as he evidently did desire it, he had to be humoured and an ultimatum was sent. A ship had already been sent to the Gulf of Akaba, and now the Mediterranean Fleet was moved eastwards and preparations made for coercive measures at the expiry of a ten-day ultimatum.

On the tenth day Abdul Hamid gave way, and finally a note was sent to the British Ambassador at Constantinople to say that the Porte did not question the telegram of April 8, 1892; that a Joint Commission would be appointed to fix boundaries so as to secure the maintenance of the *status quo* on the lines of this telegram; and that the boundary should run from Rafeh approximately straight to a point not less than three miles from Akaba.

The danger to Egypt which was revealed in the Great War is complete justification for the firmness which was displayed on this occasion by the British Government.

So the incident ended—a very tedious affair that had dragged on from January to May. There are generally some small points that bring a touch of humour even into negotiations like those with Abdul Hamid.

It has been mentioned that the line of boundary proposed by the British and Egyptian Governments was to run from a place called Rafeh approximately in a straight line to near Akaba. This line would not prejudice or indeed affect Turkish interests, and it was impossible to divine why Abdul Hamid was so intractable about it. One suggestion made to account for his obstinacy was that

he had in his mind confused Rafeh with Jafeh. The
latter name suggests Jaffa. Jaffa was far away from any
boundary that Egypt ever would claim or had dreamt of
claiming. To have mentioned Jaffa in this connexion
would have been a preposterous aggression on Turkey.
I did not credit the suggestion that Abdul Hamid had
really mistaken Rafeh for Jaffa, but the notion that such
a confusion in his mind was possible, and that the whole
trouble that had lasted for months could have been cleared
up at any moment by a conversation over a map, had an
element of comedy. Perhaps, however, Abdul Hamid
did not believe in maps, and would have regarded any
map presented to him as something designed and drawn
to deceive.

Another aspect of the Akaba trouble was peculiar and
personal: I hesitate to describe it lest it should seem too
trivial. It needs a digression that, to begin with, must
seem quite irrelevant. The serious student of foreign
policy had best perhaps pass over it unread.

There are a few days in the first part of May when
the beech-trees in young leaf give an aspect of light and
tender beauty to English country which is well known
but indescribable. The days are very few, the colour of
the leaves soon darkens, their texture becomes stiffer;
beautiful they are still, but "the glory and the dream"
are gone. Unless Whitsuntide is unusually early, Sundays
in the first half of May are the only days on which those
who have business in towns can be sure of a whole day
spent in the country at leisure. The first Sunday in May
was a little too early for the perfection of the beeches
in the country round my Hampshire cottage; the second
Sunday in May was the perfect day. In my calendar it
was known as "Beech Sunday," a day set apart and conse-

crated to enjoyment of the beauty of beech-leaves and to thankfulness for it. It was my habit on that morning, each year, to bicycle to a beech-wood some nine miles from the cottage. There I lunched once every year on that day at the foot of a certain tree. The wood was entirely of beech; the trees standing far apart, the grey boles grew up straight and clear and smooth for some distance above the ground. High overhead the branches touched and made a canopy; the blue sky just visible here and there; the sunshine coming through the tender, light-green leaves; a breeze stirring them now and then, but very gently,—such was the vision of what I had seen and known year by year that was present to me in the Foreign Office in the second week of May. I thought of it, looked forward to it, counted upon it.

The ultimatum had been delivered on May 3, it was to expire on Sunday, May 13. As the second week of May was passing and no answer came from Constantinople, it became evident that Abdul Hamid would not forgo one day of the precious ultimatum. As the hours of Saturday passed, someone in the Foreign Office, probably Eldon Gorst, with special knowledge of Turkish ways, assured me casually and confidently that Abdul Hamid would certainly give way, but that he certainly would not do so till the last day.

When the answer arrived, on the last day, a decision would have to be taken at once as to whether it was satisfactory or not. If the ultimatum expired with no answer or with an unsatisfactory answer received, the Mediterranean Fleet must be instructed to act. I must therefore be on the spot in London on the last day. As this became clear to me I expressed my feelings to one of the high authorities in the Foreign Office; he listened civilly, but,

as was told me years afterwards, expressed outside my
room astonishment that was scornful.

On the morning of Sunday, May 13, Charles Hardinge
and Eldon Gorst came to my house in Queen Anne's
Gate to await the Turkish answer and to consult. About
midday it came; it was completely satisfactory; Hardinge
and Gorst went their ways. I took a train into Surrey
and walked through some good country that I knew and
so to Guildford and back to London to be ready for the
coming week of office and political work on Monday.

I remained, so far as ultimatums to Turkey were concerned, a sadder and a wiser man. This ultimatum had
been necessary, but it was the outcome of a long-drawn-
out dispute, and there had been no need to choose even
a particular week, still less a Sunday, for its last day.
I had now to wait another twelve months to see the great
beech-wood as I knew it in its greatest beauty.

The question has already been asked, "Why did Abdul
Hamid raise this question at all, and why was he so
obstinate about it?" The obvious answer was suggested
at the time: that he acted on German instigation. It seems
improbable to me that this was so. The Algeciras Conference was peaceably over long before our ultimatum
became necessary, and there was no crisis to make the
Germans wish to distract our attention and embarrass us
at that particular moment. They did not seriously propose to support Abdul Hamid in this dispute. If they
instigated him, it was a policy of mischief so idle and
purposeless that I could not credit them with wasting
time upon it. The following letter which I wrote to
Lascelles, our Ambassador at Berlin, gives the line taken
at the time. Nothing occurred later to qualify or change
this view of the Akaba affair.

*Sir Edward Grey to Sir Frank Lascelles*

FOREIGN OFFICE, LONDON,
*May* 1, 1906.

MY DEAR LASCELLES,—I volunteered to Metternich yesterday a statement of how things stood between us and Turkey respecting the Egyptian frontier dispute. I did so on the ground that I did not desire to withhold from him in this matter what I have said to others.

I have done all this as practical proof that, now the Conference is over, we are not working against German interests as such, and do not wish to treat them in a specially frigid or distant way. Whether it has any effect I do not know, but it may be useful to you to know how it was meant.

Metternich complains of my having said that German friendship might be encouraging Turkey: he provoked the remark by a statement that it was the weakness of Russia which was encouraging the Turks. I have told him that my remark was not meant as a reproach about the Egyptian frontier difficulty, of which we were not talking at the time, and that what I did mean was that the vigorous support given by Germany to the Sultan, e.g. as regards Macedonia, might have led him to presume too far.

As a matter of fact, I do not suppose the German Embassy has done anything in the Egyptian frontier question; but Baron Oppenheim has been very thick with Mukhtar, who has stirred up the agitation in Egypt, which has led to an increase of the garrison; and if his influence with Mukhtar has been used to calm him, it has been singularly unsuccessful.

Yours sincerely,

(Signed) E. GREY.

It may be convenient to deal at this point with the diplomatic situation in Turkey. Misgovernment and ill-treatment of Christian minorities in Asia Minor was endemic, outrage and massacre were epidemic; a very brutal outbreak had occurred in 1895 which had shocked Lord Salisbury, and, as we now know from published German documents, had temporarily disgusted the German Emperor. Constantinople was a sort of cockpit of

concessionaires competing for commercial openings, especially those in Asia Minor.   To obtain concessions diplomatic support was necessary; and, for diplomatic support
to be effective, we needed prestige and influence.   Abdul
Hamid was an adept at playing off one Government
against another; influence could be acquired at Constantinople at a price.   The price was friendship to Abdul
Hamid, whatever he might do in Turkey; never to worry
him about Armenian massacres; to protect him in the
Concert of Europe from being worried by other Powers.
No British Government could pay this price.   Lord Salisbury could not have done it, if he would, and he made it
evident, after the horrors of 1895, that he would not, if
he could.   The German Government and the German
Emperor paid the price and got the position that Great
Britain had once held at Constantinople.   German influence, acquired by complacency to Abdul Hamid and
backed by the prestige of German armaments, became
dominant at Constantinople.   British influence declined.
British representations about Armenian massacres made
us hated, but not feared.   Abdul Hamid knew that without European support we could not go beyond diplomatic
worry; for the Fleet could not interfere in Asia Minor,
nor could we act alone in a matter that was of European
and not separate British interest without provoking the
jealousy and counter-measures of other Powers.   Public
opinion in Britain demanded that we should make representations; we did so, to the cost of British material
interests in Turkey.

The irony of it all was that little or no good was done.
We received some diplomatic support from France and
Russia, but always within limits that stopped short of
practical results.   Russia was not willing to push her

championship of Christian Minorities to effective lengths, unless she was thereby to get political results favourable to herself, such as the opening of the Straits to Russian ships of war.  Her championship of Christians in European Turkey in the seventies of the last century had ended in her being deprived of the fruits of victory over Turkey; and it was British policy that had taken the lead in restricting these fruits.  Great Britain no longer supported Turkey, which Lord Salisbury had denounced as "the wrong horse," but was understood to be unwavering in her desire to keep the Straits closed against ships of war.  France had her hands full with her own affairs, and could not afford to provoke friction with dreaded Germany over anything in which French interests were not specially concerned; she had trouble and apprehension enough without that.  We, as an island Power, could and did take a lead in protesting against Abdul Hamid's doings, but we could not expect, and did not receive, whole-hearted co-operation from continental Powers, who feared a European conflagration unless Germany was whole-heartedly with us too; and Germany was Abdul Hamid's friend.

Germany at Constantinople exploited the situation steadily to her own advantage.  We sacrificed our influence and material interests in Turkey; we did indeed keep our hands clean and acquit the national conscience, but to do this without effectively helping the objects of our efforts and our sympathy, the Christian Minorities in Turkey, was a very barren and unsatisfying result.

German policy seems to have been based upon a deliberate belief that moral scruples and altruistic motives do not count in international affairs.  Germany did not believe that they existed in other nations, and she did not

COUNT METTERNICH
German Ambassador in London, 1901-1911

assume them for herself.  The highest morality, for a German Government, was the national interest; this over-rode other considerations, and as such she pursued it at Constantinople.  Her policy was completely successful; ours was deadlock and failure.  Germany pushed her commercial interests in Turkey; the wealth of Asia Minor was passing into her hands; but she gained these advantages by acting on the belief that morals do not count in policy.  It was this mistaken view of human affairs between nations that lost her the war.  The very principles and views that for so many years seemed an unqualified success in her Eastern policy had the seeds of destruction in them.  Surely the conclusion is irresistible that a policy which rules out all moral purpose except national interest has a fatal lack of what is essential to enduring success.

Those who are so disposed may see, in what is written here, evidence of something that moved us to an anti-German policy.  It was not so.  The methods by which Germany pushed her policy in Turkey did indeed seem to us cynical, but her success in getting concessions and making Asia Minor a special field for German enterprise we accepted.  There was plenty of room in the world for both British and German enterprise.  When German trade was good, British trade was good too.  It was the great commercial centres of Great Britain that were most pacific and least anti-German up to the very outbreak of the Great War; and on the eve of that war we had completed an agreement with Germany about the Bagdad Railway that would have facilitated, and not hindered, that enterprise in Asia Minor on which she set such store.

One other matter in this year 1906 must be noticed.  It had no bearing on or relation directly to foreign policy, but it caused storms in the House of Commons and contributed to the feeling of uneasiness about myself in a section of the Liberal Party. This feeling had its origin in my association with what was supposed to be a forward foreign policy, when I was Under-Secretary (1892-5), and had been intensified by differences of opinion about the South African War. Such a feeling, once started, is apt to be increased by incidents that, taken by themselves, would not originate it.

The affair now to be related is an illustration of a certain kind of difficulty in which any British Government may at any time be placed in the course of governing an oriental country, where its rule depends on force and on prestige.

On June 13, 1906, some British officers stationed in Egypt were shooting pigeons at the village of Denshawai in the district of Tantah. They were unexpectedly, and, as it seemed at the time, unaccountably attacked by the inhabitants. The attack was violent and brutal: the officers received more or less severe injuries, and one of them, Captain Bull, was found dead with two severe blows on the head a mile and a half from the scene of the assault.

Arrests were made, and a trial was to take place before a tribunal of the highest competence. There was no reason for the Foreign Office to be concerned or to interfere. Lord Cromer himself reported the matter, and left Egypt for his annual holiday before the trial was concluded.

Suddenly I was confronted at the Foreign Office by the following telegram:

*Mr. Findlay to Sir Edward Grey*
(Received June 27)

ALEXANDRIA,

*Telegraphic.* *June 27*, 1906.

The Special Tribunal has been engaged during the last three days in trying the case of assault on British officers. News has just arrived that judgment was given this morning. The following are the sentences:

Four of the ringleaders are condemned to death; two are condemned to penal servitude for life; one to fifteen years; six to seven years; three to one year and fifty lashes; and five to fifty lashes. The remaining prisoners, to the number of thirty-one, were acquitted. With regard to the prisoners found guilty, the decision of the Court was unanimous. Premeditation and concerted action were clearly established by the evidence, as was also the fact that the blows which he received acted as a contributory cause of the death of Captain Bull. I am informed that any British jury would have found the first six persons guilty of murder. In the case of the four men who are under sentence of death there are no extenuating circumstances; they were held by the Court to be all equally guilty. The Court expressed its opinion that extreme forbearance and self-restraint characterized the behaviour of the officers. It was only after the latter had given up their guns that the chief attack took place. The villagers continued it in cold blood, and showed the greatest brutality. Three of the best-known native advocates defended the accused, and were given a full hearing. As laid down in the decree of 1895, the sentences will be executed immediately. After an exhaustive discussion of the whole case with the Regent, I am fully convinced that the evidence entirely justified the sentence.

In reply to a telegram from the Foreign Office the following further telegram was received:

*Mr. Findlay to Sir Edward Grey*
(Received June 28)

ALEXANDRIA,

*Telegraphic.* *June 28*, 1906.

Following was the composition of the Special Tribunal:

1. Boutros Pasha, Acting Minister of Justice, officiated as President.

2. Mr. Hayter, Acting Judicial Adviser, who was formerly a Judge in the Soudan.

3. Mr. Bond, Vice-President of the Native Court of Appeal, an office practically corresponding to that of Lord Chief Justice, whose capacity and experience are great.

4. Fathi Bey, President of the Cairo Native Tribunal.

5. Colonel Ludlow, officiating Judge Advocate, representing the Army of Occupation. His experience of Courts Martial is considerable, and he is acquainted with Arabic.

It is specially provided by the Decree of 1895 that immediate execution should be given to the sentences passed by the Special Tribunal (see Lord Cromer's telegram No. 190). Dangerous suspense and excitement would be entailed by delay in all cases such as the present, between which and death sentences in England there is no parallel. The Special Tribunal was instituted as a substitute for courts martial. It merely expedites procedure, every possible security being given to the accused. I am not aware that any other Army of Occupation has ever delegated its powers. The capacity of the members of the Court can be attested to both by Lord Cromer (whose address is 20 Mansfield Street) and Sir E. Gorst.

I am advised that no legal power to interfere with the execution of the decision come to by the Court is possessed either by the Egyptian Government or by His Majesty's Agency. As soon as Lord Cromer applied to the Egyptian Government for the convocation of the Court the matter passed out of our hands.

The execution should be carried out at two o'clock this afternoon on the scene of the outrage. Order will be maintained by troops sent for that purpose, and I submit that any interference on the part of His Majesty's Government is earnestly to be deprecated. In the present state of the country, dangerous results might be brought about by such interference. I am convinced that Lord Cromer would concur in my opinion.

You may be perfectly assured that the Court were not inspired either by panic or vindictiveness in passing sentence; that the evidence proved premeditation and concerted action on the part of the condemned men; that the death of Captain Bull was due to their action, and that they were the principal participators in that action.

The sentences were very severe, startlingly so, and were to be executed immediately. There was no time for a

Cabinet, but I consulted Campbell-Bannerman in his room at the House of Commons and we got Asquith to join us. Our decision was that we could not interfere, and the sentences were executed.

They were carried out in public on the spot where the assault had been made.

Full papers were published, and will be found in Egypt No. 3 and No. 4, 1906, presented to Parliament. They leave no doubt that the Tribunal and officials on the spot believed they were acting in accord with justice, and with what order and safety in Egypt required. But the full account of all the circumstances, when published, created a painful impression that the punishment had been excessive. My defence in the House of Commons had been based on the two telegrams quoted above. When the full facts were before me I felt that what had been done was open to question.

Technically there was no right to interfere with the sentences, but in the last resort the British Government had always the power to intervene—a power, nevertheless, which it was most undesirable to exercise, and which could only have been rightly used in extreme emergency.

Ought we to have interfered, or not?

The effect of the execution of the sentences was bad in Egypt. It intensified anti-British feeling. The effect at home was also bad. That is true, but it does not answer the question.

Egypt was in a disturbed state. The effect of overriding the decision of the Tribunal would have been incalculable. It would have spread an impression in Egypt that the officials on the spot were not to be supported from home: disorder might have broken loose, severe measures of protection and repression might have become necessary, with loss of life and many untoward results.

The problem confronts the British Government again and again. If officials on the spot commit in good faith an error of judgment, which is worse—to support them or to throw them over? To uphold the authority on the spot at the cost of making British rule open to reproach, or to override it at the risk of undermining it altogether? No general answer of universal application can be given. Each case must be judged by itself, but those who think the question easy to answer can think so only because they do not understand that there is a problem to be solved.

It is interesting to recall Lord Cromer's view of this affair. He came to see me directly he arrived in England, and had heard of the sentences.

He was greatly disturbed; he realized to the full the bad effect on public opinion. He said that if he had had any notion that such things might happen he would never have left Egypt before the trial was over.

He was very emphatic that it would have been a capital error to overrule the Tribunal when once the sentences had been pronounced, taking very strongly the view that to throw over the authority on the spot would be disastrous, especially in the state of feeling then existing in Egypt. The district of Tantah in particular was a centre of disturbance and crime. British travellers, who go to Egypt and get at the facts, are sometimes astonished at the number of murders in a bad district; and the men concerned in this affray were notoriously bad characters. Rescission or modification of sentences would, in Lord Cromer's view, have led to worse disasters.

Lord Cromer gave his own surmise of what had been at the bottom of the whole affair.

The pigeons belonged to the villagers; it was the custom of British officers to get permission from the Omdeh, the head-man of the village, to shoot the pigeons. For this a sum was paid that made the villagers well content. On these terms shooting had taken place at this very spot before. Lord Cromer's surmise was that the money paid had never reached the owners of the pigeons. They had therefore determined to resist any further shooting and to go for the officers who next attempted it. The Omdeh again gave permission to shoot, and trouble followed. The result, of course, was to put a stop to the practice of pigeon-shooting altogether.

Here it may be convenient, and not out of place, to say something of recreation and home life. Both are sadly curtailed by office. In a normal year, if there be no unusual crisis, Ministers for Foreign Affairs all over Europe get what holiday and change of air they can in the end of the summer. Like many other people, they have to wait till the fresh glory of late spring and early summer is over; then, when the days are getting shorter and the year is beginning to decline, and the air is keen, and birds are in the moult and silent, they retire to the country. At this season, after Parliament adjourned, I used to spend some time at Fallodon. The daily bulk of Foreign Office work was large, but it could be done at home, with occasional journeys to spend two or three days at the Foreign Office to consult and to keep in personal touch with those in charge there. This stay at Fallodon and two or three short visits to friends for shooting were the recreation of the Parliamentary Recess. In October residence in London again became permanent till Christmas, when there was another opportunity of getting to Fallodon. Hitherto recreation in London had consisted of two games a week of real tennis, generally in the M.C.C. Court at Lords. I saw, however, that it would be impossible to keep the fixed times necessary to play and be in practice for the game, and so it was given up entirely.

Week-ends in spring and summer were spent in the Hampshire cottage, where I would fish for some hours when free on Saturdays and at Whitsuntide. In autumn and winter I found a quiet hotel opening on to a heath in the New Forest. There I could have the same private rooms at the end of each week. On Sunday morning I might start between 11 o'clock and midday, walk off into the Forest, eat my pocket-luncheon in some wild part of it, drop into an inn at Beaulieu, Lyndhurst, or Burley for tea, and thence get back to the hotel on the outskirts of Brockenhurst in the evening, in the dusk in early spring, under moon or stars in winter. The other hours of the day were available for reading or work. Early on Monday morning I returned to London with all arrears of work done, lungs filled with fresh air, limbs stretched, mind and body refreshed. These week-end expeditions have sometimes, I am told, been questioned, as implying slackness in work; they were, it is true, planned for pleasure and not for duty, but they did in fact suit the work much better than any other way of spending the week-end out of London. The ordinary country house visit so often means neither work, rest, nor exercise; I made sure of all these, and the anticipation of these weekly escapes kept up my spirits during many weary hours of work in London. So it was till war came, when for months together an hour or two in Richmond Park or Kew Gardens on Sunday afternoon was all that was possible.

If the word "holiday" could be applied to any of the days described above, they would indeed imply a goodly amount of holiday in the years; but for a Cabinet Minister, who is head of a big Department of State, there is no real holiday; the work follows him like his shadow, presses upon him like a perennial stream. Every day given to outdoor pursuit must be paid for by working early and late hours, that day or the next.

For the first two years at the Foreign Office, 1906 and 1907, no salmon fishing, for which I had a passion, was attempted. After that, for a fortnight each April, a small fishing was rented on a Scotch river; when this eagerly-longed-for time approached it was interfered with or cut short by some exigency of work. In 1909 it was reduced to one day, and after two or three disappointments I felt that the attempt must be abandoned, or someone at least as fit for the responsibility as myself must be found to take my place for the time. John Morley was willing, and for a fortnight in April I had relief, only telegrams and papers of real importance being sent to me, that I might keep in touch. Morley dealt with all the work that was required of the Secretary of State, and had all the papers of the office at his disposal. It was a happy interval, for Morley left me in no doubt that he liked the change of work; indeed, from what I heard from officials at the Foreign Office, he enjoyed it almost as much as I enjoyed the holiday.

# CHAPTER IX

## (1907)

## GERMANY AND THE NORTH SEA

North Sea and Baltic—Negotiating with Germany—French Apprehensions—Lord Ripon's Opinion—Royal Visits—Embarrassments
and Suspicions—Self-poisoning in Germany.

IN looking through old papers, it is depressing to read
of the distrust and suspicion with which Governments and peoples regarded each other in these
years. The impression given is of an atmosphere so mis-
erable and unwholesome that nothing healthy could live in
it. Probably it was no worse than it had always been, and
it did not seem so bad at the time as it does in retrospect.
At the time one incident succeeded another; there were
intervals of comparative calm between them. In reading
the record the impression is continuous and cumulative.
Various negotiations in 1907 and 1908 were an instance of
this. There were at least four separate subjects under
discussion: a guarantee for Norway, the abrogation of
the old treaty under which Britain and France were in
effect guarantors that Russia should not fortify the Aaland
Islands, the *status quo* in the Baltic, and the *status quo*
in the North Sea. It is not worth while to explain these
negotiations. What result they had at the time has been
superseded by the war and its consequences. Nor did
they have any important influence on the course of events
before the war; but the records about them show how
suspicious everyone was. It can at least be claimed for
us that we did not, in these affairs, foment suspicion

among others nor give just cause for it ourselves, though we did not escape being suspected.

Russia engaged in a separate negotiation with Germany about the Baltic. The effect of this on France appears from the following extracts:

### From Sir F. Bertie to Sir Edward Grey
*October* 31, 1907.

M. Pichon is getting nervous as to what may be in discussion or have been already settled between Russia and Germany in regard to the Baltic. He asked me yesterday whether I had any information on the subject, and, on my replying in the negative, he said that he could not help suspecting that Germany had either done or was doing something to secure for herself advantages in the Baltic. She had been suspicious of British policy in regard to Norway, attributing to His Majesty's Government the intention, in the event of war, to occupy a Norwegian port as a basis for hostilities with Germany, and she had therefore wished to have the integrity of Norway guaranteed, and both she and Russia had appeared to attach little or no importance to the position of Sweden.

### From Sir Edward Grey to Mr. Lister
FOREIGN OFFICE,
*December* 9, 1907.

SIR,—I observed to M. Cambon to-day that the French Government had had a communication from the Russian Government about the Baltic.

M. Cambon replied that this was so. His Government understood that Russia and Sweden were discussing an arrangement, and that there must also be an arrangement with Germany.

The Russian Government had represented to them that this was like the arrangement which had been made between France, England, and Spain with regard to the Mediterranean. But the French Government could not take this view, because England and France already had treaty obligations in the Baltic.

I reminded M. Cambon that when the Aaland Islands Treaty had been under discussion in the summer I had always said it would be desirable to make sure what the arrangements as to the Baltic were to be in future before we abrogated the Treaty.

I said I saw nothing to which we could object in the proposed arrangement between Russia, Germany, and Sweden if, as I understand, it was for the maintenance of the *status quo,* and did not relate to any closing or neutralizing of the Baltic, and had as a consequence the maintenance of the Baltic as an open sea for navigation.

I had therefore thought it better to say at once that we had no desire except to see the *status quo* maintained, and that there seemed nothing in the arrangement to which we could take exception.

M. Cambon asked whether I had expressed this view to the Russian Government. And I said I had done so, and also to the German Government.

But I told M. Cambon that I thought his Government and ours should make a point of seeing the terms of the proposed arrangement before we consented to the abrogation of the Aaland Islands Treaty. I was not sure what form the new arrangement would take, but I rather thought it would consist in three separate notes exchanged by Russia, Germany, and Sweden.

M. Cambon asked what the effect would be in case of a war between England and Germany of an arrangement about the *status quo* in the Baltic. If, for instance, we were to enter the Baltic and attack German territory there, would that be a breach of the *status quo* which Russia would be bound by the proposed arrangement to oppose?

I thought clearly not. If, after the war was over, we were to attempt to annex territory in the Baltic district, that might be a violation of the *status quo.* But if Russia permitted Germany to go to war, which was in itself a sort of disturbance of the *status quo,* she could not object to the other belligerent carrying war into the Baltic too, the information given to us being that the proposed arrangement did not involve the closing or neutralizing of the Baltic.—I am, etc.,

E. GREY.

*Sir Edward Grey to Count de Salis*
FOREIGN OFFICE,
*December* 9, 1907.

I told Count Metternich to-day that I had not attempted to communicate with the Prime Minister in connexion with the information which he had given me about the Baltic and the North Sea, as I assumed there was no desire to begin negotiations of any kind at this moment.

I had nothing new to say about the Baltic Arrangement. It seemed to me that Germany, Russia, and Sweden were within their rights in coming to an agreement as to the maintenance of the *status quo*. There was nothing in such an arrangement to which we could take exception, and I might tell him, without any *arrièrepensée* that we did not object to it or regard it as likely to make difficulties between us.

### Mr. Lister to Sir Edward Grey

PARIS,
*December 11, 1907.*

In the course of conversation with the Minister for Foreign Affairs to-day, I alluded to your conversation with M. Cambon on the subject of the Russo-Swedish and Russo-German Arrangements with regard to the Baltic.

M. Pichon said that he felt convinced that the latter went considerably farther than the maintenance of the *status quo* in the Baltic. He hoped, however, very shortly to have more precise information on the subject. In any case, he believed that nothing had been signed as yet, and that we were still in time. He did not by any means intend to play the game of Germany by quarrelling with Russia over the matter, but he would not conceal from me that he was much irritated at her action. He could not appreciate too highly, he said, your attitude, which, as usual, had been absolutely loyal throughout, and he realized that the position of England was a delicate one. The position of France was very different, and he was quite determined to speak very clearly to Russia. He was, in fact, actually doing so.

I did not at the time share the French apprehensions about the Russian negotiations with Germany regarding the Baltic, and was disposed to think that the trouble arose from Isvolsky having been the reverse of prompt in keeping the French informed.

On December 4, 1908, Metternich told me that the Emperor was in favour of an arrangement to maintain the *status quo* in the North Sea, to which England, Germany, Denmark, and Holland should be parties.

It was obvious that negotiations without France about the North Sea would cause worse trouble at Paris than negotiations about the Baltic. The following extract from a record of my conversation with Metternich shows the line taken.

*Sir Edward Grey to Count de Salis*

FOREIGN OFFICE,

*December* 4, 1907.

SIR,—The German Ambassador to-day came to tell me confidentially, by the desire of his Government and of the Emperor, that discussions had been proceeding since the summer between Russia, Germany, and Sweden with a view to the conclusion of an Arrangement respecting the Baltic, similar to that which we had made with Spain about the Mediterranean, for the purpose of agreeing to maintain the *status quo,* a consequence of which would be that the Baltic remained an open sea for navigation.

The Emperor had thought of mentioning the matter to me at Windsor, but he had decided not to do so, because he regarded his visit here as a family affair, during which it might not be suitable to raise political questions, and also because at that time it was not certain that the negotiations were approaching a conclusion. It was considered now, however, that the discussion with Russia was almost ended, though the discussion with Sweden might need some time longer.

The Emperor further wished me to be told that, in his opinion, this Arrangement might with advantage be supplemented by a similar Arrangement with regard to the *status quo* in the North Sea, to which England, Germany, Denmark, and Holland should be parties. Belgium being a neutral State, it was not so appropriate that she should be included.

I first thanked Count Metternich for making the communication to me respecting the Baltic, and said that, though I could hardly speak officially about it at once, personally I saw in it nothing whatever which could cause difficulties with us. We had no desire except to see the *status quo* preserved, and freedom of navigation. I was very glad the communication had been made to me, as it was always better to know the truth about such matters before one heard of them in an inaccurate form.

I then asked Count Metternich whether the fortification of the

Aaland Islands, respecting which we had a Treaty, would be regarded as a disturbance of the *status quo*.

Count Metternich said this was a point of difficulty between Sweden and Russia, though not with Germany.   Russia felt that the Aaland Islands offered dangerous facilities for the importation into Finland of arms, etc., in revolutionary times, and she wished to be able to guard against this.

I said Russia had raised the question of the Aaland Islands Treaty in the summer on this ground, but the question had since been dropped.

With regard to the North Sea, the idea was entirely new to me. It was, of course, a thing on which I should have to consult my colleagues before I could say anything.

Count Metternich reminded me that the whole of this communication was made confidentially.

That these apparently innocent and anodyne discussions were not so simple as was supposed appears from the line taken by Lord Ripon.   As soon as he saw the record of the German proposal about the North Sea, he wrote to me about it with lively apprehension.   Lord Ripon was no Chauvinist: he was a lover of peace, desiring to avoid quarrels and to be on good terms with all foreign countries.   That he should have felt as he did shows the need there was for caution.   The correspondence with him was as follows:

*From Lord Ripon to Sir E. Grey*
*December* 15, 1907.

MY DEAR GREY,—I am very much obliged to you for replying so promptly to my letter about the proposed North Sea Convention, and very glad to find that the Germans have agreed to make a communication to France on the subject; this is satisfactory.

No doubt it is desirable to avoid refusing off-hand to consider any proposal emanating from Germany, but, on the other hand, there is a danger of some misunderstanding arising if we enter into negotiations and end by breaking off.   But there is no use troubling you further on the matter till we know what the actual proposals of the German

Government are. At present it does not seem to me that a North Sea Convention would do us any good, and it might hamper us inconveniently in the future. All that we need in the North Sea is to have our hands quite free as they now are.—Yours sincerely,

RIPON.

### From Sir Edward Grey to Lord Ripon

*December* 13, 1907.

DEAR LORD RIPON,—I am not sure that Germany has any motive except to show that she is not isolated. She may have intended to separate us and France, but if so that is over, for she has now put the North Sea proposal before France and told her that she has done so because we said that France must be a party. The French Government now know the line we have taken both about the Baltic and the North Sea, and Cambon has been very appreciative of both.

You will see the record of conversations which I had yesterday, and these will further define the line which I have taken.

If Germany is set upon appearing before the world arm-in-arm with us and France, it will not do to affront her by refusing before it is clear that there is something which is objectionable in the proposal. If we did, Germany would have some pretext for saying that we aimed at her isolation.

I hope you will agree with all that has been said so far; I think it is all in accord with the line you advise.—Yours sincerely,

E. GREY.

Metternich's last conversation seemed to contemplate that Denmark might come into the Baltic Convention: I remarked on her exclusion.

In due course the whole affair was considered by the Cabinet; the negotiations proceeded, and the agreement was concluded.

It is not worth while to quote further papers giving the history of the negotiations, which, once started, were concerned with points of detail. An even more fertile source of suspicion were royal visits. These visits were matters of civility and courtesy; as such their effect was

*Photograph by J. Candlish Ruddock*

THE SILVER FIR
Lord Grey seen beneath it in the Garden at Fallodon

good; they made a friendly atmosphere. But they caused me the greatest trouble.

In 1907 the German Emperor was to pay a visit to London; this in itself was well enough, but we heard that he was to come accompanied by a squadron and with such state and circumstance as would turn the visit into a great political demonstration. When this was deprecated he suddenly announced that he could not come at all. The cancellation of the visit would have been a demonstration the other way, equally to be deprecated. That the visit should take place at all was something that must make the French sensitive. That could not be helped. There was no reason why our relations with France should stand in the way of good relations with Germany; it would have been still more unreasonable to suppose that King Edward and the Emperor were not to meet and to be as intimate as they chose. So the visit took place at Windsor. King Edward also saw the Emperor at Homburg, and paid him a state visit at Berlin. The Germans would have been very indignant at the suggestion that any other Government should have been sensitive about these visits between the King and Emperor.

But when King Edward visited the Tsar at Reval, and when, in the course of his stay abroad, he saw the Austrian Emperor at Ischl, the Germans were as sensitive as anyone.

Again the King visited the German Emperor at Homburg, and then passed on to Ischl, where he met the Emperor of Austria. One suggestion made in Germany was that he had tried at Ischl to weaken the Triple Alliance.

The idea that King Edward was a busy intriguer who used these visits for political ends, particularly for that of "encircling" Germany, was a fiction, but it became an article of faith in Germany. There is, I believe, a medical term applied to certain unhealthy processes in the human body; it means "Self-poisoning." Some analogous process went on in the German mind about King Edward. It had no origin in truth. My impression was that King Edward enjoyed these visits, and he certainly had no desire to spoil his own part in them by going into deep political waters. He desired to have someone with him to whom he could refer any Sovereign or Foreign Minister, who wished to have serious political discussion. For this purpose Hardinge went with him, and acted just as any Ambassador would, reporting his conversations home to the Foreign Office in the usual way. The visits were not made the object of important strokes or developments in foreign policy.

# CHAPTER X

## (1907)

## PERSIA AND RUSSIA

The Necessity of an Understanding with Russia—The Persian Danger-point—"Vive La Duma!"—Benckendorff's Question—An Unfavourable Atmosphere—Sowing Mischief—Gains and Losses of the Persian Agreement—Letters to Nicolson—A Train of Minor Troubles—A Dinner to Isvolsky.

IT will be remembered that, when the Conservative Government made their first positive departure from previous policy, it was not in the direction of an undertaking with Russia by which differences between that country and Britain should be adjusted by mutual accommodation and agreement. The departure took the form of an alliance with Japan by which Russian advances in the Far East could be controlled. But this arrangement applied only to the Far East. It left other causes of friction untouched, and if the Russian proceedings in the Far East had been the most recent cause of trouble with Russia, they were not the most dangerous, the most long-standing, or the most likely to recur. Russian advances towards the Indian frontier were the most sensitive and dangerous point. If we were to get out of the old, bad rut in which we had so often come to the verge of war with Russia, we had to work for a definite agreement. Russia was the ally of France; we could not pursue at one and the same time a policy of agreement with France and a policy of counter-alliances against Russia. Nor was there any third country with interests in the region of the

Indian frontier with whom we could concert a policy to control Russian advance. An agreement with Russia was the natural complement of the agreement with France; it was also the only practical alternative to the old policy of drift, with its continual complaints, bickerings, and dangerous friction.

Persia was the danger-point. The inefficiency of Persian Governments, the state of their finances, the internal disorders, not only laid Persia open to foreign interference, but positively invited and attracted it. Teheran, the capital and the seat of the Central Government, was in the north of Persia; it was within easy striking distance from Russia, it was quite out of British reach. Russia had therefore a great and perpetual advantage in the struggle that went on between British and Russian diplomacy at Teheran. A British Minister many years ago endeavouring to encourage the Shah to stand up against Russian encroachments, was stopped by the Shah making the sign of a bow-string round his own neck to express the position of Russia with regard to himself. "What can *you* do?" said the Shah to the British Minister.

It is not suggested that Russian influence at Teheran was pressed with a deliberate design of advance to the Indian frontier; the policy of Russia was decided probably by the momentum of her own weight and by the weakness of Persia; but each new concession or extension of influence increased British apprehension. We feared that we might at any time be confronted by some *fait accompli* which British interests would require us to resist—a situation very unpleasant to contemplate.

British policy in Persia was therefore constantly in opposition to Russia; it was not a forward policy pushed for the purpose of extending British territory or influence.

Its object was to keep Persia as a buffer State and to maintain it as an independent country.

It will readily be inferred that the atmosphere at Teheran was one of dislike, and distrust between Britain and Russia; and thus, to the inevitable friction caused by policies that had opposing aims, was added imputation of motive, where perhaps no sinister motive existed, so that even trivial or accidental things were exaggerated into matters of importance and design.

The Persian Government, conscious of its own weakness, considered that its best hope lay in playing off one Government as far as it could against the other, and maintaining as far as it could an equipoise of bad relations between Britain and Russia.

Such was the situation, and it was very clear that nothing short of a cordial understanding would prevent it from getting worse. Unless the mists of suspicion were dissolved by the warm air of friendship, the increasing friction would cause Britain and Russia to drift towards war.

It was not so easy to create friendship with Russia as with France. Russian despotism was repugnant to British ideals, and something was constantly happening in Russia that alienated British sympathy or stirred indignation.

The institution of a Duma in Russia had done something to make even British Liberals more sympathetic. Representatives of the Duma visited London to take part in a gathering of international Parliamentary Representatives. Campbell-Bannerman was to give an address to the gathering, and the fact that there were Russian Parliamentary Representatives in such an assembly for the first time served to make a friendly reference to Russia by the British Prime Minister exceptionally easy. On the morning of the speech Campbell-Bannerman was confronted by the news that the Tsar had suspended the Duma. The occasion turned from one most auspicious to one extremely awkward. The one feature that saved the situation was that the Tsar had not abolished the Duma, but only suspended it. Campbell-Bannerman, with what seemed to me admirable adroitness, turned the awkward corner by the phrase "La Duma est morte; vive la Duma!"

The next day Benckendorff came to see me and said that he feared the phrase might give offence at St. Petersburg. I upheld what Campbell-Bannerman had said, pointing out that it was an adaptation of the phrase "Le Roi est mort; vive le Roi," which had a well-known historical origin and usage. The Tsar had made it evident that the Duma was now one of the permanent Institutions of Russia, and that he intended again to summon this or a new Duma. The phrase was therefore strictly applicable to the occasion, and ought not to give offence.

Benckendorff gave me to understand that this put the thing in a more favourable light, and I heard no more of it.

Later in the same year (1906) there was a projected visit of a British fleet to Cronstad. This aroused dislike and opposition among Liberals in the House of Commons, and caused great embarrassment at the Foreign Office; yet for us to cancel the visit of the fleet would have been a slight and rebuff to Russia, that must have prejudiced the relations of the two countries. Eventually the Russians themselves, with discretion and tact, asked that the visit should not take place.

These incidents were an illustration of how difficult and delicate a business it was to put relations with Russia on a footing that would be friendly.

A further illustration of the embarrassment and difficulty caused by the Tsar's attitude to the Duma appears in the following extract from a letter of mine to Nicolson on October 3, 1906. The House of Commons had very naturally desired to send a congratulatory address to the Duma, when that body was sitting; there was, also very naturally, a desire not to go back on the address, because the Duma was suspended and in difficulties. Here is what I wrote to Nicolson, who must have been even more conscious of the delicacy of the situation than we were in London:

The address to the Duma has become embarrassing. It was originally planned when the Duma was sitting, and could not be objected to by them. It was a sort of greeting from the oldest to the youngest Parliament. But the presentation of it by a deputation, when there is no Duma and nothing but chaos, is unfortunate. I could not have stopped it now; it was difficult enough to keep things straight in debate and answer in Parliament, and feeling in this free country runs too strong to be restrained by consideration for the feelings of an autocratic Government. Mr. Smeaton wrote to ask my advice as to going with the deputation, and I replied that, as the deputation was entirely unofficial, I could give no advice respecting it.

I also realize that you can do nothing by representation about pogroms, and I shall not ask you to make any, though we may send you from time to time the apprehensions that are expressed here. In some parts of Russia there is apparently civil war, carried on by bombs on one side and pogroms on the other.

The whole course of internal affairs in Russia rendered the atmosphere very unfavourable to friendly negotiations. The treatment of Poles and the treatment of Jews in Russia and kindred matters were often the subject of representations to me, and sometimes of questions in Parliament. Our interference could do no good; it would only make things worse. A British Government had once addressed some remonstrance to Russia about internal affairs, and the Russian Government had retorted with remarks about the state of Ireland. Nicolson told me that he had once, in friendly and informal talk, spoken to Stolypin, the Russian Minister, who effected a great land reform, about the disabilities of Jews in Russia. Stolypin had replied that he no more approved of these disabilities than British or other foreign critics did, but that, if he removed them, there would be pogroms all over Russia, which he would not be able to stop.

To add to these difficulties there were attempts to sow suspicion of us in Russia, as the following letter of March 26, 1906, to Spring-Rice (then Chargé d'Affaires at St. Petersburg) shows:

### Sir E. Grey to Mr. C. Spring-Rice

*March* 26, 1906.

DEAR SPRING-RICE,—Count Benckendorff has given us copies of a number of documents relating to a supposed secret agreement by which England and Japan guarantee the territorial integrity of the possessions of the Sultan of Turkey in Asia Minor, and bind themselves to help the Imperial Ottoman Government by their united forces against any attack upon the Ottoman Empire on the Asiatic side.

The most circumstantial of these documents is a supposed telegram from Musurus Pasha, the Turkish Ambassador in London, to the first Secretary of the Sultan, dated January 29, 1906, in which Musurus states that I have just communicated to him the definitive text of the secret article to the above effect.

No such article exists, there is no secret article or understanding of any kind between us and Japan; the published alliance contains everything that has been agreed upon between us. The supposed guarantee of Turkey has never been mentioned between us and Japan, nor have we ever mentioned such a proposal to Musurus or at Constantinople, and we have undertaken no new engagement of any kind with regard to the Turkish Empire. If it is possible to make a denial more categorical than this I am quite ready to do it.

What does interest me is the circumstantial character of the documents that have been supplied to the Russian Government. It has taken some trouble to invent them and there must have been a strong motive for doing this and conveying them to the Russian Government. But Count Lamsdorff is probably as well, or better, able than I am to guess their origin and motive.

You may give a copy of this letter to Count Lamsdorff.

E. GREY.

*Télégramme de Musurus Pasha au Premier Secrétaire du Sultan*

Le Ministre des Affaires Étrangères d'Angleterre vient de me communiquer le texte définitif de l'article secret additionnel au traité d'alliance Anglo-Japonais qui a été établi par lui de concert avec l'Ambassadeur du Japon. Je vous transmet la traduction turque de cet article :

"Les Gouvernements de Grande Bretagne et du Japon pour compléter les stipulations du traité conclu entre elles le 12 Août, 1905, sont tombés d'accord sur l'article suivant qu'ils prennent l'obligation de tenir strictement secret. Les Gouvernements de Grande Bretagne et du Japon déclarent qu'ils garantissent l'intégrité territoriale des possessions de Sa Majesté le Sultan en Asia Mineure et seront tenus de porter secours au Gouvernement Impérial Ottoman par leur forces réunies contre toute attaque dont l'Empire Ottoman serait l'objet du côté de l'Asie. Cet article additionnel et secret aura la même force et valeur s'il était mot par mot inséré dans le texte du traité susmentionné du 12 Août, 1905, et restera en vigueur pour la même durée."

Les textes Français et Anglais de l'article précité ont été expédiés par l'Ambassadeur Turc à Londres par poste.

I find two comments appended to the copy of this document, which was conveyed to the Prime Minister:

There is a mystery about this affair. I do not believe that Musurus invented this telegram; but someone has invented it, and given it to the Russians. This is the sort of thing that has gone on for years; now for the first time the Russians are giving us the opportunity of exposing the lies.

E. G.

This last fact is worth all the lies put together.

H. C.-B.

The last line here printed is Campbell-Bannerman's very apposite comment.

Nevertheless, it remained as essential as ever to come to some understanding with Russia.

Our interests were so important and in such intimate contact in Asia that, without an understanding, there was bound to be friction increasing to the point of danger—a friction that was an increasing cause of weakness and insecurity to the position of the British Empire.

In 1907 negotiations were seriously taken in hand, and resulted in the "Convention signed on August 31, 1907, between Great Britain and Russia containing arrangements on the subject of Persia, Afghanistan, and Thibet."

The cardinal British object in these negotiations was to secure ourselves for ever, as far as a treaty could secure us, from further Russian advances in the direction of the Indian frontier. Russia was to cease threatening and annoying British interests concerned with India. This had been a formidable diplomatic weapon in her hands. She was now, once and for all, to give it up. The gain to us was great. We were freed from an anxiety that had often preoccupied British Governments; a frequent source of friction and a possible cause of war was removed; the prospect of peace was made more secure.

What did Russia get in return? On paper it was an equal bargain. The part of Persia by which India could be approached was made secure from Russian penetration. The part of Persia by which Russia could be approached was secured from British penetration. The gain was equal—on paper. In practice we gave up nothing. We did not wish to pursue a forward policy in Persia; nor could a British advance in Persia have been the same menace to Russia that a Russian advance in Persia might

be to India. It is no wonder that the Russian Foreign
Minister had some difficulty in getting military authorities in Russia to give up something of real potential value
to them, while we gave up what was of little or no practical value to us.

No attempt was made to include the whole Persian Gulf
in the British sphere of interest: Russia had just been excluded from warm water in the Far East as a result of the
Anglo-Japanese Alliance, and it seemed to me unreasonable to try to turn the Anglo-Russian Agreement into an
instrument for expressly excluding her from warm water
in the Middle East. The Persian Gulf was kept outside
her sphere, but left in the "neutral" sphere. Russia gained
nothing as regards the Gulf by the Agreement, but her
position was not made worse. Even so, the Agreement
seemed to me one-sided. What we gained by it was real—
what Russia gained was apparent. I remember asking
someone in the Foreign Office who had special knowledge
of Russia, whether the Russian Government were really
afraid of a British forward policy and designs in
Persia. He replied that he thought Russia really did
fear them. It was difficult to believe that. I felt
sure that, if Russia gave up every movement and every
design that might embarrass us in Central Asia, she would
sooner or later expect a modification of the British attitude
towards her access to warm water. I did not expect her
to bother about the Persian Gulf, but I thought it probable
that at the first opportunity she would talk to us about the
Straits in the Near East.

Private letters of mine to Nicolson, then Ambassador
at St. Petersburg, written in November 1906 and April
1907 explain what was in my mind. I give two of them

in full, though some sentences are not relevant to the particular point that they are quoted to illustrate:

*Sir E. Grey to Sir A. Nicolson*

FOREIGN OFFICE,

*November 6, 1906.*

MY DEAR NICOLSON,—In answer to your despatch of November 4, and your private letters on the same subject, I would say I see no objection to your giving to M. Isvolsky a sketch of an agreement as you propose, and one is being sent in a despatch. You should, however, make it clear to him that it does not pretend to be in treaty form, and is rather in the nature of an *aide-mémoire* of what has been thrown out in conversation.

I do not wish the negotiations to go to sleep. But, on the other hand, we must avoid raising in M. Isvolsky's mind the suspicion that we wish to force the pace in order to take advantage of Russia's present situation.

I should, however, omit the last paragraph from the draft which you propose. It is not essential to an arrangement with Russia that we should each of us become parties to a promise to prevent third Powers from obtaining concessions in the parts of Persia in which we have each of us respectively renounced influence ourselves. It would be enough that we should each agree not to seek or maintain influence in the specified district reserved for the other. After our arrangement with Russia was completed, we could obtain from Persia an undertaking not to make concessions which would have any political character to a third Power in our specified district. Russia could do the same for herself, and it would follow, from the arrangement which we and Russia had made, that neither of us would oppose the other in making these separate arrangements with the Persian Government.

Such a settlement between Russia and us would give absolutely no opportunity or pretext to any other country for saying that the settlement had infringed the principle of the open door.

Of course, I understand M. Isvolsky's difficulty with the military party. Seistan is, no doubt, a place of strategic importance in their eyes. But it is only of such importance if they wish to attack the Indian frontier, or to put pressure upon us by making us think that they intend to attack it. The benefit which we expect from an arrangement with Russia is that we should be set free from any such apprehension, and this is precisely what we ask in the settlement.

If, as you suppose, M. Isvolsky will say at this point, "But what is Russia to get in return," you will naturally reply that she gets in a certain specified district the same security that we get in Seistan. He will then probably point out that our gain in this matter is much greater than that of Russia, who is not really disturbed by the apprehension that aggression on our part in the north and north-west of Persia is practicable; and that he must, therefore, have a further *quid pro quo* with which to overcome the opposition of the military party, or at least to convince the Emperor that the opposition of the military party is unreasonable. *But it is for him to say what it is he wants!*

Probably he already has something in his mind, but is hesitating to propose it. I think he should let us know what it is. If it is access to the Persian Gulf, that is a matter which should be referred to us for discussion. But I doubt, myself, whether any complete arrangement with Russia can be made unless it includes the Near East as well. It is the differences in the Near East that have been the original cause of the hostility and friction between Russia and us.

So far as the Russian Government are aware officially our attitude in the Near East has not been changed. But it is not for us to propose changes with regard to the treaty conditions of the Dardanelles. I think some change in the direction desired by Russia would be admissible, and we should be prepared to discuss the question if Russia introduces it. If M. Isvolsky mentions it you might, therefore, say that it is a matter on which you are at present without instructions to speak to him, but which you will refer home. I enclose for your own information only a departmental memorandum on the Dardanelles. It shows that much may be possible, but it must not be taken yet as committing even me, much less the Cabinet, who have not seen it.

The difficulty is, of course, that the question of the Dardanelles concerns the other Powers of Europe. Our settlement with Russia, when completed, will have to be published, and so important a matter as a promise on our part to give diplomatic support in favour of any modification of a European treaty could not be introduced as a secret article. The fact that this is so makes it proper that M. Isvolsky, and not we, should be the first to mention the matter; it cannot be pressed without raising a European question, which it is Russia's interest, and not ours, to raise, though we might no longer object to seeing it reopened as we should have objected a few years ago.

The sketch of a Persian agreement is founded upon yours, but the preamble was expanded by John Morley, and Hardinge has used the Anglo-Russian China Railway Agreement as a model for the rest, so as to introduce terms already familiar to Russia.

I fear the temporary ascendency of the reactionary party round the Tsar will not make the atmosphere favourable for these negotiations of ours.

E. G.

### Sir E. Grey to Sir A. Nicolson, St. Petersburg
FOREIGN OFFICE,
*April* 1, 1907.

MY DEAR NICOLSON,—My days are so full when the House of Commons is sitting that I have not written to you as I intended. I rely upon Hardinge to keep you informed.

You need not fear delay on our side about Afghanistan. I spoke to Morley about it, and when a satisfactory Asiatic Agreement is in shape, I think he will be prepared to agree and to settle with the Amir afterwards, without hanging the whole thing up for communications with the Amir.

It is important that our negotiations should be concluded practically *pari passu* with the Japanese negotiations. I have impressed upon Komura that the two ought now to proceed simultaneously, though there should be nothing tripartite about them.

It would be much better not to bring the Dardanelles and Bosphorus into this Asiatic Agreement, for the reasons I gave in my conversation with Benckendorff. I thought it better to give Benckendorff my record of that conversation, to avoid misunderstandings afterwards. The fact is, that if Asiatic things are settled favourably the Russians will not have trouble with us about the entrance to the Black Sea; but France, at any rate, must be taken into confidence before we make engagements, and we should expect Russia's support about some Egyptian and other kindred things in the Near East, which matter to us and are not important to her.

The real rock ahead is the prospect in Russia itself. If the Duma is dissolved, and there is a regime of pogroms and courts martial, feeling here will be very adverse. We could carry a settlement of

Asiatic frontier questions in any case, but I don't think we could do more if things were very bad in Russia, for there would be resentment at our choosing this time to make a concession about the Straits. But this would not be the worst consequence of reaction in Russia; the worst is that things would be said in Parliament, and in our Press, which would mightily offend the Czar and the Russian Government, and might make it impossible for you to make progress at St. Petersburg.

I see no objection to an arbitration agreement of the usual kind, of which we have made so many, being added to any agreement with Russia, if she wishes it; it would be popular here.

I will try to keep the "Knight Commander" [1] case quiet in Parliament for the present, and the other also; but they must go to arbitration eventually, if Russia will not settle them without.—Yours sincerely,

E. GREY.

The question of the Straits was not mixed up with those Anglo-Russian negotiations about Persia. The Agreement was completed and signed in August 1907 without any secret article or secret understanding whatever.

The question of the Straits was, however, raised by Isvolsky, the Russian Foreign Minister, when he came to London in the autumn of 1908, and was then carefully considered by the Government, as will be related in a further chapter.[2]

The following letter from me to Campbell-Bannerman announces the conclusion of the Agreement:

*Sir E. Grey to the Prime Minister*

*August* 31, 1907.

MY DEAR SIR HENRY,—You will have seen, by the telegrams, that the Russian Agreement is being signed. The Russians have eventually accepted the proposal which was agreed upon after consultation between Morley, Ritchie, Nicolson, Hardinge, and myself. Nicolson went

[1] A Liverpool-owned British steamer sunk by a Russian cruiser off Vladivostok in July 1904. The controversy, about compensation for her owners and crew, lasted till March, 1911.

[2] See infra, pp. 171-81.

back with it to St. Petersburg; Isvolsky would not have it at first, but has eventually found in it a compromise with his own opponents in the Council of Ministers at St. Petersburg.

Nicolson has, as usual, been invaluable, never missing a point, and with excellent judgment. So has Hardinge, with his knowledge both of the Russian Government and of Persia, and his clear view as to the good policy of an agreement.

But without Morley we should have made no progress at all, for the Government of India would have blocked every point and Morley has removed mountains in the path of the negotiations.

I am having the final text printed and translated to be circulated to the Cabinet confidentially. We hope to defer publication to give the Indian Government time to make a communication to the Amir.—Yours, etc.,

E. GREY.

The Agreement dealt with Persia, Afghanistan, and Thibet. It is unnecessary to dwell upon the clauses that refer to the two last countries: they gave no trouble afterwards, and those that concerned Persia will be found in the published papers.

In its primary and cardinal object, the security of the Indian frontier, the Agreement was completely successful. There were no more nerves or apprehensions about that. Thus was the real *raison d'être* and the achievement of it the real justification of the Agreement.

But a long train of minor troubles followed.

It had been my hope to conclude and publish the Agreement before Parliament rose; but the negotiations dragged on and were not finished till Parliament was on the eve of adjournment. When the Agreement was signed the Indian Government very naturally demanded that publication should be delayed, till they had had time to communicate it, with their own explanations, to the Amir of Afghanistan. Publication was therefore delayed for some weeks for this reason, and when it was seen that the Agreement had been concluded while Parliament was still sitting, and not published till after Parliament had risen, the charge was brought that publication had been deliberately withheld to keep the House of Commons in the dark. It was one of the instances in which a perfectly plain and straightforward account has to be given with the certainty that it will be treated as a pretext and not accepted as a valid reason.

Persia did not like agreements between Britain and Russia; she had regarded enmity between her two great neighbours as her security, and was used to playing off one against the other. The opportunity for that sport had come to an end.

The real cause of trouble, however, was that the "integrity and independence" of Persia, so tenderly cherished in the Preamble, did not in practice exist when the Agreement was made. Persia was honeycombed by concessions, particularly to Russia for telegraphs, Cossack officers, roads, and so forth; she owed money to Russia and to Britain, and some of her revenues were pledged as security; she was in want of more money; her finances were in disorder; her internal troubles frequently threatened the lives or property of foreigners in outlying districts, and thus compelled, or at any rate invited, interference to protect them. This latter consideration applied particularly to the parts near the Russian frontier and in the Russian zone of interest. I had never expected that the Agreement would diminish Russian activity in the north of Persia. It was impossible that the hands of the clock, which had already marked so much time in the lapse of Persian independence, should be put back, but I hoped that the clock might be stopped. And so in a sense it was, for the Russians kept their interference strictly to the north. Russian Foreign Ministers, freed from the apprehension of British rivalry at Teheran, were ready to be easy and to go slow, but Russian agents were apt to regard themselves as having a free hand in the Russian sphere, and in that sphere things were frequently done that were not consistent with "integrity and independence." Both Isvolsky and Sazonof, who succeeded him, did what they could to keep Russian agents within bounds; but Russian Government was a despotism without discipline. Different Ministers and different diplomatic agents pursued different politics. Russian agents were of all sorts; some were able and clever; some were not; some accepted a friendly policy towards Britain, some did not; some meant well, some did not, and some meant nothing at all. Had the Tsar been a Cæsar, a Cromwell, or a Napoleon he might have brought this chaos into order and discipline, or he might have perished in the attempt. The successive Foreign Ministers, I believe, did what they could, but incidents frequently occurred in Persia of which we were bound to complain. My remonstrances were sometimes strong, and the Russian Foreign Minister would get restive. Members of the House of Commons got restive because they thought my remonstrances were not strong enough. These were, as a matter of fact, often too strong to be published, if friendly relations were to be preserved.

Russian conduct in Persia was not different from what it had been before the Anglo-Russian Agreement; the trouble now was that this conduct was held to concern us in a way that it had not done before. In previous days British Governments had not been held responsible for Russian dealings with Persia: all they had been required to do was to guard against the defence of India being prejudiced by what happened in Persia. Now we were partners with Russia in an Agreement that purported to maintain the integrity and independence of Persia. This gave us technically a title, might indeed be said to impose upon us an obligation, to restrain or influence the conduct of our partner. There was constant trouble in the House of Commons, and sometimes it seemed as if the Agreement would end by making matters worse between Britain and Russia than they had been before. The Russian view of the situation was that, as long as they kept to their own sphere and we were secure on the Indian side, they ought not to be worried.

Very disagreeable trouble arose about Persian finance. Persian finance was hopeless without Western advice. Finance was not the strong point of Russians; a British financial adviser in Teheran, the Russian sphere, was out of the question. European advisers would be suspected, certainly by Russia and probably by us, of using influence in favour of their own countries, perhaps of furthering some political policy. I sugested the choice of an American, who would be outside all politics. The Russians did not like it, but they agreed, and Mr. Shuster was invited to Teheran. Had he accepted the situation as he found it at Teheran, and made the best of it, he would, in spite of all difficulties and drawbacks, have done much for Persian finance; but his method was that of "Hands off" to Britain and Russia. As far as we were concerned, we should not have minded. A strong, independent Persia was what we desired, though we knew it to be impossible. To the Russians, however, Mr. Shuster's method meant the destruction in their own sphere of the position to which for generations they had been accustomed. It presently became evident that, to avoid a Russian occupation of Teheran, Mr. Shuster must leave it. His departure was a loss, but it was the lesser of the two evils. His aims were admirable and just, but he had not realized that Russian interference in the north of Persia could only be ousted by force; that Britain was not prepared to embark on a great European war for that purpose, and that Britain was the only country that had any interest in seeing Russia restrained. He attempted what was good, but what could only be done by force; and there was no force available for the purpose.

Persia tried my patience more than any other subject. I once told Benckendorff that if Russia made things too difficult the policy of friendly agreement with her might become impossible. In that case I should resign, for I could not myself pursue any other policy, and if Russia made this policy impossible I should leave it to someone else to adopt and pursue another.

I have traced some of the after-history of this Anglo-Russian Agreement in order that the narrative of other events may not be interrupted later on by having to recur to it. I return now to its beginning.

When Parliament met again there was a debate on it in the House of Commons. The Agreement was accepted, but with some criticism from the Conservative Opposition, that it was not sufficiently favourable to British interests. It was explained by me and defended with force and breadth of view by John Morley.

One pleasant incident may be recalled in connexion with it. When Isvolsky was in London after its conclusion, I asked Benckendorff to bring him to dine at my house, then in Queen Anne's Gate. John Morley and Hardinge were the only other guests. We talked long and freely, and this Anglo-Russian Agreement was, so far as I recollect, the main subject of conversation. I was a little apprehensive about this entertainment; my manner of living had every comfort, but there was no state about it, no formality, no men-servants, no party, nothing to do honour to the Russian Minister for Foreign Affairs. There was a question in my mind whether he would consider the homeliness of his entertainment a compliment or a slight. I heard afterwards that he considered the informality a compliment, and said to Benckendorff when they went away together, "I believe now what you have told me; these people are really friendly."

Isvolsky ceased to be Minister for Foreign Affairs long before the war, and I had communication with him only twice after he left St. Petersburg. The impression made by what has since come to light about his doings as Ambassador at Paris is far from favourable; but, as Minister at St. Petersburg, he did his best under considerable difficulties to work the Anglo-Russian Agreement with Persia, Afghanistan, and Thibet in the spirit in which it was made and intended.

The other transaction of importance that I had with him concerned the Straits. It was dealt with when he came to London in 1908, when he was in sore trouble over the Austrian annexation of Bosnia and Herzegovina and his controversy thereon with d'Aehrenthal, then Minister for Foreign Affairs at Vienna.

# CHAPTER XI

## (1908-1909)

## THE SECOND CRISIS (BOSNIA-HERZEGOVINA)

Russia, Austria, and Balkan Policy—The Young Turk Revolution—
An Austrian Announcement—The British Attitude—The Open-
ing of the Straits—A Russian Demand—Isvolsky's Explanations at
Cowes—Serbian Demand for Compensation—A Serious Situation
—Russian Support and its Withdrawal—Consternation in Russia
—A Charge Refuted—An Ominous Parallel—The Question of
the Congo—Humanitarianism and Politics—Cabinet Differences—
The Eight Dreadnoughts.

IT would be impossible, without a whole additional
volume, to give anything like a full account of the
years that intervened between 1907 and 1914, nor is
it necessary to do this. The line in which British foreign
policy was moving has already been explained: we continued to follow that line. All that need be done is to give
a condensed account of two or three of the more striking
incidents or crises.

The various efforts to improve Turkish government in
Macedonia have little interest and no importance now.
They were intolerably wearisome, very disagreeable, and
painfully futile. We took an active part in them, but our
motive was disinterested. Had we considered our political interest, we should have left the question alone. As I
have already explained, our activity in protesting against
Turkish misrule diminished our influence and was therefore adverse to British commercial interests in Turkey.
But humanitarian feeling in Britain and the persisting
sympathy for Christian populations under Turkish rule

was so strong that British political and material interests
were overborne by it. All the sympathy of British Secretaries for Foreign Affairs was with this sentiment, and
their action was inspired by this motive, though each successive occupant of the Foreign Office may well have felt
choked by despair of achieving any measure of success.
Macedonian Reforms could be dealt with only in concert
with other Powers. Not one of the other Powers was
disinterested; not one of them believed that Britain was
disinterested. Each was conscious of some political motive of its own, and they all invented some political motive
that was attributed to us.

Prestige and influence in the Balkans were cardinal
points of Russian and Austrian policy. Neither could afford to risk its position for philanthropic reasons: each
watched the other, and their action in Macedonian diplomacy was conditioned by distrust of each other and anxiety lest one should get an advantage at the expense of
the other. Both regarded our activity as a more or less
unreasonable encroachment upon a sphere in which they
had direct political interests and we had none.

Germany was thinking only of her political influence
and the commercial expansion, that depended on it, in
Turkey. She would risk none of this for the sake of
philanthropy, and took care to handle the subject of
Macedonia in such a way that what we or other Powers
lost by annoying the Sultan at Constantinople should go to
enhance the German position there.

France, just escaped from trouble about Morocco and
apprehensive of more to come, wished to avoid trouble
elsewhere. She too had her commercial interests at Constantinople, and she was neither inclined nor could she
afford to head a crusade against the Sultan of Turkey.

In the middle sat the Sultan, Abdul Hamid, well aware of every element in the situation, resenting the worry that was caused for him, but sure that with a combination on his part of tact and obstinacy the result would always be stalemate. In these conditions the question of Macedonian Reforms was like a bog; the Powers who plunged into it soon sank up to their knees and stuck there, bickering with each other. The whole region has passed over from Turkey, and there is no need here to justify, criticize, or give an account of the part that we and others took in trying to improve or mitigate Turkish rule in Macedonia.

In 1908 came the Young Turk Revolution, and the power of Abdul Hamid and his detestable camarilla was overthrown. The first news we received of the Revolution were touching in the account they gave of joy and good-will. For a moment the subject races in European Turkey seemed to lose their hatred of the Turk and of each other. I sympathized with the enthusiasm, and was keen that the new order should have every chance. Those who knew Turkey well warned us that the "young" Turks, men like Enver and Talaat, were much like the "old" Turks, but it was so pleasant to indulge the larger hope that I would not heed these warnings. The sequel destroyed the hopes and underlined the warnings. The history of the French Revolution, the experience in our own time of the Turkish and the Russian Revolutions, show that, bad as despotism is, doomed as it is to work its own ruin, the first-fruits of its overthrow are not love and liberty.

I was still, however, in the stage of hope and sympathy with young Turks, when, in the autumn of 1908, Austria announced that she had changed the occupation of Bosnia and Herzegovina into annexation. Turkey was indeed

to be given the Sandjak as compensation, but Austria's
act and decision were quite arbitrary. Turkey had not
been consulted, or asked to consent, and the change was
therefore a blow to Turkish prestige. A cruel blow it
seemed to the budding hopes of better things in Turkey.
Besides this, it was the alteration of a European Treaty
to which other Powers as well as Turkey were parties.
To us the territorial changes were indifferent: it mattered
not to us that Austria should annex instead of merely
occupying Bosnia and Herzegovina; but, besides sympathy with the new hope in Turkey, we felt that the arbitrary alteration of a European Treaty by one Power without the consent of the other Powers who were parties to
it struck at the root of all good international order. We
therefore took a very firm stand on principle, and said
that, though our interests were not involved, we would
not recognize Austria's action, and the change she had
made, till all the other Powers, who were parties to the
treaty, were ready to do so. Russia was offended, Turkey
was protesting; we would do nothing to make it difficult
for Austria to get their consent, but she must get it, before
we would recognize the change in the treaty.

The following documents will suffice to show the line
taken by us from the first.

*Sir Edward Grey to Sir E. Goschen*
FOREIGN OFFICE,
*October* 5, 1908.

With regard to Baron d'Aehrenthal's letter of the 28th ultimo to
Sir E. Hardinge, which I have seen, His Excellency should be reminded
that Austria-Hungary is a party to the Treaty of London, and conse-
quently to the Protocol of January 17, 1871, which is attached to it.
In this it is stipulated that the engagements into which any Power
has entered can only be broken or modified with the full assent of the
Contracting Parties, and after a friendly agreement has been arrived

at. A deliberate violation or alteration of the Berlin Treaty, undertaken without previous consultation with the other Powers, of which in this case Turkey is the most affected, could never be approved or recognized by His Majesty's Government. This should be represented to the Austrian Government, and you should impress upon them how necessary it is that their decision to annex Bosnia and Herzegovina should be reconsidered.

*Sir Edward Grey to Sir A. Nicolson*

FOREIGN OFFICE,

*October* 5, 1908.

It is the general feeling here that the new Turkish regime is deserving of consideration, and that it has met with bad treatment.

The situation is complicated, and needs careful handling, and we cannot yet approach the Russian Government on the subject; but the following is the line of action which I would wish to follow:

If my expectations are not deceived, Turkey, while merely protesting against the action of Austria and Bulgaria, will claim some compensation for herself. In this case, I hope that we shall find ourselves in line with the Russian Government in adopting an attitude friendly to the Porte in the negotiations which will take place among the Powers.

*Sir Edward Grey to Sir G. Lowther*

FOREIGN OFFICE,

*October* 5, 1908.

Rifaat Pasha has been informed by me that, in regard to both the above questions, our answer will be that the alteration of an International Treaty by any one Power, without the consent of the other Contracting Parties, cannot be considered by us to be within the rights of that Power; and until we know the opinions of the other Powers, and especially those of Turkey, to whom the question is more important than to anyone else, the action of Austria and Bulgaria cannot be recognized.

I said that Turkey had, in my opinion, suffered bad treatment; that we were thoroughly convinced of the peaceful motives, devotion to internal reforms, and integrity of the new regime, which commanded our fullest sympathy. Rifaat Pasha consulted me as to whether a declaration of war was advisable. I replied that, in my opinion, the new regime could not possibly profit by war. Turkey, at present, required chiefly money and time. By going to war she would lose both. Turkey suffered no tangible loss through the annexation of the two provinces to Austria, or through the Bulgarian declaration of independence, although, as far as prestige and sentiment were concerned, both these steps were injurious; in the event of a protest, or, later on, of a demand on the part of Turkey for compensation, any proposals which secured that her interests were fairly considered would have our support. Rifaat Pasha enquired as to the possible nature of such compensation, to which I replied that I was uncertain whether it would be practicable to give a money indemnity, and if it would be acceptable to the Porte; I only wished to suggest that the matter should be considered in this light, because in my opinion Turkey had been badly treated, and, although His Majesty's Government would not suggest it, the present complications might result in the meeting of a Conference, at which we should hope to see her interests duly considered.

To this position we adhered, and in the end Turkey received compensation in money and accepted the change of the *status quo* that had been made by the Austrian annexation of Bosnia and Herzegovina and by Bulgaria's change from a Principality to a Kingdom.

Another more difficult and more delicate question for us was that of the opening of the Straits. The Tsar came on his yacht to visit King Edward at Cowes. Isvolsky came with him, and, in a long informal talk with Asquith and me, Isvolsky expounded his grievance against Baron d'Aehrenthal, the Austrian Foreign Minister. Isvolsky held forth to us at great length, and with energy and point. He spoke in English, and the performance in a foreign language was an impressive *tour de force*. Asquith commented to me on it as a remarkable feat; but we were not concerned with or required to take a hand in Isvolsky's personal grievance against d'Aehrenthal. Isvolsky came on to London and there propounded the question of opening the Straits. He may have had this in view from the beginning, and may have allowed himself to be compromised by d'Aehrenthal about Bosnia and Herzegovina, in order to raise the question of the Straits with effect; or he may have rushed to it for compensation, after finding himself compromised. It did not matter to us which of these hypotheses was correct. I had foreseen from the beginning that, if we were to maintain friendly relations with Russia, we must abandon the policy of blocking her access to the sea. I was therefore prepared to discuss the matter.

But the moment was very inopportune. Turkey was hurt and sore at the slight put upon her by Austria and Bulgaria. It was hard enough that she should suffer this at the outset of what we hoped was a new and better era at Constantinople. We could not agree to add to her hardships by forcing upon her at once the embarrassing question of the Straits. If, later on, the consent of Turkey was obtained, this must be by satisfactory voluntary agreement and not by pressure or squeeze.

There was also a difficulty not of time, but inherent in the conditions on which the Straits should be open. A simple opening of the Straits to all ships of war of all nations would enable foreign fleets to assemble in the Black Sea at any time: this would not suit Russia at all, and would in fact be very disagreeable to her. On the other hand, we would not agree to Russian ships of war having the sole and exclusive right of passage through the Straits in time of war, when Turkey was neutral.

The following documents will illustrate the course of my conversation with Isvolsky.

*Sir Edward Grey to Sir A. Nicolson*
FOREIGN OFFICE,
*October* 12, 1908.

The following proposals have been made by Russian Minister for

Foreign Affairs for subjects to be discussed in limited Conference. If they are considered acceptable by Turkey and the other Powers we are prepared to agree to them.

The Conference should not deal with Dardanelles question, which Russia and Turkey should discuss privately, Turkey's consent being necessary before any change could be made. M. Isvolsky wishes to secure for Russia and the other States bordering on the Black Sea the right of using the Dardanelles for not more than three warships at once, on the condition that they agree not to anchor or stop there. He desires a promise from us not to oppose this arrangement, but it seems to me too one-sided to commend itself to public opinion here; in time of war, at any rate, reciprocal rights would be looked for; without some such arrangements, Mediterranean shipping would be in danger from warships, which could make raids upon them from the Black Sea, and take refuge either there or in the Dardanelles, whither they could not be pursued.

It is not, we think, the moment to discuss the Dardanelles question, which might make it appear as if Russia were pursuing selfish motives in profiting by the recent events and concluding a bargain with Austria.

The attitude of Russian officials with regard to events in Persia is also unpopular here.

Matters would be facilitated if public opinion could be convinced that reform in Turkey met with the warm approval of Russia.

If Russia were to join disinterestedly in settling the Near Eastern crisis to the advantage of Turkey, public opinion here would become more favourably disposed to her. His Majesty's Government see great difficulty in securing the acceptance here of a one-sided arrangement as to the Dardanelles, though they are quite prepared to agree to the opening of the Straits under proper safeguards. I should be glad to receive any information with regard to the feeling prevalent in Russia on the subject which you may be able to supply.

*Sir Edward Grey to Sir A. Nicolson*
FOREIGN OFFICE,
*October 12, 1908.*

SIR,—After the meeting of the Cabinet to-day I saw M. Isvolsky and told him that, though I wished to examine in the Department the details of his programme for a Conference, it had been generally approved by the Cabinet.

He then discussed what the next step should be. In his opinion it was desirable that a Conference should be announced as soon as possible, and, after considering various capitals, he expressed a strong opinion in favour of Rome as the most suitable meeting-place. He also asked me what was my view as to the way in which the invitations to the Conference should be issued—for instance, should Russia, France, and England jointly send them out?

I said I thought it would be very desirable to ascertain the views of Germany before issuing any invitations. Count Metternich had told me the desire of the German Government was to secure as fair terms as possible for Turkey and to smooth things over. If we issued the invitations without consulting her we might not have her good-will. So far as I could see, there was nothing in the programme to which Germany could object reasonably; and, by first ascertaining whether the programme met with her acceptance, we should prevent an apparent division of the Powers into two camps before the opening of the Conference.

M. Isvolsky dwelt upon the difficulty of getting Austria to accept the programme, as it included the discussion of the subject of Bosnia.

I suggested that, as the German Government wished to smooth things over, they would probably be able to arrange this.

It would be necessary to ascertain whether Turkey accepted the programme.

M. Isvolsky then asked me what I had to tell him about the Straits.

I told him frankly that the opinion of the Cabinet was that it would be very difficult, if not impossible, to get public opinion here to accept a one-sided arrangement about the Straits. At the time of the Anglo-Russian Convention we had contemplated that, in the course of time, confidence would grow up between England and Russia and make a favourable arrangement possible. But I found that, for instance, the action of Russian officers in Persia in suppressing the Constitution had created an unfavourable effect on public opinion here. I heard to-day that Russian officers were being sent with Cossack troops to put down the Nationalists at Tabreez. This, again, would make an unfavourable impression. People here would be still further unfavourably impressed if Russia sought advantages to herself from the present crisis in the Near East. If we came to a one-sided arrangement, which people here would argue necessitated an increase of our naval force in the Mediterranean, and if we altered an international treaty very greatly to the advantage of Russia, and to what would be considered our disadvantage, without getting anything in return, we should be making a concession which it would be very difficult to defend here at this moment.

I therefore thought the time was very inopportune.

M. Isvolsky dwelt upon the entire change of Russian feeling towards Turkey. Russia now desired to support Turkey as a barrier against the Austrian advance.

I suggested that Russia might demonstrate her good-will to Turkey by working for such a settlement of the present crisis as would safe-guard Turkish interests without any direct advantage to Russia herself— that would create a very good impression here.

As a detail, I pointed out the disadvantage it would be to us if, in time of war, when Turkey was at peace, one or two cruisers could come out through the Straits and harry British commerce without our being able to pursue them back into the Black Sea.

M. Isvolsky again dwelt with emphasis upon the unfortunate consequences which must follow if, once more, when there was an opportunity for settling the question of the Straits in favour of Russia, England opposed, and this time her opposition alone prevented a settlement.

I could only repeat that I saw great difficulties in any arrangement which was not reciprocal.

M. Isvolsky asked me what he was to telegraph to St. Petersburg —was he to telegraph a refusal?

I told him I had explained the difficulties which the Government felt in their way. We had had only a very short time to consider the matter, and I suggested that he should turn over the difficulties in his own mind before we considered the subject as closed.—I am, etc.

E. GREY.

*Sir Edward Grey to Sir A. Nicolson*
FOREIGN OFFICE,
*October* 13, 1908.

SIR,—Late in the evening of the 12th I had some further conversation with M. Isvolsky about the question of the Dardanelles.

He told me that the point I had put to him, as to Russian cruisers being able to come out through the Straits into the Mediterranean in time of war and being able to retire again into the Straits free from pursuit, had not occurred to him. He thought it might be met by a provision that, in time of war, when Turkey was neutral, she should observe her neutrality by giving equal facilities for passage through the Straits to all the belligerents.

I impressed upon him very strongly that I had no wish to send him away with the idea that we could not entertain any proposal about the Straits.

M. Isvolsky observed that the French Press were entirely on the side of opening the Straits.

I told him I had not given him the negative answer which he had deprecated. On the other hand, it was very difficult to give a positive answer, such as he had asked, for the reasons I had stated in the afternoon. The Cabinet felt that the time was exceedingly inopportune, and that they could not get public opinion here to accept at this moment a one-sided arrangement. I could satisfy the French Press any day, by saying that we entirely agreed with their view, which was that the Straits should be open on the same terms for all. But I should not help matters between Russia and us by so doing, for this view was one which was disliked by Russia.

I again impressed on M. Isvolsky the advantage of settling the present crisis in the Near East satisfactorily without seeking advantages for Russia or England.

I admitted that the proposal he had made as to equality in time of war did introduce an element of reciprocity, which had not been before the Cabinet, and which I would submit to them.—I am, etc.,

E. GREY.

The following despatch, which covers more ground, is perhaps worth printing here:

*Sir Edward Grey to Sir A. Nicolson*
FOREIGN OFFICE,
*October* 14, 1908.

SIR.—M. Isvolsky arrived in London on the 9th instant and called upon me at the Foreign Office on the 10th instant.

His Excellency began his conversation with me by a long explanation of what had passed between him and Baron d'Aehrenthal.

It was, in substance, what I had already heard, but he spoke very frankly of Baron d'Aehrenthal as being tortuous and insincere and always wishing to compromise the person with whom he was dealing. It was not true that he (M. Isvolsky) had given his consent in advance to what Austria had done about Bosnia. He had simply exchanged views, and had intended to discuss in Paris and London, afterwards, the possibility of the annexation of Bosnia by Austria and the consequences of such an eventuality. Meanwhile, this had been sprung upon him.

He made the most of the compensation offered by Austria as regards Novi-Bazar. In Austrian hands this would have prepared the way for an advance, and have been a wedge driven into the Slav States.

He emphasized the fact that these breaches of the International Treaty should be dealt with by a Conference, and he proposed that a Conference should be announced as soon as possible with a definite programme to deal with Bulgarian independence, Bosnia, Herzegovina, Novi-Bazar and Montenegro.

But it would not be enough simply to ratify what had already been done; that would not secure enough compensation either for Turkey or the other Balkan States.

Bulgaria had shown, in this matter, no consideration for Russian wishes, and Russia was prepared to be stiff in dealing with her. It might be arranged at the Conference that Bulgaria should pay for the Eastern Roumelian tribute and the railway. Serbia might have some rectification of her frontier, but it must not be at the expense of Turkey. There might also be a revision of the regulations about the Danube which would put the Balkan States on a more favourable footing; this would be in the nature of compensation to them at the expense of Austria. For Turkey, the hope might be held out that, if things went well, the Financial Commission and the joint right of superintendence given to the Powers with regard to Macedonia and Armenia by treaty would be done away with; and that the Capitulations also would be altered, if the Turkish Government justified such a step.

Russia would not raise the question of the Straits at the Conference.

M. Isvolsky urged very strongly that, if Russia could satisfy Turkey that an arrangement about the Straits was safe for Turkish interests, England should not oppose it. He told me that there had been great opposition in Russia to the Anglo-Russian Convention. He had had to spend great energy in getting it accepted in Russia. All the Liberal and advanced elements in Russia were in favour of an understanding with England; but the reactionary elements were against it, and would like to upset the Convention. The Emperor was, by training and education, not on the Liberal side. It was possible to keep him reconciled to reforms in Russia only by proving to him that things were going better; for instance, whereas, two years ago, there was a state of active revolution, the state of affairs was now much improved. In the same way it would be fatal to a good understanding with England if, when the question of the Straits were raised, it was found that England blocked the way and that no improvement followed from good relations with England.

His proposal to Turkey would be that ships of war belonging to the Riverain Powers on the Black Sea should have a right of way through the Straits. There might be regulations that not more than three vessels should go through at a time, and that no other vessels should go through for twenty-four hours after the first. Such regulations would, of course, only apply in times when Turkey was at peace. In time of war, Turkey would be able to do as she pleased.

In other words, the closing of the Straits would be maintained, subject to a limited serviture of this kind, in favour of Russia and the Riverain States.

M. Isvolsky went on to say that the present was a most critical moment. It might either consolidate and strengthen the good relations between England and Russia, or it might upset them altogether. His own position was at stake, for he was entirely bound up with the policy of a good understanding with England, which he had advocated against all opposition.

I asked him to give me a draft of what he proposed with regard to the Conference, so that I might have something definite to put before the Cabinet; this he promised to do.

I said I realized how critical the moment was. We were most anxious to work with Russia. We were in favour of the new regime in Turkey, not in order that we might support Turkey against Russia, but because we regarded an independent and well-governed Turkey as the only alternative to anarchy and confusion.

M. Isvolsky said the Russian desire now was to be friendly with Turkey. They did not wish to have Constantinople for themselves; it was not a place which could be held like Gibraltar; it had to be made a capital; they could not make it their own capital, and they would not wish to see it in any hands but those of Turkey. Therefore they wished to have a peaceful and well-governed Turkey, with whom they could be friendly.

I told him I recognized the Russian feeling about the Straits; but the proposal he had now put before me was not the same as that which Count Benckendorff had discussed with me at the time of the Anglo-Russian Convention. The proposal then had been that, while Russia should have egress from the Black Sea through the Straits, other Powers should have liberty to send their vessels of war into the Straits without going into the Black Sea.

M. Isvolsky pointed out that, as Russia would not ask for any right to stay in the Straits, it would be useless to grant a right of access to the Straits without staying there and without going on into the Black Sea. But he was not putting the proposal before me now on the ground that I had made any promise previously. He was putting it forward from the point of view of good relations.

If Russia did not make the proposal now it might be blocked by Germany or Austria at some future time; and he hoped that, if Russia could get the consent of Turkey voluntarily to an arrangement such as he had suggested, we would not oppose it.

I told M. Isvolsky I must have time to consult the Prime Minister and my colleagues, who had seen the proposal made some time ago, but to whom this would be quite new.

I urged that some immediate proof of confidence in the new regime in Turkey and good-will to it should be shown by offering a guaranteed loan if Turkey desired it. This would at once produce a general feeling of confidence and tranquillity.—I am, etc.,

E. Grey.

Eventually a memorandum embodying our views about the Straits was given to Isvolsky; he was partially, though not completely, pacified, and the question of the Straits was for the time allowed to rest.

There came upon us all, however, another and more formidable affair. Serbia demanded compensation for the change in the *status quo* made by Austria, to the disadvantage, as Serbia considered, of her own interests. We thought a demand by Serbia for territory would not be reasonable, but that some economic concession to facilitate the transport of Serbian exports to the Adriatic might provide an innocent solution.

Serbia was obstinate and headstrong, Austria was haughty, hard and stern. How serious the situation became will appear from the following telegram from me to Nicolson—

*Sir E. Grey to Sir A. Nicolson*

FOREIGN OFFICE,

*February* 27, 1909.

Your difficulties of Russia's position, which, as reported in your telegrams Nos. 102, 103, and 104 of the 26th instant, M. Isvolsky has explained to you, have, as you will see, been put before the French and German Governments in my communications to them in terms similar to those used by M. Isvolsky.

But the facts of the situation are accurately represented by the observation made by you to His Excellency as reported in the first sentence of your telegram No. 103. M. Isvolsky must recognize that, without a successful war, no advantages, except economic concessions, can be obtained for Serbia, and that war must inevitably ensue unless claims for territorial compensation are abandoned by Serbia.

When M. Isvolsky was in London I understood from His Excellency that in the end these claims would in all probability have to be withdrawn, and I explained to him that he could rely on our diplomatic support in obtaining such redress as was possible for Serbia, but that we should be unwilling to give him armed assistance.

The position of the Serbian Government is, in my opinion, that they have announced their readiness to submit to the decision of the Powers, but that public opinion at home will not allow them to abandon of their own accord claims to territorial compensation.

I received information yesterday from Count Metternich that his Government intended to make some proposal to France and His Majesty's Government. This had not as yet reached us, but it is probable that it will take the form of a suggestion that, provided that

Serbia will abandon her demand for territorial compensation, Austria should be asked by the Powers to take into favourable consideration the granting of economic concessions to Serbia.

I have not altered my view, which I expressed to the French Government, that it is impossible to expect Russia to advise Serbia to abandon territorial claims unless Germany has previously given substantial assurance that she will support the demand for economic concessions from Austria. Russia cannot now any longer delay deciding whether she will support Serbia in the event of war or whether, when the moment for decisive action arrives, she will tell Serbia that she finds it impossible to support her demands, as being contrary to the interests of peace. It is possible that M. Isvolsky is reluctant to come forward himself and explain to the Serbian Government what are really the facts of the case, and, if so, His Majesty's Government might join with France in undertaking this task in the interests of peace. But it would first be necessary that we should ourselves be aware of Russia's intentions.

If war were to take place, it would probably in the end embroil the greater part of the Continent, and even Russia must see that such a risk for the sake of Serbia's demands for territorial compensation is utterly disproportionate to the end in view. Above is only intended as expression of our opinion, and since reading your telegram No. 105, which has just reached me, I authorize you to use your own discretion as to how much of this you mention to M. Isvolsky.

The probability is, that if Russia had told Serbia from the first that she must not expect more than economic concessions, the situation would never have become dangerous, and Russia would have emerged with the credit of having done, at any rate, something for Serbia. As it was, Russia was stiff for a time, and then suddenly threw up the sponge and collapsed unconditionally. The strain on Isvolsky's temperament had been very great, and he seemed to have had a sudden reaction at the end to despair and disgust.

It was an unpleasant finish, as the following despatch from Nicolson shows:

*Sir A. Nicolson to Sir E. Grey*

St. Petersburg,
*March* 29, 1909.

Sir,—It was only on the morning of the 27th instant that the general public became aware that the Russian Government had consented, if asked by Austria-Hungary, to the unconditional abrogation of Article 25 of the Berlin Treaty, or, in other words, to recognize the annexation by Austria-Hungary of Bosnia and Herzegovina. It had always been understood that the Russian Government were, in conjunction with the Governments of Great Britain and of France, maintaining the attitude which had been announced on more than one occasion, both officially and publicly, that the modifications of an international treaty by Austria-Hungary on her own initiative, as well as the arbitrary infractions of the same treaty by Bulgaria, would not be recognized until the matter had been discussed and examined by all the Signatory Powers in conjunction with the compensations due to other States whose interests had been directly or indirectly affected by the acts of last autumn. It was therefore with surprise, and indeed with bewildered consternation, that the public learnt that the Russian Government, who were supposed to have under their especial care the interests of the smaller Balkan States, and whose influence in the Balkan Peninsula had been endangered, had consented suddenly to abandon the position which they had hitherto assumed, and to sanction the act which Austria-Hungary had executed some months ago. It was considered not only in the Press, but also, so far as I have been able to observe and ascertain, in all classes of society, that Russia had suffered a deep humiliation, and had renounced the traditional part which she had hitherto played in South-East Europe, and in the prosecution of which she had made so great sacrifices in the past. Even among those who take but little interest in foreign affairs, and who do not feel much sympathy for the smaller Balkan States, whom they regard as troublesome and ungrateful younger brethren, there was a feeling of bitter resentment that, at a most critical moment for two of the minor Slav States, their natural protector had abandoned them to the mercy of a German Power; and that Russia had consented, without making any reservations in favour of those who had looked to her for assistance, if not material, in any case moral and diplomatic, to give her seal to an act which had been committed by Austria-Hungary to the detriment of Slav interests. I have been assured, by those who have witnessed many various phases in the recent history of

Russia, that there has never previously been a moment when the country had undergone such humiliation, and, though Russia has had her troubles and trials, both external and internal, and has suffered defeats in the field, she has never had, for apparently no valid cause, to submit to the dictation of a foreign Power.

As I am sending this despatch by post, I do not like to enter into fuller details or to draw certain consequences which may possibly follow from the step which the Russian Government have taken. I will only notice that voices are being raised whether the ally and friend of Russia have proved sufficiently strong supporters at the hour of need.

The *Golos Pravdy*, the organ of the Octobrist Party, has given expression of these doubts in no uncertain tones, and has drawn the attention of its readers to the fact that the combination of the three Powers was too weak to withstand the first shock which it sustained from the Central Powers. It is considered out of the question that Russia could have taken the recent step without previous consultation with her Ally and her friend; and, indeed, it has been spread about that it was on the advice of Great Britain that the step was taken. When this version has come to my ears, I have naturally given it a direct denial. The whole truth will doubtless gradually be known, but when it is known it is hardly likely to mitigate the feeling of humiliation which at present is weighing so heavily on the public mind.—I have, etc.,

A. NICOLSON.

There was more unpleasantness still. I was accused in Austria, and I think in Germany too, of having fomented trouble and tried to provoke a European war. The following telegram to Cartwright gives some indication of my feeling at the injustice of the charge:

*Sir E. Grey to Sir F. Cartwright*
FOREIGN OFFICE,
*December 23, 1908.*

I can only qualify as preposterous and utterly absurd the Austrian suspicions that His Majesty's Government are desirous of bringing about a European war. (See your telegram No. 104 of the 21st instant.) Both public opinion here and the foreign policy of His Majesty's Government are alike opposed to such a scheme. So far from ever having encouraged the Governments of Serbia, Montenegro, and Turkey in an attitude of opposition to Austria, we might fairly claim that it is to some extent due to our influence that the Ottoman Government has shown itself ready to negotiate with Austria. We have used all our influence in the cause of peace by discouraging impossible claims and demands and by curbing the violence of public feeling, which was outraged by the policy of Baron d'Aehrenthal himself. Our power to preserve the peace of Europe can only be weakened by the unjust accusations which Austria is bringing against us, and which, moreover, are accepted as true in the Austrian dominions.

You may speak in this sense and in that of my previous telegram on the subject when discussing the matter with Baron d'Aehrenthal or any other influential persons.

This caused me little concern, for I thought it only a personal matter. In fact, it had a much deeper significance: it was a symptom of that inveterate and ineradicable distrust which poisoned European diplomacy and made any healthy growth impossible.

The following extracts from despatches are worth quoting. The first is from my official record of a conversation with Metternich at the Foreign Office on October 9, 1908:

Count Metternich said that Austria had given no warning to Germany, who had been just as surprised by what had taken place as the other Powers had been. But, though Germany wished, as he had said, to encourage the new regime in Turkey, she would feel bound in this matter to support her ally and friend.

The second is an extract from a telegram from Goschen, our Ambassador at Vienna, dated October 17, 1908, reporting a conversation with the German Ambassador there:

Herr von Tschirsky, in discussing the annexation question, remarked on the cleverness of Baron d'Aehrenthal in not previously giving a hint to Germany of his intentions. Discussions which might have been uncomfortable for both sides had thus been avoided.

The next quotation is an extract from a telegram from Goschen at Vienna, also dated October 17, 1908:

German Ambassador presented German Emperor's reply to Emperor of Austria to-day. The Press, to whom the German Ambassador seems to have been rather communicative, reports that the letter was most cordial, congratulating the Emperor upon the annexation and promising support.

Lastly, I give an extract from a report, dated February 11, 1909, made to me by Hardinge, then Permanent Under-Secretary at the Foreign Office, of his visit to Berlin in attendance upon King Edward. The extract refers to a conversation that Hardinge had with Prince Bülow:

Turning to the annexation of Bosnia and Herzegovina, he (Prince Bülow) assured me that although he had heard of the project after the meeting at Buchlau, Baron d'Aehrenthal's intention to put it into immediate execution had come as a complete surprise to him, and that he had only learnt it at the same time as the news was communicated in London and St. Petersburg. Although he expressed his conviction that Baron d'Aehrenthal may have been justified by the Pan-Serb agitation in the two provinces in his decision to put an end to it by annexation, he did not disguise from me his disapproval of the methods by which Baron D'Aehrenthal had attained his object. It would have been so simple for the Austrian Government to have announced to the Porte that, in view of the new state of affairs prevailing in Turkey, they proposed to dispense with the guarantees, which they had hitherto possessed, for the maintenance of order on the frontiers of the provinces, by withdrawing the Austrian troops from the Sandjak, in return for which the Turkish Government might have been willing to countenance the conversion of the occupation into definite annexation. To such an arrangement Turkey would probably have agreed, and none of the

Powers would have objected. Instead of this, by his precipitate action and seemingly thoughtless procedure, Turkey had been deeply incensed, the Powers affronted, the value as a concession of the evacuation of the Sandjak thrown away, and the Austrian Government compelled in the end to pay an indemnity of two and a half millions. It had been incumbent on the German Government to support Baron d'Aehrenthal throughout this crisis, whatever might be their feelings as to his procedure, but they had, when the opportunity presented itself, given moderating advice.

It is impossible to recount these events of 1909 without being struck by an ominous parallel with the crisis of 1914. In 1908, as in 1914, Austria acted without full consultation with her Ally—so the world was told by Von Bülow in the first, and by Von Bethmann-Hollweg in the latter, crisis. In 1908, as in 1914 Germany, while deprecating the headstrong character of Austria's action, thought it necessary to support her Ally. In 1909, as in 1914, Russia felt herself challenged to support Serbia. There the parallel ends. In 1908 Russia preferred humiliation; in 1914 she faced war. Let anyone who has not been impressed by Nicolson's account of the humiliation felt in Russia in 1909 turn back to page 182 and read it again. Let him remember also that this humiliation was branded into Russian feeling by the subsequent speech of the German Emperor at Vienna —the exulting speech, in which he spoke of having supported Austria in shining armour. Prestige amongst the Slav nations of South-East Europe was as necessary to Russia as to Austria. Russia could not afford a second blow such as that of 1908. And yet in the crisis of 1914, especially after Serbia's disarming reply to the Austrian ultimatum, there was no ruler in Germany great enough to feel that what was essential to the peace of

Europe was not the support of Austria in "shining armour," but a wise and strong restraining hand.

Here it is tempting to imagine how a moralist might reflect upon the discredit of the Near East policy of the Powers most concerned in it. For many years under Abdul Hamid (and his successors proved no better) Turkish rule had been a blighting misgovernment, with outbreaks of cruel outrage upon Christian minorities. Austria and Russia, each afraid of the other, each thinking of its own prestige and influence, had let the thing go on. Neither dared risk disturbance of the equilibrium, and the equilibrium was Abdul Hamid. So jealous and fearful were they both, that each was apt to resent as an intrusion even the lone hand of Britain, when it was put forth in the direction of Turkish reforms. Germany feared to see the equilibrium disturbed, lest consequences should ensue between Austria and Russia, in which she might feel it necessary to be involved. But Germany went further. If Austria and Russia were not moved by humanitarian considerations, Germany openly disregarded them, and made a friend of Abdul Hamid to further her own material interests in Asia Minor.[1]

What has come of all this rivalry, this struggle for prestige and for gain?

The thrones of Berlin, Vienna, and Moscow are empty. Germany, to get on her feet, is receiving international help on terms that would once have seemed incredibly humiliating. The fragment of country of which Vienna is now the capital has been a suppliant to the League of Nations, happily with success, to be saved from annihilation. Russia has had years of internal bloodshed, terror, and untold misery, of which we do not yet see the end.

[1] See the analysis of German official papers at the time of the Armenian atrocities in 1895, published in *The Times* of Jan. 8, 1924.

It would be distorting true perspective to say that lack of idealism in Near East policy was the cause of all this disaster; but it may fairly be said that it was a symptom of things that were the cause, and it was from the Near East that the flash came which fired the train of dire consequences.

The meditations of a moralist on public affairs are apt to become dreamy and far-fetched; perhaps these are so. Yet they may give rise to thoughts that are worth considering by all nations with great responsibilities, and they are not irrelevant to present realities and future contingencies.

One other subject which caused me much anxiety in these days, that of the Belgian Congo, deserves a brief mention.

From the early days of the nineteenth century there have been uprisings of public opinion against glaring abuses and cruelty, when public attention was once concentrated on them. These had their roots in a religious feeling that was deep and strong, even if it was sometimes narrow. This support made men like Wilberforce, Howard, Shaftesbury, and Plimsoll, and a woman such as Florence Nightingale, forces in public life, and made Britain a pioneer in the abolition of slavery, in Factory Acts and in prison reform. But the national conscience was not satisfied by reform of abuses in British territories; it insisted that British Governments should concern themselves with matters for which they had no special responsibility in lands over which they had no control. Gladstone roused it on behalf of Italy, and made it formidable against misrule in Turkey. It bestirred itself concerning slave labour in the Portuguese colonies, and cruelty in the Congo under King Leopold of Belgium. No British

Government could disregard it, and I believe that all the Governments of which I could form an intelligent opinion, those from 1880 onwards, sincerely desired and endeavoured to give effect to it. In doing so they were beset with difficulties; only in the United States was there any similar movement of opinion demanding action outside its own country. And in that vast country the movement was too partial to cause an uprising of national sentiment about such things as Turkish misrule, or to overcome the tradition of non-interference in the old world, handed down from Washington. In other countries, whatever the humane sentiments of individuals may have been about their own affairs, they did not take the form of pressure for philanthropic action abroad that might involve their own Governments in complication with continental neighbours. It was only an island such as Britain that could safely afford to embark on diplomatic crusades. To continental countries, these British efforts were often inconvenient, as in the case of Turkish reforms, and they were often resented, because they were not understood. They sometimes ran counter to obvious British interests, but this did not predispose foreign Governments to think them sincere. On the contrary, it stimulated them to search deeply for some concealed motive, though the true one lay on the surface before their eyes. It was no wonder, then, that in some instances these efforts of British Governments resulted in friction and futility. Their endeavours brought upon them the obstruction and dislike of foreign Governments, and their want of success exposed them to the criticisms of those at home, whose earnest and conscious rectitude of purpose made them too impatient to reckon or to allow for the difficulties that had to be encountered.

Of one only of these movements will account be given here. To do more would occupy too much space with affairs that were not in the main line of foreign policy.

By the time I returned to the Foreign Office in 1905 the agitation here was running high against cruelty in the Congo under the personal rule of King Leopold. The evidence was based upon a mass of information, including British consular reports, and nobody doubted that the state of things was atrocious. The outcome had been the formation in Britain of the Congo Reform Association, whose object it was to put an end to the abuses. My own feeling was one of detestation of the system and its crimes and of the character of the man who was responsible for them. The Belgian Government and Parliament disclaimed and had, in fact, no responsibility for what was done in the Congo. This was solely the personal affair of the King; but, if he relinquished the Congo, Belgium had the option of taking it. The Congo agitation did not therefore directly affect our relations with the Belgian Government; but Belgians did not like the attacks upon their King, and the suspicion that in the agitation there was some political motive prejudicial to their future option over the Congo made our action unpopular with them.

My own view of the remedy and of the objective we should set before ourselves was clear. It was the transference of the Congo from the personal rule of King Leopold to the constitutional Government of Belgium. I was convinced that a great and beneficent change would be effected as soon as the administration was in the hands of a Government that was not concerned with trading profits and private gain; and also that the abuses, of which we heard, could not continue under a Government that had to account for its acts to a freely elected popular Assembly.

The transfer of the Congo to Belgium would therefore be a real and effective solution.

This solution was not only practicable, but it was also the only one that would be honourable and politically expedient. To promote any other would be to disregard the indisputable right of Belgium to have the Congo, whenever King Leopold relinquished it. Any other settlement would arbitrarily and forcibly pass over and deny the right of a smaller State.

To do this would also be politically unwise, for it would open up a vista of political complications. If Belgium declined to exercise her right to the Congo, France had, by treaty with her, a right to pre-emption. Neither we nor other Powers were party to that treaty, but it was in the knowledge of us all, and we had neither intention nor desire to question the French pre-emption. It would come into operation only if Belgium voluntarily resigned her own right; but it was most improbable that other Powers interested in Africa would acquiesce in seeing Belgium voluntarily set aside and the whole vast and, in some parts, valuable area of the Congo, presented to France. France, therefore, would naturally stand up for the rights of Belgium, on which her own contingent interest depended; to ignore those rights would lead to friction with France and would prompt Germany, who had important African possessions adjoining the Congo, to assert her own interest in the question. Portugal, who also had territory adjoining the Congo, might also claim to be admitted to the discussion. In fact, the future of the Congo would become an international question fraught with unpleasant possibilities.

European Powers had already enough complications on hand, and it would be the height of imprudence, and even of impolicy, to add the Congo to them. On the other hand, if the Congo were transferred to Belgium, not a finger would be stirred or a word said by anyone. The Belgian solution was therefore the only one that would be effective, expedient, and honourable to all concerned. For this we pressed.

Our action was based on the international treaties or arrangements respecting the Congo and Africa in general to which we, with other Powers, were parties. But we got no support from anyone; we were left coldly and severely alone in our representation. Neither France nor Germany desired to share in the unpopularity in Belgium that we incurred by the anti-Congo agitation. Each of them probably wished to avoid the risk of its becoming a political question.

King Leopold resented the British agitation, including no doubt my own speeches and diplomatic action; he even sent me a long personal letter of protest. We continued to make ourselves disagreeable, and we hoped we were making him uncomfortable; it was all we could do. Any sending of force by ourselves into the Congo would have been regarded with great distrust and jealousy by other Powers, and would have been taken as a sure indication that we meant to get something for ourselves; the precedent of Egypt, where we had landed with temporary intentions and stayed permanently, would have been vigorously recalled. Our contention that the Congo agitation here was disinterested would have been stultified.

It is not worth while now to examine what share we might claim in having hastened the transfer of the Congo to Belgium. King Leopold did at last relinquish it. From that moment the representations of the British Government ceased; the Congo Reform Association dissolved itself; the agitation stopped.  This should fairly be noted as proof that the stir of British public opinion about the Congo was, what it professed to be, genuinely philanthropic and disinterested.  The transfer of the Congo to Belgium was regarded not only with satisfaction, but with relief; and the expectation that Congo reform would result proved to be justified, and the hope has been fulfilled.

It is well known that there were from time to time during these years differences of opinion in the Cabinet about naval or military expenditure.  Probably they are endemic in all Cabinets, but it is only occasionally that they attain to epidemic violence.  The difference is not on the principle of national safety, but as to the margin of strength necessary to secure it.  The most acute crisis in the Liberal Government came over naval expenditure in 1909.  Were we to be committed to the construction of eight new battleships, or would six, or even four, be enough for national safety?  For some days there was a Cabinet crisis.  Eventually it was observed that all eight ships could not be laid down at once, and it was agreed that the construction should proceed in a manner that would not delay the completion of the eight ships if reflection and further knowledge proved them to be necessary, but on the understanding that reduction of the number could be made, if it became apparent that the need for them had been overestimated.  To the public and the Press at this time "eight ships" became a formula, but in the Cabinet the difference was about substance and not formula.  No one of us wanted eight ships, unless they were really required; every one of us was prepared to agree to them, if they were proved necessary to secure national safety.

The usual method by which agreement is reached in such crises is as follows:

The difference of opinion is disclosed, stated, and stoutly maintained on each side at a Cabinet. If it is so important and acute as to make resignation seem certain or probable, individual Ministers of different views seek private talks with each other outside the Cabinet. In this way the strength of their respective arguments is tested; the amount of concession that each feels he can make is ascertained. Finally, a Cabinet again meets with the knowledge that it is going to agree. This presupposes that the difference of opinion is really about the merits of the question, and is not a pretext put forward for a personal or political object. When it is a pretext for either of these things the procedure is much less pleasant and the prognosis less favourable.

There was often a wrestle, sometimes sluggish, sometimes brisk, about Army Estimates. Haldane had to argue and struggle to get what he asked for; sometimes he had to economize on what was of secondary importance, in order to get what the War Office felt to be of primary importance. On one occasion temperature rose sufficiently high to cause one of the opponents of Haldane's Estimates to speak of the War Office in conversation as "the Ministry of Slaughter"; but, in the end, what was regarded as essential was obtained without ill-feeling or rancour.

# CHAPTER XII

## (1908-1910)

### KING EDWARD AND FOREIGN POLICY

The King's Visits Abroad—Unfounded Suspicions—The Supposed "Encircling Policy"—The King's Illness and Death—An Estimate of his Character—Legend and Fact—Intangible Qualities—His Popularity a National Asset—The Value of the Monarchy as a British Institution—King George's Accession.

THE visits of King Edward abroad have been the subject of much surmise and suspicion. They were not made the occasion of any manœuvres against any Power. They were friendly when he went to Germany; the malignant suggestion that, when he visited the Emperor of Austria, an attempt was made by him, or by anyone who went with him, to sow dissension between Austria and Germany has been disposed of by the publication of the confidential report of that visit made by Sir Charles Hardinge. To this I may add that I impressed upon Sir Fairfax Cartwright, when he went as Ambassador at Vienna, that he should do nothing to make trouble between Austria and Germany. We wanted the Entente and Germany's Triple Alliance to live side by side in amity. That was the best that was practicable. If we intrigued to break up the Triple Alliance, our contention that the Entente was entirely defensive and was not directed against Germany would cease to be true. Disturbance and possible war, it was clear, would be the consequence. The Germans worked up the theory of an "encircling policy" and attributed it particularly to King

Edward. I did not think that the German Government seriously believed this theory. It seemed incredible that they should not realize that, if Germany had alliances, other countries must have them too. It seemed to me that they surely must see that the Franco-Russian Alliance was the inevitable outcome and counterpart of the Triple Alliance; that German strategic railways must beget other strategic railways. The French encouragement of Russian railways towards the German frontier was a natural consequence of the railways Germany had already made towards the French and Belgian frontiers. The consequence cannot fairly be considered more malignant than the cause. After the Triple Alliance was formed Russia was isolated, France was isolated, Britain was not only isolated, but in constant danger of war with France or Russia. German statesmen cannot seriously have thought that this situation could last. France and Russia found some comfort in an Alliance, and at last Britain found it in an Entente. It seemed to me that Germans must understand this sequence of events, and that the theory of the "encircling" policy was encouraged to keep German opinion up to high-water mark in expenditure on German armaments.

The visit of King Edward to Reval in the summer of 1908 was, and is still, made the subject of unjust suspicion and mischievous legend. As usual, King Edward was accompanied by Hardinge, and I stayed at home. The report made to me by Hardinge at the time of the visit is printed in an Appendix to this chapter. Here let it be observed, about all these reports by Hardinge of the visits of King Edward, that they are the real full, authentic, confidential record of what took place.

In May 1910 we knew that King Edward was seriously

ill. I had gone to my cottage for a week-end without expecting that anything was imminent; a private message from Hardinge told me that he had received very bad news from Buckingham Palace. I returned to London. My brother had just arrived from Africa. I told him what was impending, and we sat up together. The house I was living in is in Queen Anne's Gate, but on the farther and retired side and not facing Bird Cage Walk. Late at night, all was quiet about us. Presently the silence of the deserted street was broken; something was being cried; we leant out of the window and heard the newsvendors calling, "Death of the King."

It is not till a thing has actually happened that we know the full import of it. Prepare for it as we may, try all we may, we cannot beforehand realize all that it will mean to us. But when the event comes, an enlargement of understanding is suddenly borne in upon us on a wave of emotion. I felt that something irreparable, like a landslide, had happened. To explain what King Edward was it is necessary first to get rid of some misconceptions about him, which have obtained abroad rather than in his own country. A legend arose in his life-time which perhaps was believed more widely afterwards, that British foreign policy was due to his initiative, instigation, and control. This was not so in my experience. He not only accepted the constitutional practice that policy must be that of his Ministers, but he preferred that it should be so. He read all the important papers, and now and then a despatch would come back with some short marginal comment approving of something contained in it; but comment of any sort was rare, and I do not remember criticism or suggestion. In conversation he would show that he was aware of all that was being done and had followed it, but his comments would be on some point immediately in hand. He did not care for long and sustained discussion about large aspects of policy, though he brought strong common sense and good judgment to bear on any concrete matter of the moment. It would be a mistake to infer from this that he was indifferent to the general trend of our foreign policy. It must be remembered that the course for this had been set before I went to the Foreign Office in 1905. I was continuing a policy with which he was already familiar and in sympathy. My impression is that he had gone through the same process as many of us had done, that of getting to feel uncomfortable at dependence on Germany, and to dislike repeated quarrels with France or Russia. He was therefore staunch in his desire for friendship with these two countries. Had his Ministers reversed this policy, he would, I imagine, have made it clear to them that he disliked what they were doing and thought it unwise. As it was, he never left a doubt that the policy we were pursuing had his cordial approval and good-will. But never for a moment did he suggest that this policy should be given a point against Germany; and when he paid a State visit to Berlin he enjoyed making his presence popular there as much as anywhere else.

He took an active interest in high diplomatic appointments, such as those of Ambassadors, but it was from the point of view of their personal qualities, not from that of policy. He wished us to be represented abroad with dignity and personal prestige.

What, then, were the qualities that made him so important to the country? They are not easy to describe, because they were the intangible qualities of a personality peculiar to himself. Let the more commonplace be considered first. He had in a very high degree the gift, proper and valuable in a Sovereign, for ceremonial. No one knew so well as he how ceremony should be arranged, ordered, and carried through in the manner most effective and impressive. By his own person, and by the part he took in it, he added dignity to it. In all this he performed to perfection the function that only the Sovereign can perform for the British Empire. This, however, is expected of the Sovereign, and, however well it is performed, unless there be something else, people are left satisfied but cold; they may even come to resent the pomp and the display. King Edward had a rare, if not a unique, power of combining bonhomie and dignity. The bonhomie was warm and spontaneous, but it never impaired the dignity. His bearing was a perfect example of tact, ease, and dignity, and to this were added good sense and judgment that not only avoided mistakes, but perceived the thing that should be said to suit the occasion or please an individual. These gifts, valuable in any Sovereign, were particularly so in one who was the living centre of an Empire that included the self-governing Dominions and India.

There was, however, something more that gave a spirit and aspect to it all, and this was due to his individual personality. Warm human kindness was of the very substance of the man. The misfortune or unhappiness of anyone he knew caused him real discomfort; and he would do anything in his power to relieve it. The success or good fortune of a friend gave him lively pleasure and satisfaction. He had a capacity for enjoying life, which is always attractive, but which is peculiarly so when it is combined with a positive and strong desire that everyone else should enjoy life too. These, it may be thought, are not very uncommon qualities, but King Edward had a peculiar power of making them felt. The crowd knew and recognized them. I imagine, for instance, that the humblest devotees of horse-racing in a Derby-day crowd knew that King Edward was there to enjoy the national festival in precisely the same spirit as themselves, that he wished them to enjoy it too; that their enjoyment was part of his own. There was, in fact, real sympathy and community of feeling between himself and his people. It was the same wherever he went. I was told it was perceptible even in the short time of his visit to Berlin, though there was no political Entente to predispose to popularity.

The effect was due, no doubt, to the genuineness of his own feeling; but, when all has been said, something is required in the nature of genius to account for this remarkable power of projecting his personality over a crowd.

He became intensely and increasingly popular, and when he died, the unprecedented, long-drawn-out procession, to pass the bier of state in Westminster Hall, was a manifestation of genuine and personal sorrow as well as of national mourning.

Popularity such as this centred in a constitutional Sovereign was an immense advantage to the State. The position is one that cannot be combined with responsibility for policy. Any association, past or present, of the Sovereign with political controversy would be fatal to it. The manner in which it was filled by King Edward, and his great popularity, made him a real asset of national stability; and this, in a time of crisis or upheaval, would have been of inestimable value. His death was felt as a national loss, especially by his Ministers, who were in the exposed position of responsibility for the conduct of the nation's affairs.

Every human institution must change, if it is to last. The strength and endurance of the British Monarchy has been due to its adaptability to new conditions. The United States and France have shown that Monarchy is not essential to modern States: the British Empire to-day demonstrates that even in the most democratic country there is a place for Monarchy, that, rightly evolved, it performs a function that no other institution could accomplish. The British Monarchy to-day adds to the stability, without in the least hampering the freedom, of Britain itself or of any part of the Empire. In previous centuries such an evolution must have seemed improbable: one can imagine a successful essay to prove it impossible by the argument that the Crown must either be a check upon democracy or be reduced to futility. The answer is, *solvitur ambulando* —the thing is impossible until it exists. It has come by the most convincing of all methods, not by plan, but by practical evolution.

Certain conditions are necessary. The succession must be hereditary: no other method of choice will give a Sovereign that complete aloofness from rivalry and controversy which is essential to his peculiar position. He must, in his person, embody the traditions of the past as well as the practice of the present; his previous life must have trained and prepared him for the position. He must realize that, while the ceremonial side of the Crown has to be maintained with dignity, and even with reasonable splendour, it is in fact a democratic institution. Each Ministry in turn must in equal degree, irrespective of class or party, have the confidence, support, and good-will of the Sovereign. However much his influence may be used with the Prime Minister or other members of the Cabinet in favour of his personal opinion about policy or appointments, there must be nothing done by the Sovereign to weaken or undermine the position of Ministers. In return, their attitude to him must be one of respect as well as frankness; they must be careful to protect the Monarchy and observe its forms. The performance by the Sovereign of the duties and his observance of the limitations of the Monarchy must be repaid by perfect loyalty to him.

Everyone who was present when King George first received those who had been the last Ministers under King Edward must have been touched by the deep regret with which King George found himself so early called upon to fill his father's place: they must have been impressed, too, by the modesty and also by the earnest public spirit with which he addressed himself to the task before him. The promise of that first audience has been fulfilled: the King has been faithful to the traditions and practice of his father, and in the trying years that followed has shown a continuous example of public duty and patriotic feeling. The years that have passed do but confirm the impression that constitutional Monarchy is of the highest value in substance and in form to the unity of the Empire.

## APPENDIX TO CHAPTER XII

Report of Sir Charles Hardinge to Sir Edward Grey on the Visit of King Edward to the Tsar at Reval in June 1908

After a rough passage across the North Sea, the King and Queen arrived at Kiel on Sunday, June 7. Their Majesties were there met by Prince and Princess Henry of Prussia, and, after a short stay, left again for Reval, escorted by a division of German destroyers for some distance from the harbour.

The smart appearance of the whole of the German North Sea Fleet lying at anchor in the port gave food for reflection upon the recent German naval programme of construction, while the intricate evolutions of the torpedo flotilla, which excited the admiration of all the naval officers on board the royal yacht, served as a useful object-lesson of the efficiency of the German Navy.

I may mention that the officers of the two British cruisers H.M.S. *Minotaur* and *Achilles* were, while waiting at Kiel to escort the King in the Baltic, entertained at dinner by Prince Henry of Prussia, who made a speech to them expressing friendship towards England, disclaiming any aggressive intentions on the part of the German Navy, and asking them to make these views understood and spread throughout England. It is thought by those who know Prince Henry that he would not have spoken in this strain without direct instructions to do so.

I was able to ascertain, during our short stay at Kiel, that the work of enlarging the Canal has already been begun, and that a commission is this very week sitting at Kiel to arrange the details of the work.

The King and Queen arrived at Reval on the morning of the 9th instant, having had splendid weather in the Baltic, and there met the Emperor, the two Empresses, and members of the Imperial Family, with some of the Russian Ministers, on board the two Imperial yachts and the cruiser *Almaz,* the sole survivor of the large Russian fleet that took part in the battle of Tsushima.

During the two days spent at Reval the weather was fortunately brilliant, although only two days earlier such a gale had been blowing as would have rendered communication between the yachts almost impossible, and four inches of snow had fallen.

During the course of the visit the King had several interviews with M. Stolypine and M. Isvolsky, from which, I understand, the best possible impressions were created on both sides.

I had several opportunities of discussing with M. Isvolsky the various questions of foreign policy in which our two countries are chiefly interested, and I cannot help thinking that this direct exchange of views between the two Foreign Offices will be beneficial and facilitate the solution of most of our pending questions.

My first enquiry of M. Isvolsky was as to the impression which had been created upon him and in Russia by Sir Edward Grey's recent speech [1] in the House of Commons. He replied that it was excellent, and that what had impressed people in Russia so much was the tone of moderation and firmness with which it was inspired. He was evidently pleased with it.

The question of Macedonian Reform entailed a considerable amount of discussion, and gave M. Isvolsky an opportunity of expounding the

[1] Presumably the speech in the House of Commons explaining the Anglo-Russian Convention, Feb. 17, 1908.

general policy of Russia towards England and Germany, which I will endeavour to describe as shortly as possible.

M. Isvolsky stated that the scheme of Macedonian Reforms was one which he had deeply at heart, and upon which Russian public opinion, as shown by the Press, felt strongly. He personally would have gladly accepted the whole of the scheme as first developed by Sir Edward Grey if he had seen the slightest prospect of obtaining its adoption by the rest of the Powers, and, lastly, by the Sultan. He knew for a fact, however, that this scheme would have met with the greatest opposition on the part of Germany and Austria, and even now he anticipated considerable difficulties if any further modifications of a drastic nature were to be introduced into the scheme as defined by his last note. He reminded me that Russia is always in a difficult position *vis-à-vis* of Germany, owing to the military supremacy of the latter Power on the frontier, that in Germany there is very great nervousness as to future political developments amongst the Powers, and that the age and indifferent health of the Emperor of Austria are a source of uneasiness as to the future. It was imperative, therefore, that Russia should act with the greatest prudence towards Germany, and give the latter Power no cause for complaint that the improvement of the relations of Russia with England had entailed a corresponding deterioration of the relations of Russia towards Germany. During the past two months the German Government had formally complained to him more than once of the hostility of the Russian Press towards Germany, and, although he greatly regretted the outspoken sentiments of the Russian Press, which he fully believed reflected their true feelings, he had been obliged to confess his impotence under the present system of liberty of the Press to control their utterances. The visit of the French President to London, of the King to Reval, and the impending visit of the President to Russia, had not tended to improve matters, and he foresaw that difficulties were to be expected from Germany and Austria, especially in the adoption of the scheme of Macedonian Reforms. He therefore expressed the hope that his last note, which he had reason to believe the German Government might be induced to accept as it stands, would be adopted by Sir Edward Grey as the limit to which the rope could be strained without breaking, and that the King's visit to Reval might be consecrated by the announcement of the complete agreement of England and Russia upon the scheme of reforms to be adopted in Macedonia.

I told M. Isvolsky that when I left London the text of his last note had not been received by Sir Edward Grey, only a telegraphic summary having been sent by Mr. O'Beirne. Sir Edward Grey had therefore been unable to give me complete and definite instructions, although he had authorized me to make suggestions for a solution of some of the points still at issue. When at Kiel I had received the text of his note, and, although I realized that a complete agreement had almost been arrived at, it would be impossible to make such an announcement as he had suggested unless he was ready to accept the compromise which I had been authorized to suggest. As for the attitude of Germany towards England and Russia, and towards the recent improvement of relations between them, His Majesty's Government were inspired with no hostile feelings towards Germany, with whom they were anxious to maintain the most friendly relations, and they realized that every action should be avoided which would unnecessarily irritate or exasperate feeling in Germany. Such an attitude was probably even more necessary for Russia, but in the case of His Majesty's Government this did not mean that they would be ready to sacrifice their legitimate interests or those of humanity at large to escape the ill-will of Germany, since this would be the course best calculated to provoke it. Although the attitude of His Majesty's Government towards Germany was, and had been, absolutely correct, it was impossible to ignore the fact that, owing to the unnecessarily large increase in the German naval programme, a deep distrust in England of Germany's future intentions had been created. This distrust would be still further accentuated with the progress of time, the realization of the German programme, and the increase of taxation in England entailed by the necessary naval counter-measures. In seven or eight years' time a critical situation might arise, in which Russia, if strong in Europe, might be the arbiter of peace, and have much more influence in securing the peace of the world than at any Hague Conference. For this reason it was absolutely necessary that England and Russia should maintain towards each other the same cordial and friendly relations as now exist between England and France, which in the case of England and Russia are, moreover, inspired by an identity of interests of which a solution of the Macedonian problem was not the least.

So, also, as regards the King's visit to Reval, which could not possibly be interpreted as a provocation to Germany, since it could not be admitted that the German Emperor should enjoy a monopoly of State visits to other Sovereigns, and Sir Edward Grey had been very explicit in his statement in the House of Commons that it was not proposed to negotiate any *new* treaty or convention at Reval. I explained that this statement had been expressly made with a view to preventing any trouble between Germany and Russia owing to the King's visit to the Emperor of Russia. . . .

In raising the question of the Balkan railways he (M. Isvolsky) complained bitterly of Baron Aehrenthal's action in springing upon him the Sanjak Railway concession without any warning whatever—a proceeding which had seriously disturbed the *status quo* in the Balkans, and had shaken his confidence in him. It was clear that, in spite of Baron Aehrenthal having spent seventeen years in Russia, he had not grasped the real feeling in Russia towards the Slav population in the Balkans, since he had imagined that there could be only a short flare up in the Russian Press, and that Austro-Russian relations would then return once more to their former groove. In this he was entirely mistaken, since the relations between Austria and Russia in connexion with affairs in the Balkans could not be the same again. M. Isvolsky said that he felt considerable anxiety about the Balkan Railway questions; he was convinced that the Sanjak Railway would be pushed by Austria with the utmost energy, and he considered it absolutely necessary that the Danube-Adriatic Railway should be pushed forward *pari passu*. The Russian Government had only a very small financial interest in the proposed railway, but they realized that the completion of the Austrian schemes would mean a monopoly of railway construction in Macedonia, and, if this rumour should be confirmed, he would not hesitate to take strong measures to prevent what he would consider to be an infringement of the spirit of the Treaty of Berlin. Although he regretted that His Majesty's Government had been unable so far to support the Serbian Railway scheme, he appreciated their reasons for not doing so; but he hoped that, as soon as an agreement had been arrived at on the scheme of Macedonian reforms, His Majesty's Government would be able to lend their support to it.

I told M. Isvolsky that His Majesty's Government are not at all opposed in principle to the construction of railways in Macedonia, which must necessarily have a civilizing influence, but that they had deprecated the opportuneness of the action of Austria at a moment when the Powers were devoting their whole attention to the question of reforms. I was, however, able to state that, as soon as the scheme of reforms had been put forward by the Powers at Constantinople, Sir Edward Grey would be ready to instruct His Majesty's Ambassador to impress upon the Porte the necessity for granting similar treatment to the Danube-Adriatic Railway as has already been granted to the Sanjak Railway. We were, I said, of the opinion that either no concession, or both concessions, should be granted.

M. Isvolsky entirely concurred, adding that the Russian Government would prefer that none should be granted.

The conversations which I had with M. Isvolsky, of which the above is a summary, lasted about three hours altogether, and although I have known M. Isvolsky personally for a great many years, they gave me an interesting insight into the official side of his character which I had not previously had an opportunity of seeing. He struck me as very able and adroit, but extremely timid. Although he tried hard to make me commit myself on the Macedonian question beyond the limit of the authority which was given to me, any suggestion which I made to him was at once set aside as requiring careful study. He was, however, very friendly throughout.

I had several opportunities of short conversations with the Emperor, who looked extraordinarily well, and in the best possible spirits. On the first occasion that His Majesty spoke to me he warmly praised Sir Edward Grey's speech in the House of Commons, which, he said, showed a remarkably true appreciation of the real political situation in Russia, and which had made the best possible impression. He asked me to convey to Sir Edward Grey his warmest thanks, and to say that he endorsed and accepted every word that his speech contained. He was extremely glad that the debate had taken place, since it had shown to the world that the two great political parties in England shared the same friendly feeling towards Russia, and, the dissentients having had free scope to say all that they wanted against him and his Government, the air had been cleared as after a thunderstorm.

He hoped very much to have the opportunity, before long, of making the personal acquaintance of Sir Edward Grey, who had so largely contributed to the realization of his dearest hopes in achieving a real improvement in the relations between England and Russia.

The Emperor repeatedly expressed his great satisfaction at the visit of the King and Queen, which, he said, sealed and confirmed the intention and spirit of the Anglo-Russian Agreement, and he expressed his profound conviction that the friendly sentiments which now prevail between the two Governments could only mature and grow stronger with the progress of time to the mutual advantage of both countries. There might be occasional divergence of views in small matters, but the identity of the national interests of England and Russia in Europe and Asia would far outweigh any possible results from such trivial differences of opinion. A glance at the Russian Press of all shades and opinions showed conclusively how extremely popular throughout Russia the King's visit had become, and how it was welcomed as the visible sign of a new era in Anglo-Russian relations. On my expressing my surprise that such papers as the *Novoe Vremja,* which I had always regarded, when in Russia, as the bitterest foe of England, had now become the ardent supporters of an Anglo-Russian understanding, His Majesty admitted that he also was astonished at the rapidity with which the feeling had spread, and that he had never been so surprised as when he had read recently in a Chauvinistic "rag" called the *Sviet* a warm article in praise of England, and urging closer relations between the two countries. Since the liberty of the Press had been established in Russia, the Press had really become the reflex of public opinion, and it was astonishing to see the complete unanimity that prevails as to the necessity of warm and friendly relations with England. The idea had taken firm root amongst the people, and it only required now to be carefully fostered to bear fruit in the future. The Emperor admitted that, from the point of view of the relations of Russia to Germany, the liberty of expression now enjoyed by the Press had caused him and his Government considerable embarrassment, since every incident that occurred in any distant province of the Empire, such as an earthquake or thunderstorm, was at once put down to Germany's account, and serious complaints had recently been made to him and the Government of the unfriendly tone of the Russian Press. He was, however, quite unable to remedy this state of affairs, except by an occasional official *communiqué* to the Press, and this had generally but slight effect. He wished very much that the Press would turn their attention to internal rather than to foreign affairs; but this was too much to expect.

The Emperor alluded to the recent Baltic and North Sea Agreements, and said that he could not see at all the reason for them, nor the advantage. As far as he could judge, the situation remains practically the same as heretofore, the only result being much waste of time and

LORD HARDINGE OF PENSHURST, K.G.
British Ambassador in St. Petersburg, 1904-1906, and Permanent Under-
Secretary for Foreign Affairs, 1906-1910

energy, and considerable anxiety during the negotiations amongst smaller Powers as to the intentions of the Great Powers. They seemed, however, to have given some satisfaction to the German Emperor, and he did not therefore grudge it to him.

I seized the opportunity to say to the Emperor that I presumed that it would always remain a cardinal principle of Russian policy to keep the Straits between the Baltic and North Sea open, to which His Majesty warmly assented as a matter of vital interest to Russia. I said that the free entry into the Baltic was also a matter of great importance to England, and that, if ever the question of closing the Straits were raised in the future, Russia could count on our co-operation with her to keep the Straits open. The Emperor remarked that this is one more instance of the identity of our interests.

*July* 12, 1908.

The remainder of this record deals with the details of the proposed Macedonian Reforms, sundry questions arising out of the Anglo-Russian Agreement in regard to Persia, and the measures to be taken in Crete on the withdrawal of the international force. The above are the only passages touching the relations of the Great Powers.

# CHAPTER XIII

## (1911)

### THE THIRD CRISIS (AGADIR)

Death of George Grey—Trouble in Morocco—The French March to Fez—The German Retort—The *Panther* at Agadir—The British Attitude—The Silence of Berlin—Lloyd George's Speech—German Protests—German and French Bargaining—British Efforts for Peace—Some Moments of Relief—A Theory of German Action—German Policy Reviewed—Some German Ambassadors.

EARLY in 1911 George Grey, the brother next to me in age, was killed by a lion in East Africa. His work and his pleasure had been as a pioneer and explorer in new and in unmapped countries. Our work had been on different lines and in separate continents, but Fallodon had remained his home when in England. He had spent several months with me there or in my house in London in 1910, and we had planned to make permanent home together, when he should have given up travel and when I should be out of office. He had encountered exceptional difficulties in early life, and had surmounted them by great qualities. His thought on all practical sides of human work was clear and strong, and he had the power of decision and resolute action. He was a most excellent judge of men. To this was added an innate contempt for anything that was not straight, and courage, both physical and moral, that was impregnable. In times of danger, and in wild places, he was a leader of men. In these last years I had known also his unspoken tenderness and sympathy, a quality that is so particularly attractive, when combined with strength of character and courage.

His sudden death was a great shock and an irreparable blow to his family and near friends.

In the spring of this year there was great internal disturbance in Morocco; Fez itself was in danger, and it was evident that the hand of France might be forced and that it might even be necessary for her to send troops to Fez to relieve the situation and prevent catastrophe, in which her own or other European subjects might be involved. Spain was the other Power with a special position in Morocco: she was very sensitive about her own prestige and very apprehensive lest, as the weaker Power compared with France, her prestige should suffer. If France took action, Spain was sure to do something in order to assert her influence. The whole Moroccan question would then be reopened. As long as it was possible, I deprecated any action by either Power, but things got worse in Morocco and eventually France sent a force to Fez and Spain landed troops in her zone. Then suddenly the Germans sent a ship, the *Panther,* to Agadir. Agadir was a port not open to commerce; it was said to be suitable for a naval base. The German action at once created a crisis, and for weeks the issue of peace or war hung in the balance. We were bound by the Anglo-French Agreement of 1904 to give France diplomatic support. This engagement we fulfilled in letter and spirit, while doing all we could to steer for peace, not war.

The German contention was that French action in going to Fez had altered the *status quo,* as settled by the Act of Algeciras, and that if that *status quo* was not restored Germany must have compensation. To this we could not demur, and France accepted negotiations on this basis. In what followed I took the line with Metternich that, if trouble came, British public opinion would side with France and that German demands on France for compensation should not be such as it was impossible for any French Government to concede. On the other hand, I urged on France the expediency of withdrawing from Fez as soon as possible, and I deprecated the sending of British and French ships to lie alongside the German ship at Agadir, or even to occupy other Moroccan ports as a counter-stroke. Such action by us or by France, taken while there was hope of peace, would weigh the balance on the side of war. As regards compensation I told the French in reply to their enquiries that we would raise no objection to anything they decided to give Germany in the French Congo, and that, even in Morocco, British interests did not, in our opinion, require us to object to concessions to Germany, short of anything that might be a naval base on the flank of our trade route. Concession to Germany in Morocco would not have been an agreeable solution, but it was for the French, not for us, to exclude it. It was, of course, made clear to the French that we should not suggest or hint at anything that they disapproved of, and that we should give them diplomatic support in resisting German demands that they felt to be excessive. This time there were no scares, such as there had been in 1906, that we were going to leave France in the lurch diplomatically. My relations with Cambon were such that I could discuss every possible method of conciliation with him, without his becoming apprehensive that we meant to throw the French over.

The despatch of the *Panther* to Agadir was a very brusque way of opening negotiations with the French: the Germans followed it up by a disregard of us that led to a dramatic incident. At the risk of somewhat confusing the order of the general narrative I will quote the documents that explain and comment on the incident.

Here is the original announcement made to us of the despatch of the *Panther*:

### Minute by Sir A. Nicolson

SIR EDWARD GREY,—The German Ambassador called this morning and said he had been instructed to make a verbal communication, which is recorded in the above *aide-mémoire*.[1]  A similar communication was, Count Metternich said, being made to the French and Spanish Governments by the German Ambassadors at Paris and Madrid.  I merely remarked that Agadir was not an open port, and that I was unaware that any German or foreign subjects resided there or in its neighbourhood.

Count Metternich continued by saying that he wished to make an explanatory statement: the advance of France to Fez, in regard to the necessity of which German reports differed from those of the French, and also the establishment both by France and Spain of military posts in various parts of Morocco, had created a new situation, and one which rendered the provisions of the Act of Algeciras illusory.  By that Act France and Spain were only authorized to organize police forces in certain open ports.  The German Government had no desire to pass any criticisms on the above action of France and Spain, but they were bound to lend an ear to the requests of German subjects and protected subjects in districts in the south where no organized police forces existed.  It was the duty of the German Government to afford the necessary protection to the lives and properties of their subjects in the south, and to continue to afford such protection until a condition of normal peace and tranquillity had been re-established.  The German

---

[1] The *aide-mémoire* is as follows: Des maisons allemandes établies au sud du Maroc et notamment à Agadir et dans ses environs, se sont allarmées d'une certaine fermentation parmi les tribus de ces contrées que semblent avoir produite les derniers événements dans d'autres parties du pays. Ces maisons se sont adressées au Gouvernement Impérial pour lui demander protection pour leur vie et leurs biens. Sur leur demande le Gouvernement a décidé d'envoyer au port d'Agadir un bâtiment de guerre, pour prêter, en cas de besoin, aide et secours à ses sujets et protégés ainsi qu'aux considérables intérêts allemands engagés dans les dites contrées. Dès que l'état de choses au Maroc sera rentré dans son calme antérieur, le bateau chargé de cette mission protectrice aura à quitter le port d'Agadir.

Government were ready to endeavour to find with the French and Spanish Governments a definite solution of the Morocco question. They were well aware that there were difficulties in the way of reaching a solution, but, owing to the friendly relations between Germany, France, and Spain, they did not consider that such difficulties were insurmountable. If the British Government were ready to assist towards this end their aid would be gladly welcomed.

I said that I would repeat to you as faithfully as possible what he had said to me. He could understand that the communication was one of great importance, and would have to be very carefully considered.

A. N.

Foreign Office, *July* 1, 1911.

P.S.—I should add that Count Metternich said that a return to the *status quo ante* was out of the question.

On July 4 I had the following conversation with the German Ambassador in London:

*Sir Edward Grey to Count de Salis*

Foreign Office,

*July* 4, 1911.

Sir,—I informed Count Metternich to-day, on behalf of His Majesty's Government, that I must tell him that our attitude could not be a disinterested one with regard to Morocco. We must take into consideration our treaty obligations to France and our own interests in Morocco. We were of opinion that a new situation had been created by the despatch of a German ship to Agadir. Future developments might affect British interests more directly than they had hitherto been affected, and, therefore, we could not recognize any new arrangement which was come to without us.

Count Metternich asked me whether he might take down the exact words. I therefore dictated them to him, observing, however, that he must take this as a conversation and not as a written communication.

He remarked that the new situation.had been created by French and Spanish action.

I said I understood the view of the German Government to be that the French and Spanish action had made it necessary for them to calm German public opinion by showing that Germany was not disinterested

in the question of Morocco.  They had taken the overt step of sending
a ship to Agadir.  We had not taken any overt step, though our commercial interests in Morocco were greater than those of Germany.  It
was therefore the more incumbent upon us to make it clear that we,
no more than Germany, could let things develop without taking an
interest in them.

Count Metternich then said that the attitude of our Press towards
the sending of a German ship to Agadir was not likely to foster that
favourable atmosphere for discussion for which I had expressed a wish
in conversation yesterday.  The German Press, on the other hand, had
been very calm.

I said that I had stated yesterday that the action of Germany in
sending a ship to a closed port, where it was not known that commercial
interests existed, was sure to excite the Press here and elsewhere.  If
we, instead of the German Government, had sent a ship to Agadir
while the German Government did nothing, the German Press would
have been equally excited.

In commenting upon the communication which I had made, Count
Metternich said that he was sure the German Government would under-
stand that it was natural for us to take an interest in the question.—
I am, etc.,                                                    E. GREY.

It will be observed that this was a communication made
after consultation in the Cabinet: the first paragraph was
what I had been authorized to say.  Days passed, and
Metternich was apparently left without any instructions
from Berlin, and could tell me nothing from his Government when I saw him.  It is true that we had not addressed any direct question to the German Government,
but it was unusual for any Government completely to
ignore a communication such as I had made.

On the afternoon of July 21 I was suddenly told that
Lloyd George (then Chancellor of the Exchequer) had
come over to the Foreign Office and wanted to see me.
He came into my room and asked me if the German Government had given any answer to the communication I

had made on behalf of the Cabinet on July 4. I said that none had reached me, but, to make sure, I had enquiry made in the Office whether anything had come that day which had not yet reached me. There was nothing. Lloyd George then asked whether it was not unusual for our communication to be left without any notice, and I replied that it was. He told me that he had to make a speech in the City of London that evening, and thought he ought to say something about it; he then took a paper from his pocket and read out what he had put down as suitable. I thought what he proposed to say was quite justified, and would be salutary, and I cordially agreed. I considered there was nothing in the words that Germany could fairly resent. Lloyd George spoke as he had proposed that evening. What follows is the important part of it:

But I am also bound to say this—that I believe it is essential in the highest interests, not merely of this country, but of the world, that Britain should at all hazards maintain her place and her prestige amongst the Great Powers of the world. Her potent influence has many a time been in the past, and may yet be in the future, invaluable to the cause of human liberty. It has more than once in the past redeemed continental nations, who are sometimes too apt to forget that service, from overwhelming disaster, and even from national extinction. I would make great sacrifices to preserve peace. I conceive that nothing would justify a disturbance of international good-will except questions of the gravest national moment. But if a situation were to be forced upon us in which peace could only be preserved by the surrender of the great and beneficent position Britain has won by centuries of heroism and achievement, by allowing Britain to be treated, where her interests were vitally affected, as if she were of no account in the Cabinet of nations, then I say emphatically that peace at that price would be a humiliation intolerable for a great country like ours to endure. National honour is no party question. The security of our great international trade is no party question. The peace of the world is much more likely to be secured if all nations realize fairly what the conditions of peace must be.   And it is because I have the conviction that nations are beginning to understand each other better, to appreciate each other's points of view more thoroughly, to be more ready to discuss calmly and dispassionately their differences, that I feel assured that nothing will happen between now and next year which will render it difficult for the Chancellor of the Exchequer in this place to respond to the toast proposed by you, my Lord Mayor, of the continued prosperity of the public purse.

The speech was entirely Lloyd George's own idea.   I did nothing to instigate it, but I welcomed it.   The effect was much greater than any words of mine could have been. There was a section, and a considerable section, of opinion in this country that looked upon the Foreign Office in general, and myself in particular, as being unduly anti-German, just as in 1893, for instance, they looked upon Rosebery and the Foreign Office as being anti-French. Anything that I said was therefore liable to produce a certain reaction of antipathy in this section.   The Germans knew this well enough, and no doubt prepared to make some discount of what I said.   But Lloyd George was closely associated with what was supposed to be a pro-German element in the Liberal Government and in the House of Commons.   Therefore, when he spoke out, the Germans knew that the whole of the Government and House of Commons had to be reckoned with.   It was my opinion then, and it is so still, that the speech had much to do with preserving the peace in 1911.   It created a great explosion of words in Germany, but it made Chauvinists there doubt whether it would be wise to fire the guns. The speech certainly had the effect of making the German Government keep in touch with their Ambassador in London and send him instructions, as the following records of conversation show:

*Sir Edward Grey to Sir E. Goschen*

FOREIGN OFFICE,
*July 24, 1911.*

SIR,—Count Metternich asked to see me to-day, and when he came informed me that he had fully reported to his Government what I had said to him on Friday, the 21st. He was now instructed to make a communication to me. It was as follows:

From the beginning the German Government had sent a ship to Agadir in order to protect German interests, and for no other reason. The special cause was the attack of natives on a German farm.

At this point I observed that I had not, I thought, heard of this attack before. I had understood that the despatch of the ship had been due to apprehension as to what might happen, not to what had actually happened.

Count Metternich remarked that he had not been told of it before.

He then proceeded to say that, so far, nothing had happened to give reason for thinking that the German intentions were changed. Not a man had been landed; and he could inform me, though this was very confidential, that the German commander had strict orders to land men only in case of extreme necessity—when the lives of Germans were menaced.

I observed that I thought there were no Germans in this region, and that I supposed, therefore, the term "German" must mean German-protected persons.

Count Metternich said that he had no information on this point.

He went on to say that his Government regretted the credence which was given to insinuations as to the intentions of Germany that came from hostile quarters. Germany never had thought of creating a naval port on the Moroccan coast, and never would think of it. Such ideas were hallucinations. She had no intentions on Moroccan territory, but demanded that France should keep strictly to the Act of Algeciras, or else come to explanations with Germany. The German Government thought that the latter course would be more in the interests of France, and they had proposed, quite generally, that Germany should be given compensation in colonial matters, in order that she might give up her right to object to French action in Morocco. Negotiations had been begun with France, and both parties had promised to keep the strictest secrecy. On the German side this had seriously been done; not even the Allies of Germany were informed of what had passed.

France, on the contrary, to Germany's regret, had given partial information to the Press, and also to her friends, the information being incorrect and incomplete, and calculated to mislead as to the intentions of Germany.

Herr von Kiderlen had declared to M. Jules Cambon that he could not go on with negotiations and make positive and detailed proposals (a thing which he had not done hitherto) until secrecy was guaranteed. In order to avoid misrepresentation, he had proposed that information should be given, when mutually agreed upon, to mutual friends and to the Press. M. Jules Cambon's answer to this was expected yesterday.

If the German demands were rather high, Germany was ready to make concessions in Morocco as well as in colonial matters. But the Chauvinistic tone of the French, and part of the British Press, menacing Germany with the interference of the friends of France, did not tend towards a settlement. Should the present negotiations be wrecked, even then Germany would have no designs upon Moroccan territory; but she would have to demand from France, with determination and emphasis, that the Algeciras Act should be fully carried out, in spirit as well as in letter. Germany could not, as one of the Great Powers, let the French presume to encroach upon her rights, contrary to written treaties. Germany still hoped that things would not come to that point, and that a friendly exchange of opinions à deux would avoid this. If, however, France should not wish to come to an understanding on the basis proposed, Germany would have to demand a return to the status quo ante in Morocco, and in doing so would count on the support of the other Powers who were parties to the Algeciras Act, and especially of England.

Count Metternich told me confidentially that his Government had made no demand as to the right of pre-emption in the Belgian Congo.

I said that I would communicate this statement to the Prime Minister. But, as I was likely to be asked in Parliament what was happening at Agadir, I should like to know whether I might say that the German Government had informed me that not a man had been landed.

Count Metternich requested that I should make no public statement with regard to this conversation until he had had time to communicate with his Government.

I further observed that the question of what was the status quo ante was a matter of interpretation, in which I assumed that all the Powers who signed the Algeciras Act would have a say, and, if so, what Germany had said seemed to me to point to a conference in the last resort.

Count Metternich said that no doubt there were sometimes in treaties dark points which it was difficult to interpret, but there were other points which were clear. In this case it was very clear that France ought to withdraw from any occupation of Morocco extending beyond what was contemplated by the Algeciras Act, and the question was not one to be submitted to a vote, nor was it open to serious discussion. Germany, he repeated, hoped for our support.

I observed again that the question as to the *status quo ante* was a matter for interpretation, and it would have to be discussed if the time came to raise it.—I am, etc.,

E. GREY.

The following despatch shows the next stage:

*Sir Edward Grey to Sir E. Goschen*

*July 25, 1911.*

SIR,—The German Ambassador came to see me to-day, and, in reply to my question of Monday as to whether I might make use in Parliament of the information which the German Government had given that no men had been landed at Agadir, he gave me the answer of the German Government.

The information was confidential, and they must request me to treat it as such. They could not consent to its being used in Parliament, after the speech of the Chancellor of the Exchequer. That speech had been interpreted without contradiction as having a tone of provocation for Germany, and the German Government could not let the belief arise that, in consequence of the speech, thy had made a declaration of intentions about Morocco.

I observed that I must say at once that the fact that the Chancellor of the Exchequer's speech, which seemed to me to give no cause for complaint, had created surprise was in itself a justification of the speech, as it could not have created surprise unless there had been some tendency to think that we might be disregarded.

The German Ambassador said that he had a further communication to make about the speech, but meanwhile he went on to say that, if an understanding with France fell through owing to French resistance,

Germany must demand that the Treaty of Algeciras be kept, and the *status quo ante* be restored, whether that were agreeable to France or not.

The German Government did not think that a Conference would be necessary. Germany, as one of the signatories of the Treaty of Algeciras, was entitled by herself to vindicate the rights of the treaty. If, in that endeavour, Germany found the support of third parties, it would be very welcome, and would facilitate her action. But if, after the many provocations from the side of France and her free-and-easy manner in Morocco, as if neither Germany nor a treaty existed, France should repel the hand which was proffered to her by Germany, German dignity as a Great Power would make it necessary to secure by all means, and, if necessary, also alone, full respect by France for German treaty right.

This communication was read to me by Count Metternich, and he then proceeded to read to me a further communication.

The text of the speech of the Chancellor of the Exchequer had given rise, in part of the British Press, and in nearly the whole of the French Press, to attacks on Germany. The German Foreign Secretary could not say how far this was intended by the British Government. The effect of the speech had made a bad impression in Germany, as, owing to utterances made by me to Count Metternich, the effect of the speech could not have been unforeseen.

Negotiations were in progress with France to put an end to the difficulties which had arisen owing to the free-and-easy way in which she had thought it right to disregard the obligations of Algeciras. Germany had explicitly and repeatedly declared that she would like, without recriminations on the past, to come to a peaceful and amicable understanding directly with France. France had accepted this, and had agreed to carry on negotiations for the time being secretly. Germany had made propositions to France that seemed to the German Government quite loyal and acceptable. Those propositions concerned territories in which English interests were neither directly nor indirectly engaged.

If notwithstanding that, England thought that she ought to express some wishes, it might have been expected that these wishes would have been transmitted to Germany in the usual diplomatic channel. Instead of this, the British Government had, through one of their members, given public declarations which, to say the least, *could* have been interpreted as a warning to Germany's address, and which, as a matter of fact, had by the British and French Presses been interpreted as a warning bordering on menace.

Germany could not see by what reasons the British Government had been guided. The British Government could not have been in any doubt that, by that proceeding, the friendly understanding between Germany and France could not be furthered. Considering the tone which for some time had been adopted by part of the British Press, and by the whole of the French Press, the British Government could hardly doubt what effect the speech of the Chancellor of the Exchequer would have. If the British Government, assuming this as a hypothesis, should have had the intention to embroil the political situation and lead towards a violent explosion, they could not have chosen a better means than the speech of the Chancellor of the Exchequer, which took so very little into account, with regard to Germany, the dignity and place of a Great Power, which the Chancellor of the Exchequer claimed for England in that speech.

I said that I could only repeat what I had already said about the speech of the Chancellor of the Exchequer. The speech had not claimed anything except that we were entitled to be considered as one of the great nations. It had claimed no pre-eminence, and it had not even indicated that there was a crisis. It had dealt in general terms with remote contingencies. The German Government had said that it was not consistent with their dignity, after the speech of the Chancellor of the Exchequer, to give explanations as to what was taking place at Agadir. I felt that the tone of their communication made it not consistent with our dignity to give explanations as to the speech of the Chancellor of the Exchequer.

This, however, I could genuinely say. It was not intended, by anything that had been said, or would be said, to embroil Germany's negotiations with France. On the contrary, we sincerely desired that they should succeed. The Foreign Office Vote was to be taken in the House of Commons the day after to-morrow, and I would then make this clear. But the tone of the German communication was very unfavourable also as regards France, and made it more than ever evident that a very difficult situation would arise if the German negotiations with France did not succeed.

From this Count Metternich did not dissent.—I am, etc.,

E. Grey.

That was the end of this incident, but the negotiations dragged on for many weeks yet to come, and there were very anxious periods.  The Germans at first made such huge demands on the French Congo as it was obvious that no French Government would concede.  The fact was that both Governments had got into a very difficult position: each was afraid of its own public opinion.  The German Government dared not accept little.  Their own Colonial Party had got their feelings excited and their mouth very wide open.  If the mouth was not stopped— and it would need a big slice to fill it—there would be great shouting.  The French Colonial party would revolt if their Government gave up much.  Probably after a time the German Government was as anxious as the French to get out of the business by a settlement, but neither dared settle.

I was accused afterwards of having been more French than the French, and of having made things more difficult, because I observed to Metternich that some very large demand made by Germany on the French Congo was more than France could possibly concede.  It was supposed that I was urging the French to resist.

The following two documents will illustrate the line taken by me with the French:

*Sir Edward Grey to Sir F. Bertie*
FOREIGN OFFICE,
*July* 19, 1911.

Your telegram of July 18.

Since France considers that the demands made upon her by Germany are greater than she can consent to, it is evident that the French Government should now make counter-proposals which will embody what concessions in the French Congo she is prepared to grant.  Any concession there considered reasonable by France could not be objected to by us.

I shall telegraph again as to the course developments may take in the event of a refusal by Germany to reduce her demands on French Congo.

*Sir Edward Grey to Sir F. Bertie*

FOREIGN OFFICE,

*September* 5, 1911.

SIR,—M. Cambon showed me to-day a telegraphic summary of the conversation of yesterday between the French Ambassador and Herr von Kiderlen in Berlin.

Herr von Kiderlen had, after some discussion, accepted in principle the project for what was virtually a French protectorate over Morocco. He had made difficulties about the limitation of economic equality to thirty years, about the French protectorate over Moorish subjects abroad, and about the judicial organization; and he had protested against the proposals about German protégés. He was, however, ready to agree to a secret understanding as to the establishment later on of a French protectorate, really and technically. He had said that the Germans could not give anything in Togoland, and that he must refer all the proposals to the Chancellor.

M. Cambon asked me what I thought of this.

I said that I expected Herr von Kiderlen would reply that what was offered in the French Congo was not enough. Personally, it seemed to me that, geographically, climatically, and generally, Morocco was of so much greater importance to France than the French Congo that it would be a pity for France not to increase her offer of territory in the French Congo, if necessary, and if she could get a clean and definitive arrangement as to Morocco. Could she not, for instance, give the triangle for which Germany asked up to the river Alima?

M. Cambon said that this was impossible. He said that it must be remembered that, after the experience of the arrangement with Germany of 1909, the French Parliament would be apt to say that what was given up in the French Congo was solid, while nothing was being obtained from Germany except a bit of paper which might be worth nothing.

I remarked that any cessions of territory in the French Congo might be made dependent upon the agreement with Germany being accepted by all the other Powers who were parties to the Act of Algeciras. This would give France an assured position in Morocco.

THE FOREIGN OFFICE

I observed how important it was that, if there was trouble, it should be quite clear that it was Germany who forced it. I hoped, therefore, that the French would not break off the negotiations. M. Cambon replied that the French Ambassador at Berlin was fully aware of the importance of this.—I am, etc.,

E. GREY.

All my effort was to get Germany to moderate her demands as much as she could and to get France to go as far as she could in increasing her offers. Whatever influence we had was used in this way to promote a peaceful settlement.

It was my opinion, and that of the Cabinet, that in the last resort we should propose a Conference to avert war. I spoke of the possibility of this to Metternich: he did not hold out much hope that it would find favour at Berlin. I sounded the French; they were not inclined to it, at any rate not yet. Cambon asked me what we should do if Germany refused a Conference. This I could not tell. I could only say that public opinion here would be stronger if a Conference were refused. No man and no Government could pledge this country in advance to go to war.

Eventually France and Germany came to terms. France got her free hand in Morocco, and Germany got concessions elsewhere. The Moroccan question was at last out of the way, and was not to threaten the peace of Europe again. The storm was over, but a ground-swell continued, sufficient to give the German Government a tossing in their debate in the Reichstag and to excite the Crown Prince to a demonstration of feeling on that occasion. But the French and German Governments had made up their minds to peace. The French took care to make the Yellow Book that they published as much of an anodyne as possible. It was said at the time that the French

Ambassador and the Secretary for Foreign Affairs at Berlin arranged together that this should be so.

Two other quotations will show the views I expressed to Ambassadors of less interested Powers:

*Sir Edward Grey to Sir E. Goschen*

FOREIGN OFFICE,

*July* 13, 1911.

Italian Ambassador having asked my opinion about Morocco, I said that Germany had opened the question in the worst possible way. Having given it to be understood that her interests were only commercial, she had gone to a port which was closed commercially; she has thus made it clear that commercial interests were only a pretext. Agadir happened also to be the port most suitable for a naval base. Germany had thus at the outset mobilized the whole of British public opinion, and made it certain that our interests would be engaged on the side of France.

It is now for Germany, if she wishes to make conversations easy, to do so by removing first impression created by her action.

We do not wish to impede a settlement between her and France, but we must wait to know what Germany's object is before we can decide whether British interests require us to intervene in discussions.

You should adapt your language to these views when the occasion demands it, or if it becomes necessary to repeat or supplement what I said to German Ambassador on July 4.

*Sir Edward Grey to Sir G. Buchanan*

FOREIGN OFFICE,

*September* 4, 1911.

SIR,—The Russian Ambassador asked me to-day what I thought of the prospects of the conversations between France and Germany.

I said that the outcome was very obscure. The Germans had changed their ground so often that it was very difficult to form an opinion. There would certainly not be war unless Germany intended to have it. If the conversations came to a deadlock, everything would depend upon what Germany did. If she took some action to rush matters, either by landing a force in Morocco or by sending to France a communication in the nature of an ultimatum about the Algeciras Act, such as Count

Metternich had foreshadowed in a conversation with me some weeks ago, it would of course mean that she intended war. But otherwise some settlement would be patched up. I said that I understood the Russian Government were being kept informed of everything, and I asked whether he had any news from St. Petersburg.

He replied that he had none.

I told him that Sir Fairfax Cartwright had not been cognizant of the articles in the *Neue Freie Presse*,[1] and the attacks upon him had been worked up from German sources. There must have been some object in this. It might be that Germany intended to make a settlement with France, and to explain that this settlement was not satisfactory owing to the action of England. The German Government might intend to cover their retreat by giving this explanation to German public opinion. It might be one way of securing peace, though it would tend to an increase of naval expenditure.

I observed that the whole matter might have been settled if the Germans had gone to the French, when the latter reached Fez, and told them quietly that Germany must have a settlement. But when the Germans opened the proceedings by sending a warship to Agadir they mobilized public opinion here, in France, and in Germany. The Germans were now hampered by the public feeling which they had themselves created.

Count Benckendorff expressed himself very decidedly to the effect that the sending of a German warship to Agadir was very unfortunate, and indeed immoral.—I am, etc.,

E. GREY.

One more despatch may be worth quoting to show that even in Berlin there was sometimes a lighter side to the discussions, and that our Ambassador there was not without a sense of humour:

*Sir E. Goschen to Sir Edward Grey*
(Received August 28)

BERLIN,
*August* 25, 1911.

SIR,—I had to-day some conversation with Herr Zimmermann on the subject of Morocco, and particularly on the subject of the despatch

---

[1] An alleged interview with him published by that journal.

of the *Panther* to Agadir.  He complained bitterly about Mr. Lloyd George's speech, which, he said, had done untold harm both with regard to German public opinion and the negotiations.  I said that for what had done most harm one must go back a little further than Mr. Lloyd George's speech, namely, to the despatch of the German warship to Agadir.  He said that he had never understood why public opinion in England had been upset by that event.  "When we informed Sir Edward Grey that we were going to send a ship to Agadir——" I here interrupted and said, "You mean that you had sent a ship to Agadir."  He acquiesced in my interruption, and continuing, said, "When we informed Sir Edward Grey that we had sent a ship to Agadir he took the news quite quietly, and we had no idea that there was going to be all this trouble about it."  I said that it was in my recollection that you had spoken strongly to Count Metternich on the subject.  He said, "Well, at all events, we had no idea that public opinion would feel so strongly about it, and Mr. Lloyd George's speech came upon us like a thunderbolt."  He added that the whole trouble arose from the fact that it was not recognized in England that the despatch of a ship to Agadir, which had been the Emperor's idea, was really meant to make it easier for the French Government to defend any compensation they might be ready to give, and which they had expressed readiness to give, before the French Parliament.  I could not help saying that it seemed to me to be a somewhat dubious method of facilitating the negotiations, and that I could scarcely fancy a French Minister of Foreign Affairs standing up in the French Parliament and saying that he had to yield to German demands for compensation because Germany, as a hint that she meant business, had sent a warship to a closed Moroccan port.  Besides, I added, I thought that the *Panther* had been sent to protect the lives and property of the employees of certain Hamburg merchants.  "Ah!" said Herr Zimmermann, "that was the primary reason, and the reason for the urgency which prevented us from informing the Powers of our intention.  But it was thought, all the same, that it would have a good effect on the negotiations in the way I have just stated."  I am bound to say that even Herr Zimmermann smiled when I mentioned the Hamburg merchants.  I said that I was glad to know the real reason why the ship had been sent to Agadir, but I thought, if he would allow me to say so, that it might have been wiser if, before M. Cambon left Kissingen, he had been consulted as to whether the despatch of the *Panther* would have the salutary effect on the negotiations which the Imperial Government anticipated.  To this Herr Zimmermann replied that he was not at Berlin at the time, or perhaps——.  Here he broke off his sentence, which would seem to imply that he agreed with me.

Herr Zimmermann went over a lot of old ground, and spoke at some length as to the disappointment Germany had felt at our attitude, the growing excitement in German public opinion, the irritation of the Emperor, and many other things which you have repeatedly heard from Count Metternich, and which I have reported as having been said by the Emperor.  I need not, therefore, trouble you with the rest of his observations.

The reasons, however, which he gave me for the despatch of a ship to Agadir are, as far as I am aware, quite new, and therefore may be of some interest.—I have, etc.,

W. E. GOSCHEN.

The summer of 1911 was one of splendid heat; such a summer as comes seldom in England; it surpassed anything known in this generation.  If my memory is correct, there were not less than thirteen days distributed through the summer when the temperature was 90 degrees or more in the shade—Greenwich reported 100 degrees on one day, but I have always doubted this figure: no other place got within 3 or 4 degrees of the 100.  Still, it was very hot, and even when Parliament was not sitting, the prolonged Agadir crisis prevented me from enjoying the glorious weather at Fallodon.  One other colleague, not tied to London by official work, kept me company for love of the crisis.  Winston Churchill was then at the Home Office, but he followed the anxieties of the Foreign Office with intense interest and, I imagine, saw much of Sir Henry Wilson, then at the War Office—at any rate, he insisted on taking me once to see Wilson, and their talk was keen and apparently not the first that they had had.  Let me not be supposed to imply that Churchill was working for war, or desired it: he followed all the diplomacy closely, but never either in Council or in conversation with me did he urge an aggressive line. It was only that his high-metalled spirit was exhilarated by the air of crisis and high events. His companionship was a great refreshment, and late in the afternoon he would call for me and take me to the Automobile Club, which was but thinly populated, like other clubs, at that season. There, after what had been to me a weary, perhaps an anxious, day he would cool his ardour and I revive my spirits in the swimming bath.

What was the real motive that underlay the despatch of the *Panther* to Agadir?

Whoever has been inside British foreign policy is familiar with the emotion of indignation, amusement, or contempt with which he reads of the deep motives and the clever schemes that are invented for present-day British diplomatists and attributed to them by ingenious writers in foreign, and sometimes even in the British, press. One who is conscious of this may well be cautious in attributing deep and sinister designs to the action of foreign Governments. I therefore give, with all reserve, the theory that seemed to me best to fit the facts.

One thing seems to be certain. The appeal of Hamburg merchants, the original reason given by the German Government for the despatch of the *Panther* to Agadir, was not the real reason; there was something behind that, at any rate. We had assumed that the forced dismissal of Delcassé in 1905 and the dragging of France to a Conference at Algeciras in 1906 were an attempt to break the newly formed Anglo-French Entente by demonstrating to France that friendship with Britain would bring France more trouble than help. On this assumption Agadir would be a second attempt to effect the same

object.   It would, in my opinion, be contrary to evidence
and reason to suggest that the Bosnia-Herzegovina Crisis
of 1908-9 was engineered by Germany to shake the relations between Britain, France, and Russia; but the result
of it had been to damage in Russia the prestige of the
alliance with France, and to lower Russian opinion of the
value of British friendship.   This may have encouraged
the notion that another crisis directed against France was
not an entirely hopeless project.   On this theory Germany
must have contemplated the contingency of war with
France, if need be.   Had the crisis led to war, this would
have come at the very season that we know was favoured
for the purpose by German military leaders in 1870, and
that was selected for the menace to France in 1905, and
that we believe was decided by the military authorities
for war in 1914.

If this theory be correct, if the Agadir Crisis was
intended to end either in the diplomatic humiliation of
France or in war, why was it allowed to end without
effecting either object?   One answer would be that in
1911 the German Fleet was not so strong as in 1914,
nor the German Army at the same height of equipment
to which it was subsequently brought by her capital levy.
Germany had, therefore, decided not to risk war with
Britain, and when it became apparent that there was this
risk she switched, difficult as it then was to do so, on to
a policy of certain peace.   Before the crisis she may have
been encouraged to think the risk of war with Britain
negligible, or even remote.   My own conduct of Foreign
Affairs had become very unpopular with part of the
Liberal Press and was the subject of open criticism.   The
writers of these criticisms made the mistake, as is so often
done, of attributing all that they disliked to the influence

of one man, not realizing that all important telegrams to and from the Foreign Office were circulated every day to the Cabinet, and that it is impossible for any Secretary for Foreign Affairs to continue in his post unless he has the general approval of the Cabinet. How much the impression made in Germany by these Liberal critics was increased by sources with which the agents of the German Embassy in London were bound to be in touch I never knew or enquired. The surmise is that Germany thought, for one reason or another, that we should be less firm in 1911 in a Morocco Crisis than we were in 1906. If so, the speech of Lloyd George must have upset the whole of their calculations.

We were told at the time, with what truth I do not know, that, when it seemed possible that war might come, the great financial interests in Germany strongly opposed it, urging that they had not been warned in time to make suitable arrangements. If this be true, the fact that the German Government had not warned their financiers can only be accounted for in one of two ways: either they had overlooked the necessity for warning them, or else this theory that the German Government had contemplated and deliberately provoked the contingency of war is not correct. Some day perhaps the Germans will tell us—if they really know, or have still the means of finding out the truth.

The end was almost a fiasco for Germany; out of this mountain of a German-made crisis had come a mouse of colonial territory in tropical Africa. France was left with her prestige intact and free of the Morocco thumb-screws. Happily there was sufficient criticism of what France had ceded to prevent the end being regarded in France as a triumph. Colonial Parties in France, as in

Britain and elsewhere, are apt to estimate portions of tropical Africa by their extent in square miles and not by their real value.   Lloyd George, of course, made no speech about having supported France in shining armour. But the consequences of such a foreign crisis do not end with it.   They seem to end, but they go underground and reappear later on.   The militarists in Germany were bitterly disappointed over Agadir, and when the next crisis came we found them with the reins in their hands at Berlin.

So also with the consequences of the Bosnia-Herzegovina crisis; in 1914 Germany and Austria found a Russia that would not collapse to order a second time.

Since 1906 I had made no enquiry whether the British and French military authorities were remaining in close touch, though I had assumed that they were doing so. Agadir made it certain that their preparations would be kept up to date.   This reflection suggested to me in later years a train of thought that took shape in imagining the indictment that Bismarck, could he have been a spectator of it all, might have brought against his successors, particularly in their dealings with Britain.

"I left you," he might say, "predominant in Europe with a strong Triple Alliance.

"It may be that the Franco-Russian Alliance could not be prevented; the very strength of the Triple Alliance was almost bound to call that counter-Alliance into being. But when it was made there was no chance of England joining it; indeed, the Alliance seemed directed more against England than against Germany, so bad were the relations of England with both France and Russia.   At length England, in her discomfort, publicly through Chamberlain offered us an Alliance.   You rejected it, and added to English discomfort by starting a naval programme, which everybody considered a challenge to the British Fleet. At last England and France, tired of their quarrels, perceived that these were a danger to themselves and an advantage to Germany, and English statesmen, weary of the discomfort of their isolation and apprehensive for the future, found French statesmen ready to make up their quarrels in the Anglo-French Agreement of 1904. Thereupon you threatened France; she gave up Delcassé; you saved that point, but in doing so you turned the Anglo-French Agreement into an Entente. Meanwhile, you made no attempt to check the hatred of England that was felt in Germany, not understanding that, to indulge hatred is sure to spoil wise policy and sound statecraft. And those speeches of the Emperor, who thought, even while I lived, that he could do better, without than with me; those 'shining armour' and 'mailed fist' speeches, those rattlings of the sword, which, though he personally never desired to draw in great conflict, nevertheless made other nations look nervously to the state of their own weapons. You increased the naval competition and rejected, sometimes even resented, English overtures for a naval agreement. As if England could possibly give up the naval competition, the Navy being to her all that the Army was to Germany.

"Meanwhile, as if to make sure that English and French military as well as naval authorities kept their arrangements up to the mark, you got up the crisis of Agadir. What purpose did that business serve, except to bring England and France closer together?

"And finally, you let your military staffs prepare a war plan, of which the unprovoked invasion of Belgium was a cardinal point, and you think to this day that the invasion of Belgium had nothing to do with England's entry into war against you. I will tell you what I would have done. After the Franco-Russian Alliance was made I should have foreseen that, in spite of an English Minister's boast about 'splendid isolation' the discomfort of England's position must bring her to Germany, and when the offer came, as come it did to you, I would have made sure that it did not come to nothing. There would then have been no agreement with France, or, if there had been, it would have been conditioned by the Alliance or previous Agreement with Germany. I should have had my hand in it, and known all about it; and I should also have known all about the relations between England and Russia, just as you knew when Austria and Russia joined in the Mürzsteg programme about the Balkans. Then, when the Russian Fleet had been destroyed by the Japanese, I should have made the German Fleet strong enough to over-match the French, telling England my object and stopping naval expenditure there. England in this policy would have been no obstacle to German commercial expansion; even as it was, she practically came to agreement with you about the Bagdad Railway.

"Then, if I thought the time had come for war, I should have remembered how, in 1870, the British Government required me, as a condition of neutrality, to sign an agreement to respect Belgium, and what English statesmen said about it at the time. I should have made sure whether English feeling was still the same, and have told the General Staff that they must have a plan that did not involve Belgium, or else they must have no war. With England neutral, I should have been sure of Italy; with France and Russia unable to maintain supplies of munitions, or even to purchase them from abroad, the war would not have been long and victory would have been certain. Then easy terms for France and Russia, as for Austria in 1866, and Germany would have been supreme on the Continent. England would, meanwhile, by the development of modern weapons and aircraft, have lost much of the safety she once had as an island: she would have had no friend but Germany, and Germany could have made that friendship what she pleased."

Germans can judge whether such a policy as is here suggested for Bismarck was possible for them. Had such a policy been pursued by Germany, I think it not only possible, but almost certain, that British Ministers and British opinion would have reacted to it as described. The result would have been German predominance and British dependence, but this would not have been foreseen in London till too late.

It was shortly after the Agadir Crisis that a change was made in the German Embassy in London. Metternich left. He had been rigid in upholding the German view against ours. Over and over again he had covered the ground in the way of which some records of conversation printed in this book are examples. I used to compare these conversations to well-known movements on a parade-ground. But I always felt, with Metternich, that whatever I said would be faithfully reported by him; that no chance and unintentional slip of mine in our many conversations would be turned to unfair advantage; that nothing would be distorted or misrepresented. In the whole of our transactions I never found reason to complain of any unfairness. It was also my impression that, however stiff Metternich might be in upholding the views of his Government to us, however little disposed he seemed to concede anything, yet in his own reports to Berlin he put the British view in the most favourable light that he thought could fairly be placed upon it.

I regretted his departure, and the farewell dinner given to him at the Foreign Office was not a political gesture, but a genuine expression of personal regard.

Metternich was succeeded by Baron Marschall von Bieberstein. He had been Foreign Secretary at Berlin when I had become Under-Secretary at the Foreign Office in London, nearly twenty years before. The impression I had then got from reports to the Foreign Office was that of a very able Foreign Secretary, but not very friendly to us. He had now for many years been German Ambassador at Constantinople, where he had furthered the pro-Abdul Hamid policy of his Government with conspicuous ability and with great success in enhancing German political influence and commercial interests in the Turkish Empire. We respected his ability, but regarded this German policy at Constantinople as unscrupulous and detestable. We therefore felt his coming to London to be a somewhat formidable and not altogether auspicious event. We expected him, as an able diplomatist, to begin by making himself agreeable, but we were prepared to be on our guard.

When he arrived he told me that he did not wish to enter upon any discussions at present; he had come to take up his post formally; when this was done he would return to Germany and come back to take up the work permanently. I gathered that he desired to gain first impressions of us and of the situation in London, and then to consult his own Government as to the opening line he should take. He came to lunch with me quietly that we might make further personal acquaintance and began very pleasantly by telling me he had noticed in some speech of mine a sentence with which he entirely agreed. The sentence he had selected was (I quote from memory) : "It is not hard to tell the truth; the difficulty is to get it believed." This he endorsed with great approval, but what impressed me most was the emphasis with which he spoke of the need for upholding civil authority and law against forces that are disposed to disregard them. He did not specify militarism as one of these forces, but it may well be that it was in his mind. At any rate, the manner and substance of what he said set me wondering whether he was thinking of forces that had caused his own removal from the Foreign Office at Berlin. I never knew what had brought this about; it was certainly not incompetence on his part.

He gave the impression of a man whose life had been given without relief to hard work. His strength was now ebbing, and it was touching as well as admirable to see the energy with which he addressed himself to his new and important work here. He evidently understood English well, but it appeared to be an effort for him to speak it. It was an effort that he would not spare himself; to make it was to him part of the thorough performance of his work in London. After a short stay he left us, as had been intended, to prepare for his return to take up the heavy and continuous work of his post; but his strength was spent and he died.

The impression he made was of a man old and worn with toil, but so devoted to his country that he was determined to serve it thoroughly and strenuously to the end. This impression was so strong and remarkable that it has remained outstanding in my memory. This, I suppose, is why it has been given space here out of all proportion to the political importance of my dealings with him; for we met only a very few times, and transacted no business with each other.

He was succeeded in London by Prince Lichnowsky of whom more will be said later on. He came desiring to see the peace of Europe kept, and for that he worked earnestly and sincerely, till the events of 1914 over-whelmed him, and everyone else who had tried to prevent war.

The sentence quoted above as to the difficulty in getting the truth believed recalls a saying, attributed, whether rightly or not I do not know, to Bismarck. It is to the effect that the most certain way in diplomacy to deceive people is to tell them the truth; for they never believe it. And this suggests the reflection that in Foreign Affairs generally more mischief and loss has been incurred owing to incredulity than credulity. Perhaps because the former is so much more common.

# CHAPTER XIV

## (1912-1913)

## THE FOURTH CRISIS (THE BALKAN WAR)

Haldane's Visit to Berlin—Advantages and Drawbacks—An Unaccept-
able Formula—Continuance of Naval Rivalry—The Attack upon
Turkey—Victory of the Balkan Allies—Bulgaria Dissatisfied—
Second Balkan War—Defeat of Bulgaria—Treaty of Bucharest
—Its Consequences—Complications between the Powers—The
Ambassadors' Conference—Questions at Issue—Albania, Scutari,
and the Ægean Islands—Servian Claims and Austrian Opposition
—The Importance of Djakova—A Peaceful Settlement—Cambon,
Benckendorff and Lichnowsky—A Neglected Precedent.

DURING all this period, whenever we seemed to
be in sight of improved relations with Germany,
we were thrown back by the continued expansion
of the German Fleet. It has since been made clear that
Germany was aiming at a position on the sea which must
have been a most serious danger to the British Empire;
and so well aware were German statesmen of that fact
that they habitually spoke of the period of their naval
construction as "the danger-zone"[1] for Germany, thus
implying that Great Britain might have been expected to
anticipate the danger by attacking Germany, and destroy-
ing her fleet before it became too strong. Germany was
undoubtedly within her rights in challenging our sea-
power, but in so doing she compelled us to find safety both
by increasing our naval construction and by a policy
which would not leave us exposed to the hostility of other
naval Powers. A desire for peace and friendship entered

[1] See von Tirpitz, *My Memories*, p. 195.

THE RIGHT HON. VISCOUNT HALDANE OF CLOAN, O.M.

largely into our relations with France, but German action made them in this sense a practical necessity.

We were always ready for accommodation, but the results of our overtures had been so disappointing and the successive German Navy Bills [1] seemed to indicate so persistent an intention that scepticism on our side was justifiable. So, when I was informed, at the beginning of 1912, that the German Emperor would welcome the visit of a British Minister to discuss the question at Berlin, I was willing but not hopeful.

The intimation had come through an unofficial channel; it had not come to me, but had reached members of the Cabinet who were likely to be most favourable to it. The information was very vague. I did not feel at all confident that the Emperor had taken any initiative in the matter. I never knew whether the suggestion had really emanated from a British or a German source. It was, however, put before me by some of my colleagues as something on which the German Emperor had expressed a wish; if so, it would be a wanton rebuff to refuse it. At the time I thought it was possibly one of those petty, unofficial manœuvres that could be avowed or disavowed at Berlin, as best might suit German convenience. If a British Minister did not go to Berlin, the inaction might be represented as an uncivil rebuff on our part of a friendly German invitation. If a Minister did go, the visit would be represented as a voluntary British overture, which Germany had not invited, but to which the Emperor had graciously responded. Thus Germany would get some advantage either way; but it seemed preferable that she should have the credit of being gra-

[1] For a convenient summary of these Bills see Asquith's *Genesis of the War,* chapters x and xii.

cious to us rather than that we should be accused of discourtesy to her.

One objection was that the visit might arouse suspicion and distrust at Paris. I did not consider that this ought to prevent the visit, for an Entente is not worth much unless the nations who are parties to it can trust each other, and by this time France ought to have felt that she could trust us. There was nothing in the Anglo-French Entente that made it inconsistent for us to be on friendly terms with Germany. We could not, of course, enter into any engagement with Germany that would prevent us from giving France the diplomatic support promised in the Anglo-French Agreement of 1904; it would also be the height of dishonour to make an agreement with Germany that would tie our hands and oblige us to remain neutral in a war between France and Germany. We had not, indeed, pledged ourselves to support France in such a war. On the contrary, we had preserved our freedom not to participate in it; but we were bound to preserve the freedom of Britain to help France, if the country so desired. According to my recollection, for no record of the conversation has been found, I informed Cambon of the projected visit and assured him that we should do nothing with Germany that would tie our hands. As long as that condition was observed I considered that the French had no reason to be anxious, and ought indeed to be well content: for good relations between Britain and Germany ought to make things more, and not less, pleasant for France.

The question of French susceptibility was therefore not a valid reason against this British visit to Berlin. But I had no great hope that anything would come of it. There had been no preparation of the ground: there was nothing to indicate that a substantial agreement with Germany about navies was possible, and without that there could be no agreement that would really be a *rapprochement*.

It was therefore desirable that the visit of a British Minister should be private and informal, so that, if nothing came of it, there should be no sensation and little disappointment to the public. Accordingly, we agreed that Haldane should go. He was in the habit of visiting Germany; he had friendly personal relations with the Emperor and other important personages; his visit could be made more natural and less artificial than that of any other Minister. If nothing came of it, it would not have the appearance of an unusual effort and great failure; if the time was opportune for *rapprochement,* Haldane better than anyone else would be able to discover and improve it.

I agreed without demur and with good-will to Haldane's visit. I always felt that the pro-German element here had a right to demand that our foreign policy should go to the utmost point that it could to be friendly to Germany. That point would be passed only when something was proposed that would tie us to Germany and break the Entente with France. Not only were people entitled to demand this of British foreign policy, but it was essential that those who set most store by the Entente with France should concede it. To do so was the only way to preserve unity of support in the Cabinet and in the Liberal Party for the Anglo-French Entente.

Haldane has given his own account of the visit. The upshot was that the Germans were not really willing to give up the naval competition, and that they wanted a political formula that would in effect compromise our freedom of action. We could not fetter ourselves by a promise to be neutral in a European war. We had, indeed, no intention of supporting France, and still less Russia, in a war of aggression: we had a very real determination not to support any aggressor, and we were ready to say so. But there was no formula that could be trusted to define the real aggressor in advance. The revelation of Bismarck's methods in the notorious Ems despatch was a warning against the futility of such formulæ. We were bound to keep our hands free and the country uncompromised as to its liberty of judgment, decision, and action.

The section at home that was most distrustful of Germany, that was in fact anti-German, were unfavourable to the Haldane visit. Von Tirpitz and the naval authorities probably detested it. They were determined to pursue their naval policy, and the visit was bound either to interfere with this policy or to come to nothing. We discussed the result of the visit in the Cabinet on Haldane's return, but we had to realize that political formulæ are not safe, and that a substantial naval agreement, such as would relax tension and give security, was not to be obtained.

On the question of the naval competition and our relations with Germany generally, the following three private letters to Sir E. Goschen, our Ambassador in Berlin, may be inserted here, though they belong to various dates. They show the interchanges of views that took place from time to time between 1910 and 1913 and the difficulties that attended them:

*From Sir E. Grey to Sir E. Goschen*
FOREIGN OFFICE,
*May* 5, 1910.

MY DEAR GOSCHEN,—I have not seen the Prime Minister for three weeks, but even if I had seen him I am sure he has been far too busy, during the last weeks of the part of the Session just closed, to be able to go into Bethmann-Hollweg's proposals. So what I send you now are my own personal reflections; but you may use them as such at your discretion if you are pressed in further conversation with the Chancellor or Schoen.

I entirely understand the Chancellor's difficulty in giving us the southern end of the Bagdad Railway without getting in return something which Germany will look upon as a *quid pro quo*. I have the same difficulty here in giving what he asks: for British public opinion is not less exacting than German.

Crawford, of the Turkish Customs Service, tells me that 65 per cent. of the trade with Mesopotamia is British. On this trade, in the first instance, will fall the burden of the 4 per cent. increase [1] (in Turkish Customs) until it is passed on to the Turkish consumer. There will be a great outcry when the increase is made, and I shall have all I can do to get public opinion here to recognize that participation in the Bagdad Railway is an adequate *quid pro quo* for a new burden upon British trade, only a part of which is interested in Mesopotamia. This is my first difficulty. It would be insuperable if I had to make another set of concessions as well.

In the next place, with regard to any understanding with Germany: the attention of public opinion here is concentrated on the mutual arrest or decrease of naval expenditure as *the* test of whether an understanding is worth anything. In the first overtures of Bethmann-Hollweg last year I felt that the naval question was not sufficiently prominent. Since then it has receded into the background, and the perspective of his last proposals is therefore even less advantageous. This is an important point.

In the third place, there is this difficulty with regard to any general political understanding: we cannot sacrifice the friendship of Russia or of France. There is no intention of using either for aggressive purposes against Germany. When Germany settled her difficulty with France about Morocco, not only was I free from jealousy, but I had a sense of absolute relief. I had hated the prospect of friendship with France involving friction with Germany, and I rejoiced when this

---

[1] The general idea of the negotiations on the Bagdad Railway was that the Germans should cede the southern section of the railway to us, and that we should consent to a 4 per cent. increase in Turkish customs to enable the Turks to make good their kilometric guarantee for the construction of the line.

prospect disappeared. My attitude is the same with regard to Germany's difficulty with Russia about Persia. Also, I am quite sure that neither France nor Russia wishes to quarrel with Germany: indeed, I know that they wish to avoid a quarrel. So on this ground I am quite easy. But I cannot enter into any agreement with Germany which would prevent me from giving to France or Russia, should Germany take up towards either of them an aggressive attitude such as she took up towards France about Morocco, the same sort of support as I gave to France at the time of the Algeciras Conference and afterwards until she settled her difficulty with Germany. Any agreement which prevented the giving of such support would obviously forfeit the friendship of France and Russia, and this is what makes me apprehensive of trouble in finding a political formula.—Yours sincerely,

(Signed)  E. GREY.

FOREIGN OFFICE,
*October* 26, 1910.

MY DEAR GOSCHEN,—I must defer comments upon the Chancellor's proposals about the Navy and the political understanding until we have had time for consideration.

But meanwhile I wish to say that the German suggestion that France and Russia ought to become parties to a naval agreement is very welcome: for it opens the way for our saying, at an opportune moment, what I have always thought to be the only possible solution, that France and Russia must be parties to a political agreement. Further, with the present prospect of great naval expenditure by the Allies of Germany, Austria-Hungary and Italy, I think we may have to say that a naval agreement will be of no use unless they also are parties to it. That would bring into the naval and political understanding all the six greatest Powers of Europe.

If we can avoid treading upon French corns with regard to Alsace and Lorraine, I believe that five of these Powers would welcome such an Agreement, and a diminution of naval expenditure; for not one of these five Powers has designs of aggrandizement, and they all desire peace. But on Germany's part such an Agreement would mean the renunciation of ambitions for the hegemony of Europe. The way in which she receives the proposal, if it is eventually made, will be a test of whether she really desires peace and security from all attack for herself, or whether she has ambitions which can be gratified only at the expense of other Powers.—Yours sincerely,

E. GREY.

MY DEAR GOSCHEN,—Nicolson showed me your private and personal letter to him, from which it appears that you did not understand my motive in writing to you about Tirpitz's naval statement.[1] The fault is mine, because I had not time to explain all the circumstances.

For seven years some of the Pan-Germans in Germany have been working upon Pro-Germans in this country. The Pan-Germans are Chauvinists; our Pro-Germans are pacifists; but the latter are, nevertheless, very subject to the influence of the former.

It came to my knowledge that Professor Schiemann, one of the Pan-Germans aforesaid, had written to one of the Pro-Germans here after Tirpitz's speech, emphasizing the friendly nature of the statement, and saying that everything would depend upon whether we responded to it.

I had no intention of responding by proposing a naval agreement.

In the first place, I had been given to understand, indirectly, that when Lichnowsky came here he hoped that I would not raise the question of naval expenditure with him.

In the second place, if I were to do so, the naval Press Bureau in Germany would, if it suited it, construe my action as an attempt to put pressure on Germany to reduce her naval expenditure; and Tirpitz might, at some future time, say that his moderate statement had been abused for this purpose, and that therefore he could not say anything again of which similar advantage might be taken.

But, if Lichnowsky were to say anything to me about the statements of Tirpitz and Jagow to the Budget Committee as reported in the Press, or if Jagow were to say anything to you, and we made no response at all, it seems to me that we might be represented as having put our hand behind our back in a repellent fashion. Of this the Pan-Germans would take full advantage with the Pro-Germans here.

I think, therefore, that you might say, but only if you are obliged to

[1] Statement to the Budget Committee of the Reichstag, February 6th and 7th, 1913.

say something, that the statements reported in the proceedings of the German Budget Committee will have a favourable effect upon the tone of Churchill's statement in Parliament here. This will, of course, be the case. They will not affect the substance of the statement as regards our own naval expenditure, but I hope that they will enable the tone of the statement to be less stiff than it has been before, when we have been continually faced with fresh increases of German naval expenditure.

I hope that this will make clear to you the motive of my previous letter to you.

The Pan-Germans have worked upon the Pro-Germans here with varying intensity, but with unvarying want of success so far as influencing the foreign policy of the British Government is concerned. But this is no reason why we should give them more material than we can help.

I do not, however, wish you to say anything about Tirpitz's statement, unless something is said to you, because I agree that what Tirpitz said does not amount to much, and the reason of his saying it is not the love of our beautiful eyes, but the extra fifty millions required for increasing the German Army.

Nevertheless, our relations with Germany have improved because Kiderlen worked for peace in the Balkan Crisis and Jagow has done the same, and I shall do my part to keep relations cordial as long as the German Government will also do their part in good faith. To be sure of each other's good faith is all that is wanted to make our relations all that can be desired.[1]—Yours sincerely,[1]

E. GREY.

I must now pass to the Balkan War and the Ambassadors' Conference which were the main events of the years 1912-13.

Abdul Hamid has already been called the Equilibrium in the Near East. He had understood perfectly the forces by which he was surrounded; he knew the trend

---

[1] This letter was written on the assumption that von Tirpitz's statement was not intended to lead to negotiations for a naval agreement. There is nothing in what had preceded or what has become known since to suggest that this assumption was incorrect.

of each, its strength and its limitations.  He knew the
aspirations of Russia as regards the Straits and Constantinople, but he knew also that, if Russia pressed him too
hard, she would find Europe once more arraigned against
her to set bounds to her action, as in the Treaty of Berlin
in 1878.  He heard, probably with anger, but without
anxiety, the loud indignation of British public opinion,
aroused by Armenian massacres or Macedonian atrocities:
for he knew that the British Fleet could not come to the
mountains of Armenia, and that, if Britain went so far
as to raise the question of Constantinople and the Straits,
Europe would intervene and prevent the upset of the
*status quo*.  The Great Powers dared not allow that *status
quo* to be disturbed, lest they should fight amongst themselves.  Lord Salisbury, once the partner in Disraeli's
pro-Turkish policy, but since those days shocked to the
extreme by the iniquities of Turkish misrule, had swung
right away and declared that in backing Turks Britain
had put her money on the wrong horse.  Even this did
not disturb Abdul Hamid.  He had lost Britain as the
champion of Turkey, but he had made an active friend
of Germany.  He took pains to foster and attach this
friendship by commercial concessions and the attractive
prospect of the development of Asia Minor.  French
financiers, too, had considerable interests in Constantinople.  Behind all these vested interests and counter-
balancing political forces Abdul Hamid sat securely
entrenched.

The pressure for Macedonian Reforms worried him;
but he knew that Austria and Russia would not let outside
Powers deal with this question alone, and that Britain
was the only outside Power that was much stirred by it.
He relied upon the rivalry between Austria and Russia

to prevent them from agreeing upon anything that would be very thorough. Their rivalry with each other would limit their agreement to press him for Macedonian Reforms; their united jealousy of the interference of any outside Powers in Macedonia would be a bulwark to him against Britain.

As for internal affairs, Abdul Hamid could rely upon the hatred of his Christian subjects for each other. United in creed, they were divided in race; and the repulsion of race hatred was stronger than the attraction of religious affinity. These hatreds he fostered and used, and on them, and on his skill in playing upon them, he relied to prevent internal upheavals and even a combination of Christian Balkan States against him.

All the forces, external and internal, the play of them, and how to manipulate them for his own purposes Abdul Hamid understood to the utmost limit of human ingenuity. But all men must decline, and when Abdul Hamid's powers began to fail there came the internal upheaval, the Turkish Revolution that deposed him.

The change was great. Crafty, ruthless, unscrupulous ability had been concentrated to an extraordinary and malignant degree in Abdul Hamid—concentrated, that is to say, in one person with supreme authority. Now this was gone. The leaders of the Revolution had ability, and they were not more hampered by pity or by scruples than Abdul Hamid had been; but they were several persons, and not one with supreme authority. Their force was dispersed among many, and soon became dissipated in personal rivalries and intrigues. Then the European neighbours of Turkey began to move to their own advantage, as it seemed at first, but, as it proved later, to their own great distress, and, in some cases, ruin.

It was as if Abdul Hamid, in playing, for his own evil purposes, upon the weaknesses of his neighbours to keep them quiet, had been wiser in their interests than they themselves proved to be when he was gone.

First Austria moved, and annexed Bosnia-Herzegovina. Then Italy conquered Tripoli. Finally Greece, Bulgaria, Serbia, and Montenegro made a league, and fell upon Turkey. The cause was just: it was the emancipation of the Christian subjects of Turkey in South-East Europe. But, in acting thus, the members of the Balkan League liberated forces the full effect of which they did not foresee, and set in motion rivalries among themselves which they could not control.

Austria's annexation of Bosnia-Herzegovina was the first disturbance of the *status quo* of Turkey; Italy's conquest of Tripoli was a shock to it; the Balkan Allies destroyed it. The enhanced position of Serbia, consequent upon the victories of the Balkan Allies, made Austria sensitive and apprehensive. Finally came the murder of the Archduke Franz-Ferdinand, and Austria, in the excitement that followed, launched the ultimatum to Serbia that precipitated the Great War. This was the chain of events that began with the Turkish Revolution and led straight to the catastrophe of 1914; but the cause of the Great War lies deeper than this chain of events, and must be discussed elsewhere.

Turkey, weakened by the Revolution and the dissensions that followed it, could not stand against the attack of the Balkan Allies. The pent-up hatred of generations was combined for the moment against her. The Bulgarian onset was particularly vigorous. By December the Balkan Allies had victories and conquest sufficient to force Turkey to an armistice and to the discussion of humiliating terms of peace. The belligerents chose London for the meeting-place, and their delegates assembled there in December 1912.

Rooms were set apart for them in St. James's Palace, and on behalf of the British Government I met them there to give a formal but cordial welcome and express our good-will to their efforts to arrange a peace.

Turkey, it appeared, could be brought to terms that would give Greece and Serbia what they wanted; but it was more difficult to satisfy Bulgaria. Bulgarian claims came nearer to the heart, to Constantinople. She insisted on the cession to her of Adrianople, which was not yet conquered. Turkey would not yield this: Bulgaria pressed for it, and claimed that her Allies, who were all pledged with her to wage war together and to make peace only in common should, if need be, continue the war. It appeared that peace would be wrecked on this point. I had taken no part in the negotiations; they did not touch British interests, and were not our affair; but occasionally some of the delegates paid me an informal visit at the Foreign Office. At this crisis I had thus an opportunity of conversing with the chief Bulgarian delegate and ventured to speak a word or two in favour of making peace. It was probable that, if the war were resumed, Bulgaria would take Adrianople; but in war there were always risks. Bulgaria and the Allies had now in their grasp the certainty of a favourable peace. If war were resumed in order to add Adrianople to the great aims already assured there must be some, even though it were a remote, risk. Such, according to recollection, was the tenor of my remarks. These were but tentative, for it was not my affair; and they were vague, for I could not foresee what form the risk might assume. The Bulgarian delegate replied confidently that they were prepared to take the risk. Their Peace Conference broke up, and the war was resumed.

It is not necessary to do more than summarize what followed. Adrianople was taken, but Bulgaria and Greece fell out: Bulgaria accused Greece of exploiting the common victory to her own advantage. Greece and Serbia probably considered that Bulgaria, by her insistence about Adrianople, had prolonged the war, from their point of view, unnecessarily. The racial animosities that had been suspended in order to combine against Turkey reasserted themselves when the Turks were no longer to be feared in Europe. Roumania took advantage of the opportunity to intervene against Bulgaria. In the summer of 1913 there was a second Balkan War, of which Bulgaria was the victim. The Turks retook Adrianople, and the war ended in the Treaty of Bucharest. By this Greece, Serbia, and Roumania were left with all the spoils of victory. Bulgaria, whose army had been so effective and essential to the defeat of the Turks, was allowed no access to the sea. Roumania got some territory that had belonged to Bulgaria, and Greece and Serbia got territory and ports that had been hitherto looked upon as legitimate objects of Bulgarian aspiration if Turkey were driven out of Macedonia.

The Great Powers saw no reason to intervene, except to satisfy Austria and Italy about Albania and to make sure that the gains of the Balkan Allies were not pushed to a point that would raise the question of the future of Constantinople; for the rest, they were not prepared to go beyond mediation, wherever this might be useful; and they sat still while the Treaty of Bucharest was signed. This treaty had in it the seeds of inevitable future trouble.

It left Bulgaria sore, injured, and despoiled and deprived of what she believed should belong to her. Any future Balkan peace was impossible as long as the Treaty of Bucharest remained. Turkey, of course, was also sore and despoiled. Thus when the Great War came, a year later, there were two Powers, Bulgaria and Turkey, hungering for a *revanche* and ready to take whichever side would give them a prospect of obtaining it. This naturally was the side of Austria and Germany: for Serbia was at war with Austria, while Greece and Roumania were sympathetic to Serbia or to the Western Powers.

The settlement after the second Balkan War was not one of justice but of force. It stored up inevitable trouble for the time to come. To make peace secure for the future, it would have been necessary for the Great Powers to have intervened to make the settlement of Bucharest a just one. This they did not do. They dared not do it, being too afraid of trouble between themselves. They were afraid to move lest they should come in contact with each other, and yet their very care to prevent falling out among themselves in 1913 was, in fact, going to render peace more precarious in the year that followed.

The victory of the Balkan Allies over Turkey opened the Balkan Question, and the risk of consequent trouble between the Great Powers most concerned became appreciable. Constantinople itself was not in question; the Great Powers were agreed that Constantinople must be left in possession of the Turks; they were united in not raising that question between themselves and in agreeing that they would not let it be raised by the victorious Balkan Allies. The latter showed no disposition to raise it in their peace discussions with Turkey. Their gains were so enormous as to be sufficient to content them without Constantinople. The Balkan War, therefore, did not endanger European peace by throwing open the question of Constantinople and the Straits; nor were Austria and Russia, the two Great Powers most directly concerned, disposed to take an active part or to play rival hands in influencing the terms that Bulgaria, Greece, and Serbia might impose on Turkey as regards Macedonia. The point of friction and danger was Albania. Turkish rule in Albania was smashed by the war; the Balkan Allies were flushed with victory; Serbia wanted access to the Adriatic on commercial grounds, and she and Montenegro might regard portions of Albania as part of the prize and spoil of war.

Austria was determined that if Albania ceased to be Turkish territory it should not pass into the hands and form part of the aggrandizement of Serbia. Serbia, borne on the tide of her own victories, might easily reach the point of inevitable conflict with Austria. If this happened, and if Russia felt that she was required to support Serbia, European war was inevitable. To prepare in advance against this danger, and to avoid catastrophe, I proposed a Conference of the Powers. Germany and Austria agreed, and Russia was willing; this being so, the consent of France and Italy was assured. I did not press for London to be the meeting-place; personally I was inclined to Paris. The French would be pleased by the choice of Paris, and the Conference would start with that asset of good-will. Also I was not anxious to have the great addition to work, already heavy, of sitting in the Conference personally. London, however, was chosen, and early in December the Conference met.

There were six of us: Lichnowsky, Mensdorff, and Imperiali, the Ambassadors respectively of Germany,

Austria, and Italy; Cambon and Benckendorff, the Ambassadors of France and Russia; and myself for Britain. Such responsibility as there was of presiding fell to me, but we made the proceedings as informal as those of a committee of friends, which in fact we were. We met in the afternoons, generally about four o'clock, and, with a short adjournment to an adjoining room for tea, we continued till six or seven o'clock. The Conference did not have its last meeting till August 1913, and during all that time we remained in being as a Conference though we only met when occasion required. The friendly personal relations between us could not prevent our proceedings from being protracted and sometimes intolerably wearisome. It was said after the first few weeks that Cambon, when asked about the progress of the Conference, had replied that it would continue till there were six skeletons sitting around the table.

The question of greatest difficulty, and even danger, was the determination of the boundary on the north and north-east of Albania, where Serbia claimed more than Austria was willing to allow. There was an acute crisis when Montenegro got hold of Scutari, which Austria was determined that Montenegro should not have. Later on, Italy was interested in the limits to be set to Greek acquisitions of territory on the south side of Albania. During a great part of the time first the war and then the resulting peace negotiations between the Balkan Allies and Turkey were in progress, and these from time to time occupied the attention of the Conference. But when differences between the Balkan Allies and Turkey were discussed the music of the Conference was more subdued and less harsh than when we were endeavouring to set the tune to which Serbia and Montenegro should keep step

*Photograph by Reginald Haines*

COUNT ALBERT MENSDORFF
Austro-Hungarian Ambassador in London, 1904-1914

on the frontiers of Albania.   Indeed, at one time there
was a tendency to busy ourselves with peace negotiations
between Turkey and the Balkan Allies, when we were
making no progress with the Albanian question that
threatened to disturb our own peace.   At one such moment
I said that it would become misleading and undignified
to continue our sittings unless we could deal with the
question of the Albanian frontier and make an agreement
about it.   It was almost ridiculous, I urged, for us to be
attempting to make peace between Turkey and the Allies
if the question of the Albanian frontier was to remain in
suspense, causing increasing anxiety and difficulty between the Great Powers.   That, however, was said in
February, after the Conference had been in existence for
some two months and a half.

The start of the Conference in December was easy.
The Austrian contention was that Albania must be kept
as an independent and substantial entity, but Austria was
willing to let a commercial access to the Adriatic, through
Albania, be secured to Serbia by international arrangement.   These were the cardinal points and, if they were
not accepted, there could be no agreement.   I had ascertained that Russia would in principle accept them.   At
our first meeting Mensdorff stated the Austrian contention
as the basis for discussion.   Benckendorff replied at once
that he accepted it.   Mensdorff's manner gave the impression of one who heard news that is almost too good to be
true.   There was a note of interrogation from him; and
Benckendorff, who had clear instructions, reported the
Russian acceptance without qualification.   The life of the
Conference was then assured; it was not still-born; but
the troubles of life were yet before it, and European peace
would depend upon the settlement of frontier details.

These have no importance now. The records of the Conference have been examined for me; I am told that they make exceedingly dull and confused reading. I can well believe it; even the short analysis made to refresh my memory has little interest for a post-war reader. From time to time the ship of negotiation stuck on some shoal, but it was always, though often after much difficulty, floated off and onwards on some little rising tide of opportune concession, or on some buoyant formula. The sort of difficulty we had to solve was this: Serbia would claim for herself something more, something that had been part of Turkish Albania; then Austria would object. Serbia would say it was by population mainly Serbian; Austria would deny the fact; there were villages where even experts might differ about racial affinities. We did not set much store by territorial merits in these details. Our efforts were concentrated on getting something to which both Austria and Russia would agree. Russia would support Serbia in claiming some village as Serb; Austria would contend that it must be Albanian. If the Conference could not get an agreement Austria might launch an ultimatum, or even take peremptory action against Serbia. Then the whole prestige of Austria and Russia in the Balkans would be at stake, and so would the peace of Europe. The details with which we dealt were insignificant—in themselves mere sparks; but we were sitting on a powder-magazine.

One instance shall be recounted as a good illustration of the difficulties the Conference had to overcome, and also of the spirit in which we worked. It has remained fresh in my memory.

Serbia claimed a village called Djakova. Austria made a point of its being kept for Albania. Russia would not give way about Serbia's claim; Austria was stiff and positive. There was deadlock. Nothing more could be done till either Mensdorff or Benckendorff could get instructions that would ease the situation. The Conference ceased to work on the Albanian frontier; the diplomatic safety-valve, for to this the Conference might be compared, was for the time shut down. Days, even a week or two I think, passed: we could do nothing, and we knew that pressure might be rising all the time. Probably I saw Mensdorff and Benckendorff separately, and perhaps Lichnowsky too, to explore the possibilities of concession, but of this I have no certain recollection. One morning a message was brought to me, at my house in London, that the Austrian Ambassador wanted to see me on an urgent matter; I sent back a message asking him to come to my house at once. In a few minutes Mensdorff arrived. The room in the house that I occupied then was small; on a table in the middle stood daffodils and other spring flowers sent to me from Fallodon and placed in tall glasses of water. Mensdorff entered briskly, even a little breathless with haste, delighted with the good news he brought and exclaiming, "We give up Djakova!" As he bustled quickly into the room, his full-skirted frock-coat, swaying as it passed the flower-table, brushed the heads of some daffodils; the resentful daffodils tilted their glass and emptied the water down the skirts of Mensdorff's coat. Some perturbation ensued; I fetched a towel and swathed the coat as best I could. Then we fraternized over Djakova. Mensdorff was genuinely pleased to bring the news. He wanted peace; he knew that we all wanted peace; and the block was removed, and the Conference could go on again.

The Austrians, while agreeing that Djakova should be

assured to Serbia, stipulated that Serbia should cease hostilities and evacuate territories assigned to Albania. I at once urged strongly at St. Petersburg that Russia should accept this condition. Russia did so, and I then prepared for immediate collective representations to Serbia and Montenegro.

This incident was over; the Great Powers were in agreement. More trouble remained about other things, but by these methods, and in this spirit, we got through.

Another storm there was about Scutari. The Great Powers having decided that, in order to preserve peace among themselves, they must take in hand the frontier of Albania, we warned Serbia and Montenegro that it was of no use for them to continue to fight the Turks in that region. Serbia and Montenegro would get without further fighting all that Austria, in agreement with the other great Powers, was willing to let them have. On the other hand, Serbia and Montenegro, however much of Albania they conquered, would not be allowed to keep more than the Powers were agreed to concede to them.

For instance, on March 11, 1913, it appears that I told the Serbian Chargé d'Affaires that the question of Scutari would be decided by the Powers; that "for Serbia and Montenegro to pursue operations there is so useless that it appears to me to be criminal!" The Serbian contention was that to discontinue these operations would release Turkish troops to fight against Serbia elsewhere. I urged that this contention was not applicable to Scutari, and the conversation was repeated to the Montenegrin delegate in London.

The advice was of no avail. I do not remember that any advice of the kind was ever of any use even when it represented a consensus of opinion of the Powers and was

backed by irrefutable arguments.    Montenegro continued
the siege of Scutari, and took the place in April.

Then Austria demanded that Montenegro should be
made to evacuate Scutari by international action: if not,
Austria would act alone, and that might be the beginning
of trouble that would threaten Europe.   None of the
Powers thought it reasonable to support Montenegro in
the occupation of a position which Austria considered
strategically menacing to herself.   We had, therefore, no
difficulty in coming to an agreement in principle in the
Conference; but the various methods to be employed to
induce Montenegro to evacuate Scutari gave rise to
tedious discussions.   At one extreme was the suggestion
to land troops and to compel the evacuation; at the other
was a proposal to give Montenegro money compensation
—in other words, to bribe the ruling authority to leave
the place.   We ourselves would not co-operate in the use
of troops, but were ready to join in a naval demonstration.
Eventually a blend of the threat of coercion and the offer
of money compensation settled the matter to the satisfaction of Austria, perhaps also to the satisfaction of the
King of Montenegro, and this danger to European peace
was laid to rest.

It is needless to describe questions that arose about the
southern frontier of Albania.   My own part was mainly
to discover whether we might ease the general situation
and facilitate peace in the Near East by restoring to
Turkey certain Ægean Islands.   Italy held these islands
as a pledge for the fulfilment by Turkey of the terms of
peace arranged after the Turco-Italian War about
Tripoli.   The Italian Ambassador told us that no Italian
Government could stand if these islands were evacuated
while the terms of the Turko-Italian Treaty were unful-

filled. The following extract gives my comment on treaties with Turkey:

> I observed that if the fulfilment of a treaty by Turkey was the condition for the continuance of the occupation, as Turkey never fulfilled a treaty entirely, occupation might be indefinitely prolonged. Indeed, I said subsequently to the Austrian Ambassador alone, that, to make a thing dependent upon the fulfilment of a treaty by Turkey, though it was not exactly equivalent to a freehold, might almost be regarded as equivalent to a 999 years' lease.

This was at the end of July. On August 1, I seem to have said that certain changes in the situation, notably the occupation of Adrianople by the Turks, would justify the Powers in reserving their decision about the islands. The Russian Ambassador "seemed to think the idea of using the islands as a lever to get the Turks out of Adrianople not unattractive."

After August 1913 the Conference did not meet again. There was no formal finish; we were not photographed in a group; we had no votes of thanks; no valedictory speeches; we just left off meeting. We had not settled anything, not even all the details of Albanian boundaries; but we had served a useful purpose. We had been something to which point after point could be referred; we had been a means of keeping all the six Powers in direct and friendly touch. The mere fact that we were in existence, and that we should have to be broken up before peace was broken, was in itself an appreciable barrier against war. We were a means of gaining time, and the longer we remained in being the more reluctance was there for us to disperse. The Governments concerned got used to us, and to the habit of making us useful. When we ceased to meet, the present danger to the peace of

Europe was over; the things that we did not settle were not threatening that peace; the things that had threatened the relations between the Great Powers in 1912-13 we had deprived of their dangerous features.

My own part in this Conference seems very drab and humdrum in recollection. British interests were not affected by the destiny of Djakova or Scutari, and my part was not to initiate or to shape a policy, but to serve as a useful and patient mediator between Russia and Austria, to be diligent in finding the point of conciliation, and burying the point of difference.

I believe I got the confidence of all the Ambassadors in this Conference, for they felt I was not in pursuit of triumph or prestige for British diplomacy, and that Britain's one paramount interest in the whole affair was that peace should be preserved. If this was done British interest was served. We did indeed wish to preserve also the Entente with France and Russia; but France did not want trouble to come upon her from a Balkan dispute in which French interests were not concerned; and Russia, though she would not stand a second humiliation like that of the Bosnia-Herzegovina dispute, was conciliatory and anxious only to maintain her position in the Balkans without striving to increase it at the expense of Austria. Germany had evidently determined, after the Agadir business of 1911, that she did not want trouble again so soon, and this no doubt influenced Austrian policy to be moderate. The rôle of mediator was therefore consistent with the maintenance of the Entente. If a concession was made by Russia or by Austria, it was never exploited as a diplomatic "score" or used like a victory to press a further advance. On the contrary, if a concession was made, as by Austria in the case of Djakova, it was used as a reason for urging moderation and concession on the other side. To this end the Conference worked as quietly as it could; the Press was never exploited or inspired in the interest of any individual or Government. Had this been done, it would have been fatal to our work. An atmosphere of reticence, even to the point of dullness, is favourable, provided there be at work good faith and a living desire to keep the peace. Sensation and *éclat* produce the atmosphere that is favourable to storms. To avoid creating that atmosphere will be the great difficulty of "open" diplomacy, if by that phrase is meant daily publicity.

The wisdom and experience of Cambon were very helpful in our discussions, but his rôle was not an active one. France as an Ally felt bound to support Russia; but she followed, and did not wish to lead. Cambon's help in drafting was invaluable, and he sat through all our proceedings and took part in the drudgery of drafting without a sigh of impatience; but I felt that he was not altogether satisfied with my conduct. My impression was that he feared that Russia might again suffer in prestige and that this might react unfavourably upon the Franco-Russian Alliance and the Entente with us. To guard against this he would have liked a little less neutrality, even a little more partisanship, in my attitude. He may also have thought me somewhat wooden and wanting in resource to make the Conference move when it stuck on some trivial difficulty. Certainly I have the impression that he was critical, but the grounds for this are mere surmise; he never expressed them.

Benckendorff I felt to be entirely approving. He showed no apprehension that Russian prestige would suffer from the way things were going, and seemed to be content with the line I took, to understand that it was taken solely to get fair terms and to secure peace, not at all from indifference to Anglo-Russian friendship or in order to effect a British *rapprochement* with Germany and Austria at the expense of Russia and France. The spirit in which Mensdorff worked has been described above. Both he and Benckendorff had to carry out the instructions of their Governments and did so faithfully and, when necessary, firmly; but they worked for agreement, and were delighted when they could help towards it.

In the most acute matters, such as Scutari, Italy was concerned as a Member of the Triple Alliance. She was therefore on Austria's side; but Austria's fears for her position in the Adriatic did not touch Italy's heart. Italy did not feel called upon, to put it mildly, to be more Austrian than Austria in dealing with Montenegro. Except, therefore, when Italy's interest in Southern Albania or in the islands was touched upon towards the end of the Conference, Imperiali, the Italian Ambassador, had not to take a leading part. But Imperiali had a natural disposition to friendship and good-will that was both pleasant and helpful, and this he never failed to contribute.

Very important was the attitude of Germany. I believe that from the beginning Germany intended the Conference to succeed; otherwise she would not have agreed to it at all. She was not prepared to hustle Austria, and often she allowed things to drag. But Germany was determined that war should be avoided, and for this purpose she had a whole-hearted representative and agent in Lichnowsky. He hated the notion of war, and, Russia having at the outset conceded fairly the principle of an independent Albania, Lichnowsky made it evident that he considered the details in dispute not worth a European war. His official rôle was to support Austria, but he would sometimes show contempt for the importance attached to, and the time spent upon, the allocation of some village on the Albanian frontier.

It did not occur to any of us to suggest that we should be kept in existence as a Conference, as a body ready to be called together at any moment, to which future Balkan, or indeed any troubles between the Great Powers, might be referred. We could not have suggested this officially ourselves: it was not for us as a body to magnify our own importance. Still less could the British Secretary of State for Foreign Affairs have proposed that there should be a permanent body in London, with himself as President, to settle continental troubles. Such a proposal would have been resented as giving Britain an undue predominance and advantage: the very fact that London had been accepted as the place for this Conference would have been a reason why some other capital should have had its turn for the next one. So far as I know, the good faith, the good-will, the single-mindedness, the freedom from all egotism and personal rivalries that had been characteristic of this Conference, of all its members individually and collectively, made no impression, or none but a passing impression, upon the Governments in Europe. These qualities were of little value before the war, not because they did not exist, but because hardly anybody believed in their existence.

The members of the Ambassadors' Conference of 1912-13 were all alive, available, and at their posts in 1914; but no one in Berlin or Vienna seems to have remembered the past or found in the recollection of 1912-13 any hope for the future. So, when the crisis came in

1914, although the suggestion of settling by the same machinery as in 1912 was made, it was dismissed peremptorily by Germany and Austria. Had there been two men, one in Vienna and one in St. Petersburg, wise enough to foresee their perils, one great enough to propose and the other great enough to accept the suggestion of making the London Conference, or something like it, a permanent machine, future Balkan disputes might have been settled with increasing ease. But there were no such statesmen in St. Petersburg or Vienna. Austria was fascinated by the strength of the German Army and felt secure, and Russia and France were preoccupied by fear of it. In 1912-13 the current of European affairs was setting towards war. Austria and Russia were drifting with it, and dragging the other Powers in the same fatal direction. In agreeing to a Conference, and forming one in 1912, it was as if we all put out anchors to prevent ourselves from being swept away. The anchors held. Then the current seemed to slacken and the anchors were pulled up. The Conference was allowed to dissolve. We seemed to be safe. In reality it was not so; the set of the current was the same, and in a year's time we were all swept into the cataract of war.

# CHAPTER XV

## (1914)

### THE LAST DAYS OF PEACE

King George's Visit to Paris—A Reminiscence of the Review—A Request from the French—Naval Conversations with Russia—Reasons for Consenting—The French Motive and the Russian—Questions in Parliament and the Answer—Explanatory Despatches—Sazonof's Visit to Balmoral—Bethmann-Hollweg's Allegation and the Facts—An Unwarranted Suggestion—The European Situation in June 1914—Failure of Proposals to Abate Armaments—Germany and the "Naval Holiday"—An Apparently Improving Situation—A Conversation with Lichnowsky—Opinion in France, Germany, and Russia.

I N April 1914 the King paid a ceremonial state visit to Paris. It was customary for Sovereigns, in the years after their accession, to take opportunities of paying these visits to other Sovereigns and heads of States in European capitals. Human nature seems everywhere and in all races to have created and to observe rules of etiquette. Every class has them. They are generally upheld, and the observance of them seems to give mutual satisfaction. Few people affirm that they enjoy them, but the neglect or breach of them is resented, though they take up much time that might otherwise be given to work or pleasure.

King George had not yet paid any of these complimentary visits. The year 1911 had been taken up with his Coronation; 1912 and 1913 had been overshadowed by the trouble that threatened war between Austria and

Serbia, and the condition of European politics had not
been suitable for planning State visits.  These must be
arranged some weeks or even months in advance, and if,
when the date fixed for one of them approaches, a crisis
has arisen in Foreign Affairs the visit adds an inconvenient complication.  It may be inopportune and inconvenient to the two Governments concerned, who may
at the time be preoccupied with difficult or dangerous
points of policy; or it may add to the suspicions of other
Governments.  Yet to cancel the visit may emphasize the
danger of the crisis and make it seem worse than it really
is.  So it is necessary to study the international weather-
chart very carefully, and to make the most accurate fore-
cast possible for some time ahead.  In the early months
of 1914 the international sky seemed clearer than it had
been.  The Balkan clouds had disappeared.  After the
threatening periods of 1911, 1912, and 1913 a little calm
was probable, and, it would seem, due.  Surely after so
much disturbance there would be a general wish to enjoy the finer weather.  There seemed to be no reason why
King George should not, in 1914, begin the practice of
complimentary visits that had been observed by King
Edward and other contemporary or preceding Sovereigns.

France was Britain's nearest neighbour; she was also
the country with which our relations had become most
cordial and intimate.  The French wished for the visit.
To make the first visit to France seemed as natural as to
make it elsewhere would have been questionable.  So in
April 1914 the King went to Paris, and this time, as
Secretary for Foreign Affairs, I went in attendance.  All
the circumstances of the visit were auspicious.  The
weather was such as April alone can give, and of which
she gives so little.  It was bright without being hot, the

glorious brightness of summer combined with the freshness of spring. The horse-chestnuts in Paris were in flower; the foliage was a tender green. The cold months were over, and all things growing were opening to the early warmth. Men, women, and children were out of doors to enjoy it.

A Review was held at Vincennes in honour of the King. We drove slowly in State procession through the streets, which were lined with crowds of spectators. All the people seemed happy, and at ease. There was not one Chauvinist cry. The reception was most friendly, but there was nothing that gave it the character of a bellicose gesture or defiant demonstration.

A review is indeed a display of arms, but a review of troops on occasions such as this is too usual an affair to be warlike; the firing of the guns is scarcely more suggestive of war than it is on the occasion of a royal birthday. It is external, and intended to be ornamental; it strikes the ears but does not touch the spirit.

What did touch my spirit was the study of the two French cavalry soldiers, who rode beside the carriage, in which was my place in the procession. The King and the President (M. Poincaré) were in the first; in one of the carriages behind I was seated by the Premier, M. Doumergue. Cavalry rode in line on each side of the procession. We went slowly; the same two cavalry soldiers rode close beside me all the way out and all the way back. They were of two very different and opposite types. One was of swarthy complexion, with dark brown hair, a snub nose, and stolid expression; thick-set, sturdy body; a typical son of the soil; a fellow to break up the clods of stiff land, to sow, to reap, to harvest, to do all manner of work on the land; one who would carry on through all changes of weather unaffected in body, unmoved in spirit, the very man to "stub the oxmoor," with whom readers of *Tristram Shandy* are familiar. The other was fair, slender, almost frail in body; a sensitive face, suggesting a possible artist or poet; perhaps rather a dilettante. His helmet sat uneasily upon him, and every now and then he jerked his head, to keep it in place.

Each was doing, the dark one doggedly, the fair one somewhat listlessly, the duty imposed upon him by conscription. Each must be trained to kill or be killed, in defence of his country. Conscription was the burden laid upon France by the danger of war, by the lessons of history, and by present conditions. Each of these two young men, at the age when life should be developing in different ways, according to talent and temperament, was bearing his individual share of this common burden.

It brought home to me, as I had never felt it before, what conscription meant. I thought of what it was in the affairs of mankind that made conscription necessary; how unnatural it was that all this should be accepted and taken as a matter of course. The thought stirred in me restlessly but aimlessly, like something ill at ease and yet not seeking ease, for was not conscription accepted generally on the Continent, and was it not futile to expect there would be any change? We, at any rate, with our small army and with no conscription ourselves, could not bring about a change in continental armies and military systems. These great armies and alliances and counter-alliances had come into being independently of us and of British policy. We could not influence them.

And yet, what an injury it was that in great nations young men in the prime of their youth should be taken from their homes, from useful, productive or congenial occupations for which they were fit, and for three years trained to something for which they were not either by talent or temperament disposed! Surely relations between civilized nations that made such a system necessary were contrary to all good sense and reason.

And these crowds of people enjoying the fine April day, why should they wish to disturb the peace that made enjoyment possible? And why should anyone wish to disturb them? Such reflections I pursued in the long, slow drive out from Paris and back to it. The French Premier did not speak English; my French was soon exhausted; we were each occupied in acknowledging from time to time some greeting from the crowd; and after the first few minutes we conversed but little with each other.

The contrast of that peaceful day, with apparent happiness and content about us, was often present to me after the catastrophe came; and the faces and figures of the two cavalry soldiers were clear-cut in memory. Were they taken from the cavalry and put into the trenches? Were they killed, or are they still alive? There is often some quite trivial thing that stands out clear in memory for no apparent reason, however momentous or terrible are the things with which it is associated.

All the arrangements for the visit were excellently planned and executed by the French. There was nothing that departed from the ordinary routine of such occasions. There was a great banquet at which complimentary speeches were made, carefully prepared to emphasize friendship between France and Britain, without giving offence to anyone else.

Was this all? Had France and ourselves been concerned alone it would have been all. The State visit was not a long one; the time was nearly all allocated to cere-

COUNT BENCKENDORFF
Russian Ambassador in London, 1903-1917

monies; there was little opportunity for serious discussion of anything. Serious business between France and Britain was transacted by me with Cambon in London, or through Bertie in Paris, who were both entirely trusted by each Government. No special opportunity was needed for discussion, and, if it had been needed, the State visit would not have provided one.

On the last morning, however, I was asked to go to the Quai d'Orsay. Bertie and Cambon were present, and I think one or two of the staff of the French Foreign Office besides myself and the French Minister for Foreign Affairs. As far as I recollect it was Cambon who mainly conducted the conversation with me, as he was used to conversing with me in London. The French said that there was nothing in the relations between France and Britain of which they felt it necessary or wished at that moment to· speak. But there was something they wished to ask as regards Russia. Russia knew of the conversations between the British and French General Staffs, and, in order to make Russia feel that she was not kept at arm's length, it was very desirable that there should be something of the same kind with Russia. There was no question of our undertaking any obligation whatever; this was not asked. Nor was there any reason for the General Staffs of the British and Russian Armies to communicate. Geographical separation made it impossible for British and Russian armies to fight side by side in war against Germany, as the British and French armies might do. If Britain decided to participate in such a war, it would make no difference to the use of her Army, whether the British and Russian Staffs had consulted together or not. The part to be taken by the British Expeditionary Force, if it did take part, was settled by what had passed between the British and French General Staffs. There need be no suggestion of military conversations with Russia.

There was, however, reason why British and Russian naval authorities should have some previous consultation as to the parts to be played by the respective fleets in the event of Britain taking part in a war. The French did not themselves attach great importance to this from the point of view of strategy; they did not estimate very highly the value of the Russian Fleet in a war against Germany. But they did attach great importance to it for the purpose of keeping Russia in good disposition, and of not offending her by refusing.

I could see little if any strategic necessity or value in the suggestion. To my lay mind it seemed that, in a war against Germany, the Russian Fleet would not get out of the Baltic and the British Fleet would not get into it; but the difficulty of refusing was obvious. To refuse would offend Russia by giving the impression that she was not treated on equal terms with France; it might even give her the impression that, since we first agreed to military conversations with France, we had closed our minds against participation in a war. To give this impression might have unsettling consequences, as well as being untrue. On the other hand, it was unthinkable that we should incur an obligation to Russia which we had refused to France. It was as impossible as ever to give any pledge that Britain would take part in a continental war. The fact that we remained unpledged must be made quite clear. On this understanding we agreed to let the British and Russian naval authorities communicate, as the French asked. I never enquired at the Admiralty afterwards, but I imagine that the practical result of the consultations between the two naval authorities was not great. The Cabinet agreed to the naval authorities communicating on the lines laid down in the letter of November 1912 to Cambon, and I was cognizant of the fact that such communications did proceed. But neither these nor the preceding parallel consultations between British and French military or naval authorities ever amounted to anything like a convention or political agreement entailing any obligation on the Governments; and subsequent attempts to make them appear so are directly contrary to the express stipulations recorded in the Cambon-Grey letter.

What was the motive of the French Government in making this request to us? The Russo-British naval conversations were to be further provision for a war with Germany. That, of course, is true. Did the French Government urge them because they thought war with Germany was imminent, or because they contemplated aggression upon Germany? There was not the slightest hint or sign that anything of the sort was in their minds. I felt sure at the time that they had no thought of aggression; I feel sure of it still. The idea of the *revanche* —of retaking Alsace and Lorraine—though not publicly disowned, had been tacitly given up.

In 1914 the French did not desire war with Germany—they feared it, and every preparation made was a precaution against a great peril which they desired to avoid, but which they feared might be inevitable. Had they, it may be asked, at this moment in April a feeling that the inevitable might be imminent?

There was no sign, no word to suggest that this was so. In the crisis of 1906 and again in 1911, when they had thought war to be possibly imminent, they had pressed for some undertaking or promise of help from us. We had explained that we could not give it; there was no attempt, suggestion, or request made in the visit to Paris that we should depart from our position of non-committal. There was no word of warning; no expectation of a crisis.

What, then, was their motive? I took it at the time, and I believe it now to have been, simply a desire to reassure Russia and to keep her loyal. The French nervousness about Russia's loyalty and their alliance was very marked at the time of Russo-German negotiations about the Baltic. I do not suppose they distrusted Sazonof, the Russian Foreign Minister, but there was no such thing as a Cabinet policy for Russia. Different ministers might be in favour of different policies. Each was responsible separately and solely to the Tsar. Everything depended on the Tsar; he was an honourable and conscientious man, but not one of such ability and grasp as to be beyond the influence of suggestion or misrepresentation. The French had told the Russians, some time ago, of the Franco-British military conversations. It is possible that, to give these an encouraging importance in Russian eyes, an impression of some binding effect had been allowed to take root and that their political value had been thereby magnified.

Or it may be that the Russians themselves magnified the political character of what was done for their own purposes without any encouragement thereto from the French. That there was undoubtedly a tendency in this direction appears from the private letters of Russian Ministers and Ambassadors which are printed in de Siebert and Schreiner's *Entente Diplomacy and the World*. In these the military and naval arrangements between the British and French or Russian Governments are constantly referred to as "conventions." How the military and naval authorities themselves described them I do not know, but they never had the character of conventions or of anything that had a binding effect on any of the Governments. But the extent to which the editors of this book themselves go in endeavouring to give them this interpretation comes out incidentally in their reference to a visit of Prince Louis of Battenberg to Paris in pursuance of these conversations. In a foot-note they explain that Prince Louis was "First Lord of the Admiralty, but by no means a naval expert, so that the co-ordination in question was probably of a political character."[1] This statement is just the opposite of the facts. Prince Louis of Battenberg was not First Lord of the Admiralty, he was First Sea Lord and Admiral and a naval expert; he never held any political post at the Admiralty, nor was he employed, so far as I know, in any political work.

It is certain that this new step of Russo-British naval conversations was instituted by Russia, who asked the French Government to approach us on the subject. The French were willing, seeing in the proposal a means of enhancing the value of the Franco-Russian Alliance in Russian eyes; though they did not think that co-ordination of British and Russian Fleets would add much to effective naval strategy. In any case, the French could not safely refuse the Russian request to put the matter before us. The Russians knew of the Franco-British naval and military conversations. If France had discouraged or repulsed the Russian desire to have something of the same kind between Russian and British naval au-

---

[1] *Entente Diplomacy and the World,* English translation, p. 78 footnote.

thorities, the consequences might have been untoward and even serious. It would have seemed to Russia that France was cultivating intimate relations with Britain from which Russia was to be excluded. Suspicion would have taken root and grown. France would have been suspected of a design to strengthen her own position with a support that Russia, her Ally, was not to share. It is easy to imagine how unfavourably this might have been represented to the Press by those in Russia who leant towards Germany and away from France. Such are the reflections that occur when looking back on what passed at the time.

Anyhow, the Russians asked for it, the French pressed it, and we saw no reason to refuse, provided that the whole transaction was kept strictly within the limits laid down in the Cambon-Grey letter of November 1912. This was secured by the communication to the Russians of copies of those two letters.

The thing became known to Germany, and reports of it appeared in the Press. The result was that questions were put in Parliament. There had previously been questions about military arrangements with France, and I was now called upon to say if there were naval arrangements with Russia. I give the questions and my answer in full:—

Mr. King asked whether any naval agreement has recently been entered into between Russia and Great Britain, and whether any negotiations, with a view to a naval agreement, have recently taken place, or are now pending, between Russia and Great Britain.

Sir William Byles asked the Secretary of State for Foreign Affairs whether he can make any statement with regard to an alleged new naval agreement between Great Britain and Russia; how far such agreement would affect our relations with Germany; and will be lay papers?

SIR E. GREY: The Hon. Member for North Somerset asked a similar question last year with regard to military forces, and the Hon. Member for North Salford asked a similar question also on the same day as he has again done to-day. The Prime Minister then replied that, if war arose between European Powers, there were no unpublished agreements which would restrict or hamper the freedom of the Government, or of Parliament, to decide whether or not Great Britain should participate in a war. That answers covers both the questions on the paper. It remains as true to-day as it was a year ago. No negotiations have since been concluded with any Power that would make the statement less true. No such negotiations are in progress, and none are likely to be entered upon, as far as I can judge. But, if any agreement were to be concluded that made it necessary to withdraw or modify the Prime Minister's statement of last year, which I have quoted, it ought, in my opinion, to be, and I suppose that it would be, laid before Parliament.[1]

The answer given is absolutely true. The criticism to which it is open is, that it does not answer the question put to me. That is undeniable. Parliament has an unqualified right to know of any agreements or arrangements that bind the country to action or restrain its freedom. But it cannot be told of military and naval measures to meet possible contingencies. So long as Governments are compelled to contemplate the possibility of war, they are under a necessity to take precautionary measures, the object of which would be defeated if they were made public. This was a necessity in Europe before the war, and it will remain a necessity after it, if the system of competitive armaments continues. If the question had been pressed I must have declined to answer it, and have given these reasons for doing so. Questions in the previous year about military arrangements with France had been put aside by the Prime Minister with a similar answer.

[1] House of Commons, June 11, 1914.

Neither the Franco-British military nor the Anglo-Russian naval conversations compromised the freedom of this country, but the latter were less intimate and important than the former. I was therefore quite justified in saying that the assurances given by the Prime Minister still held good. Nothing had been done that in any way weakened them, and this was the assurance that Parliament was entitled to have. Political engagements ought not to be kept secret; naval or military preparations for contingencies of war are necessary, but must be kept secret. In these instances care had been taken to ensure that such preparations did not involve any political engagement.

The record of the two conversations that is printed below will show that the Russians were given clearly to understand exactly what the nature and scope of the naval conversations were to be. Those conversations also show that the understanding with France remained exactly the same as it had been defined in the letters exchanged with Cambon in 1912.

*Sir Edward Grey to Sir F. Bertie*

FOREIGN OFFICE,
*May* 21, 1914.

SIR,—I told M. Cambon on the 14th instant that the Government had considered the question of making some communication to Russia, as I had suggested in my conversation with M. Doumergue in Paris last month, and I was now prepared to communicate to the Russian Government a copy of my letter of November 22, 1912, to M. Cambon. In doing so I would point out to Count Benckendorff that, as he would see from the letter, conversations had taken place from time to time between the French and British naval and military staffs. With regard to conversations between military staffs I would say that, if ever the British Army was engaged on the Continent, what force we could spare would be allocated to the French frontier, and, therefore, we could not enter into any military engagement, even of the most hypothetical kind, with Russia. I understood that Russia did not desire a military arrangement. But I should suggest that the Russian naval authorities should ascertain from our naval authorities what had passed between the French and British naval staffs—and I suppose that the Russian authorities could also ascertain this from the French naval authorities. They would then be able to see what scope there was for any conversations between the Russian and British naval staffs. I said that I assumed that M. Cambon would communicate to Count Benckendorff the letter of November 23, 1912, which he had written to me in reply to mine of the 22nd,[1] in the same sense.

M. Cambon said that he must apply to his Government for definite authority to agree to the communication of the letters to Count Benckendorff. As soon as he had received their consent he would let me know, and I could then make to Count Benckendorff the communication that I proposed.—I am, etc.

E. GREY.

*Sir Edward Grey to Sir F. Bertie*
FOREIGN OFFICE,<br>*May* 21, 1914.

SIR,—M. Cambon and Count Benckendorff came to see me together on the 19th inst.

I observed to Count Benckendorff that, as he knew, M. Doumergue had spoken to me in Paris on the subject of relations with Russia.

I had suggested that we might communicate to the Russian Government exactly how things stood between France and ourselves; and I was now authorized by His Majesty's Government to give Count Benckendorff a copy of the letter that I had written to M. Cambon on November 22, 1912.

M. Cambon at the same time gave Count Benckendorff a copy of the letter that he had written to me on November 23, confirming my letter of the 22nd.

I said that Count Benckendorff would see from the letters that the French and British Governments were not bound to each other by any alliance, and remained free to decide in a crisis whether they would assist each other or not, but that there had taken place between the

[1] See supra, pp. 94-95.

naval and military staffs certain conversations which, should the Governments decide to assist each other in a crisis, would enable them to do so. The reason for these conversations had been that, unless something of the kind was arranged beforehand, however anxious the two Governments might find themselves in a crisis to assist each other, they would be unable to do so when the time came.

I observed to Count Benckendorff that I understood that the Russian Government did not wish for conversations between the Russian and British military staffs. The conversations that had taken place between the French and British military staffs left no room for any other arrangement, even a conditional one, so far as England was concerned. We thought, however, that the Russian Government might be informed of what had passed between the French and British naval staffs. They would then see what scope there was for conversations between the Russian and British naval staffs, and we should be prepared that such conversations should take place, on the footing of the letter that I had written to M. Cambon and of which I had just given Count Benckendorff a copy.

Count Benckendorff raised some question of whether the conversations between the naval staffs should take place in London through the Russian naval attaché or in St. Petersburg through the British naval attaché.

I said that I assumed that the conversations would be in London with the Russian naval attaché, but this was a matter to be settled by the convenience of the Russian and British Admiralties.

Count Benckendorff further asked me whether the Russian Government should not be informed of the conversations that had taken place between the French and British military staffs.

M. Cambon said that there was presumably no objection to this.

I did not see any objection, but I said that, as Russia was the Ally of France, presumably there were complete arrangements between their military authorities for a *casus fœderis* under the alliance. In Paris, of course, the authorities knew these arrangements and also the conversations that had taken place between the French and British military staffs. In London, we knew nothing of the military arrangements between France and Russia. While it seemed to me quite natural that the Russian military authorities should wish to know from the French military authorities what military arrangements they had made with any country besides Russia, it seemed to me a matter to be dealt with by the Russian Government in Paris rather in London.—I am etc.,

E. GREY.

The incident had its reactions in Germany, as the following despatch from our Ambassador at Berlin will show:

*Sir E. Goschen to Sir Edward Grey*
(Received June 23)

BERLIN,
*June* 16, 1914.

SIR,—Herr von Jagow, who, in view of his forthcoming marriage, is leaving Berlin to-day, came to see me yesterday afternoon, and conversed on a variety of subjects connected with the international situation. After deploring the unsettled state of French internal politics, and touching lightly on what he characterized as the extremely maladroit and tactless article on that subject which has appeared in the Russian Press, he said that the only thing which had given him real pleasure of late days was the declaration you had made in Parliament with regard to the rumoured naval understanding between Great Britain and Russia. Though he had always been inclined to disbelieve the rumour, he had, he admitted, been rather shaken by the categorical and reiterated statements of the *Berliner Tageblatt* on this subject, and your declaration had come to him as a great relief. He added that, in making its statements, the *Berliner Tageblatt* had always pointed out that they were sure to receive official denial, and that such denial need not be taken too seriously; he, however, had no such ideas, and had so much confidence in your loyalty and straightforwardness that his mind was now completely at rest. If the rumour had been true he thought the consequences would have been most serious. Anglo-German relations would have, of course, lost that pleasant cordiality which he was glad to say characterized them at the present moment, but an even worse result would have been that there would at once have been a revival of the armament fever in Germany. And rightly so, he said, because Germany, from her geographical position, could afford to run no chances. In the case of war she would have to face huge Russia and France "practically alone," and if she had to take into account also that the British Fleet would be against her, the naval authorities would be perfectly justified in appealing to the country to make every sacrifice in order to meet that emergency. I said that no one wished to attack Germany. He said that he was quite aware, and even confident, that no Government wished to do so. But the Russian Government was weak, and at any moment Pan-slavism might get the upper hand. Moreover, there was no getting over the fact that the great mass of the Russian people hated the Germans, and that a war against Germany would be popular. As for France, he was sure that M. Poincaré was in favour of good relations with Germany, but in a democratic country like France foreign policy did not stand by itself, but was apt to become an instrument in the hands of politicians anxious to obtain votes, and to carry out the aims of their own particular party. A war-cry against Germany was, for instance, a certain vote-catcher, and it was, he said, used far too frequently. He could not help fearing that some day the cry would be raised once too often. The frequent change of Ministries was really a great misfortune. It was always a source of preoccupation to him how long a Ministry with whom he had made arrangements would last, and whether arrangements he had made with one Ministry would hold good with the next.

The Russian article to which Herr von Jagow referred appeared in the *Birshevia Viedomosti*. It was reproduced here in the *Lokalanzeiger,* under the heading, "Russia is ready; France must also be ready."

In commenting upon it the *Lokalanzeiger* merely said that the closing words of the article to the effect that neither Russia nor France desired war, but that Russia was ready, and expected France to be the same, a result which she could only achieve by the three years' service system, showed clearly that Russia's colossal military preparations had been begun two years ago at the direct instance of France.—I have, etc.,

W. E. GOSCHEN.

I must leave the reader to decide whether von Jagow was in fact misled by my answer in the House of Commons, or whether he was taking advantage of it to improve the occasion in a diplomatic way. To me it seems probable that he knew pretty well what the real state of our relations to the Franco-Russian Alliance were. Di-

rect consultation had now been going on between the
British and French General Staffs for more than eight
years.  German intelligence agencies, especially the military, must have become well aware that the relations between the two staffs were intimate.  The disposition of
the British and French naval forces—the latter being in
the Mediterranean, leaving all the north coast of France
exposed to the German Fleet—was evidence that there
was some arrangement between British and French naval
authorities.  There must have been frequent speculation
at Berlin as to whether we were committed to an alliance;
whether, in the event of war with France and Russia,
England was certainly to be reckoned with.  This must
have been to Germany a preoccupation and anxiety, and it
was from this point of view that von Jagow would naturally have studied my statement most carefully.  If so,
his relief was genuine, and it was justified, for, if Germany had not invaded Belgium, she would not have had
to reckon with Britain, at any rate not at the outset of
war, as will be shown in due place.

But if von Jagow was relieved that we had not undertaken obligations to France and Russia, the more would
he have been anxious that Great Britain should not commit herself to action by turning the Entente into an
Alliance.  If so, the real object of his words to Goschen
was to warn us against the consequences of such a commitment and to prevent it.

This despatch from Goschen is marked in the print at
the Foreign Office as received there on June 23.  Whether
I had read it or not before I saw the German Ambassador
on June 24 I cannot remember; but, at any rate, on that
date I gave the Ambassador a warning that my reply in
the House of Commons must be taken as meaning just

what it said, and that it did not preclude some intimacy on our part with France and Russia that was like that of Allies. This conversation with Lichnowsky will be given in full a few pages further on, as it was not confined to this one point.

A much more serious matter than questions in Parliament was the fact that copies of some (apparently) private letters of Russians about these naval conversations—letters of which we knew nothing at the time—reached the German Government. As has already been observed, these letters gave the affair a political importance that it did not in fact possess. Germany may thereby have been led to think that British relations with France and Russia had an aggressive character, and that the affair had an importance that neither we nor the French ever attached to it. It is possible that these letters were in von Jagow's mind when he spoke to Goschen. Whether it would have been possible, and, if so, whether it would have been desirable to dispel suspicion, by making it publicly known that military and naval authorities of the Entente had consulted together, will be dealt with later on in a chapter discussing what more could conceivably have been done to avoid war, and whether anything conceivable would have avoided it.

This is perhaps the most suitable place in which to deal with the statement that during Sazonof's visit to Balmoral in 1912 I made a promise to Russia going far beyond anything promised to France in communications with the French Government. The suggestion that we should have been more forthcoming to Russia than to France is in itself unreasonable, but the following quotation from a statement made by Bethmann-Hollweg requires some notice:

STATEMENT OF HERR VON BETHMANN-HOLLWEG TO THE FIRST
SUB-COMMITTEE OF THE GERMAN PARLIAMENTARY COMMITTEE
OF ENQUIRY, MARCH, 1920.[1]

In the fall of the year 1912, Russia, urged by France, gave England official notice of the compact between Serbia and Bulgaria and of her co-operation. It is not understood that England raised any objection to the tenor or object of this agreement. On the other hand, it was just about this time that that episode took place at Balmoral Castle in which Sazonof informed the Tsar in the words "Grey declared without flinching that if the occurrences in question [i.e. the European War] should take place, England would make every effort to deal German power the most decided blow." . . . It is worth laying stress on the fact that England held out the prospect of her taking part in the war against Germany without any regard as to who might be responsible for the war.

It is natural that Bethmann-Hollweg should have made this comment on the statement attributed to Sazonof in his report to the Tsar, but if that report were made without giving the Tsar clearly to understand that Britain could make no promise and come under no obligation, it was in effect an untrue report.

The record of our conversation which I made at the time is quite clear on this point, and I give it exactly as it was written:

BALMORAL CASTLE,
*September 24, 1912.*

M. Sazonof asked me what our Fleet would do to help and protect Russia if by her alliance with France she was involved in war with Germany. It was understood by Russia that France would keep ships based in Bizerta to prevent the Austrian and Turkish ships operating against Russia, but all that Russia could hope to do with her Baltic fleet when ready was to close the Gulf of Finland, and some of her towns must be left exposed.

---

[1] *Official German Documents relating to the World-war.* Carnegie Endowment Translation, vol. i, p. 18.

I said that the question of the use to be made of our Fleet if we were at war was rather one for naval experts. I doubted our sending ships into the Baltic unless we were sure of the control of the entrance, and this, if Germany could overrun Denmark, it might be difficult to ensure. But of course our Fleet (if it could not get the German Fleet to come out and fight, which was what we should like) would shut up and blockade the German North Sea coast, and would, if we went to war, do all it could against Germany and to help whoever was at war with Germany. Our superiority over the German Fleet, which we should maintain at all costs, would in this event set the French Fleet entirely free for the Mediterranean.

The question of whether we went to war would depend upon how the war came about. No British Government could go to war unless backed by public opinion. Public opinion would not support any aggressive war for a *revanche,* or to hem Germany in, and we desired to see difficulties between Germany and other Powers, particularly France, smoothed over when they arose. If, however, Germany was led by her great, I might say, unprecedented strength, to attempt to crush France, I did not think we should stand by and look on, but should do all we could to prevent France from being crushed. That had been our feeling at the time of the Algeciras Conference in 1906 and again last year.

Germany had shown a desire for some agreement with us to ensure that we should under no circumstances take part against her if she was at war. But we had decided to keep our hands free. If Germany dominated the policy of the Continent it would be disagreeable to us as well as to others, for we should be isolated.

E. G.

Sazonof stayed at Balmoral for some two days. According to my recollection the main subject of our discussion was Persia; a definite time was set apart for long discussion of that wearisome subject. But, besides, we met frequently and talked informally, as guests on a country visit must do; and I have a very distinct recollection of what must have been the foundation of Sazonof's report. From time to time in those years from 1905-14

I was sounded as to how far Britain could be committed, or I was pressed to make some promise. When questions were asked formally or officially a record was made and the most important of these records are printed in these volumes. The subject, however, was liable to crop up anywhere or at any time, and I remember very well being asked whether, supposing Britain did go to war with Germany, we should restrict action to the use of our Fleet. I remember being asked the question and being irritated, not only by its hypothetical character, but because it seemed unnecessary and unreasonable. I replied with some impatience that of course *if* Britain decided to enter into a war against Germany she would use fleet, army, men, money, and every resource she had. That this would be so if we were in any great war should have been obvious to anyone.

To construe these words as a declaration of an intention to go to war with Germany, and still more as an obligation to do so, would have been unpardonable. Sazonof never for a moment understood it in this sense; neither he nor Benckendorff nor anyone ever suggested such a construction to me afterwards, or referred again to what I had said, and when the 1912 letter to Cambon was given to the Russians in 1914 as defining British attitude, it was accepted without the faintest suggestion or hint that I had ever said anything that went beyond the terms or the spirit of that letter.

It may be convenient to sum up here the situation in Europe as it appeared to me in 1914 before the great crisis came upon us. No progress was being made towards reduction, or even towards arrest of competition in armaments. Churchill's proposal for a "naval holiday," though made in all good faith and good-will on our side, had met with no response. It is told in the *Life of Campbell-Bannerman* how his earlier suggestion for arresting the growth of armaments had been regarded in Germany almost as a threatening ultimatum. "I speak unto them of peace," Campbell-Bannerman might well have said, "and they make themselves ready for battle." The proposal for a naval holiday was not welcomed in Germany; if it was not regarded as an unfriendly act, it was far from being regarded as a friendly one. It was hard to understand then why such proposals were so unfavourably received. We did not credit Germany with really entertaining a policy of fleet superiority to Britain, and, unless this was her policy, surely a cessation of naval competition, an arrest of the growing burden of naval expenditure, was to the advantage of Germany as well as of ourselves. We were surprised that she could not see this, we simply could not understand why the proposal should make people in Berlin angry.

It is easier to understand it now that the publication of contemporary documents from the German Foreign Office has shown the extraordinary suspicion with which the most innocently well-meant proposals of Lord Salisbury about Turkey were regarded by German Ministers and officials in 1895-6. We did not realize then how inveterate and deep-rooted at Berlin was the habit of attributing a sinister and concerted motive to any proposal from another Government. Nor was it understood, as it should be now, how certainly competition in armaments leads to war. If we had understood that, we might have regarded Germany's refusal of a naval holiday with more anxiety; if Germany had understood that, she might not have repelled so curtly our proposals to arrest naval expenditure. Unless, indeed, her authorities had already made up their minds that war was to come and were premeditating it, a belief for which there was some evidence later.   On this I will only say here that the refusal of a naval holiday does not go to prove that Germany had at that time determined on war.   To have agreed to suspend naval shipbuilding for 1914 would not have diminished her naval strength in August of that year, or have impaired her preparations and readiness for war. To have accepted the naval holiday would have allayed anxiety and would have made us less likely to make preparations for war, while it would not have slackened or affected her own as far as 1914 was concerned.   That some, at any rate, of the military element in Germany considered early in 1914 that the time to strike had come is probably true; but the refusal of a naval holiday does not in itself point to there being a co-ordinated and settled purpose for war in 1914.

At any rate, the failure to arrest expenditure in armaments was but a negative feature, and there was nothing new about it.   Europe had grown used to such expenditure, and to failures to arrest its growth.   There seemed no reason to suppose that it would cause a crisis this year any more than it had done in previous years.

Some new troubles there had been early in the year, such as the friction between Germany and Russia about the military command at Constantinople; there was also trouble between Turkey and Greece.   But we had come through worse crises than these: the Algeciras Conference in 1906, the Turkish Revolution with its temporary upset of German policy in Constantinople, the Bosnia-Herzegovina crisis in 1909, Agadir in 1911, and, last, the most dangerous and difficult of all, the complications resulting from the Balkan War of 1913.   European peace had weathered worse storms than any that now were visible above the horizon. I had been more than eight years at the Foreign Office, in the centre of all the troubles; it was natural to hope, even to expect, that the same methods which had preserved peace hitherto, when it had been threatened, would preserve it still.

Something else there was, too, that may have, unconsciously or sub-consciously, affected my outlook. Each time that there had seemed to be danger of war I had been more and more impressed with the feeling of the unprecedented catastrophe that a war between the Great Powers of Europe must be under modern conditions. So impressed with this was I that it seemed impossible that the rulers and ministers of other countries should not be impressed with it too. Was it not this that had, in the difficult years from 1905 till now, made the Great Powers recoil from pressing anything to the point of war?

Our own relations with France and Russia made it certain that they would not enter upon an aggressive or dangerous policy. We had, indeed, made preparations for the contingency of German aggression; but, even in that event, we were free and uncommitted. They might hope for our help, but they knew that any aggressive policy on their part would destroy that hope.

The peril of German aggression was possible, but seemed less likely than in 1905 and 1911. Germany showed no sign of attempting again to break or test the strength of the Franco-British Entente. We had shown our readiness to meet her over the Bagdad Railway, and (as far as we could honourably do so) in the matter of the Portuguese Colonies; and an agreement on those subjects had practically been completed in the early months of 1914.[1]  In spite of the rebuff about the naval holiday, relations with Germany seemed to be really improved.  Such feelings found expression in the following conversation with the German Ambassador reported in a despatch to Sir Edward Goschen:

*Sir Edward Grey to Sir E. Goschen*

FOREIGN OFFICE,

*June 24,* 1914.

SIR,—I saw the German Ambassador to-day, before he went for ten days or so to Germany.

He spoke at some length about my reply in the House of Commons the other day, referring evidently to the reply I had given to a question about an alleged new naval agreement with Russia, though the Ambassador did not mention such an agreement by name.  He said that the statement that I had made had given great satisfaction in Berlin, and had had a reassuring effect.  There was anxiety in Germany about the warlike intentions of Russia.  The Ambassador himself did not share this anxiety, as he did not believe in the hostile intentions of Russia.  But there had been an article in the *Novoe Vremya* lately very hostile in tone to Germany.  The Pan-Germanic element was really apprehensive, and, though Herr von Bethmann-Hollweg did not share these views any more than Prince Lichnowsky himself, he did feel that there was danger of a new armaments scare growing up in Germany.  Herr van Bethmann-Hollweg had instructed Prince Lichnowsky to tell me that he hoped, if new developments or emergencies arose in the Balkans, that they would be discussed as frankly between Germany and ourselves as the difficulties that arose during the last Balkan crisis, and that we should be able to keep in as close touch.

[1] I felt that the combination of the secret agreement with Germany about Portuguese colonies with our alliance with Portugal had from the first placed the British Government in an ambiguous position.  I therefore told the German Ambassador that we had assured the Portuguese Government that the Anglo-Portuguese Alliance was regarded as still in force; and, to make everything plain, I proposed that this assurance to Portugal should be published as well as the revised form of the agreement with Germany about Portuguese Colonies.  The latter had been initialled, but I was not prepared to sign it, unless it was to be published.  The suggestion was not welcome at Berlin, and the revised agreement about Portuguese colonies was therefore never completed.  This agreement was left as I found it on entering office.

I said to Prince Lichnowsky that I felt some difficulty in talking to him about our relations with France and Russia. It was quite easy for me to say, and quite true, that there was no alliance, no agreement committing us to action, and that all the agreements of that character that we had with France and Russia had been published. On the other hand, I did not wish to mislead the Ambassador by making him think that the relations that we had with France and Russia were less cordial and intimate than they really were. Though we were not bound by engagement as Allies, we did from time to time talk as intimately as Allies. But this intimacy was not used for aggression against Germany. France, as he knew, was now most peacefully disposed.

The Ambassador cordially endorsed this.

Russia, as he himself had said, was not pursuing an aggressive anti-German policy, or thinking of making war on Germany. It was quite true that Russia was much interested, and often anxious, concerning developments in the Balkan Peninsula; but anti-German feeling was not the motive of this anxiety. For instance, when the Emperor of Russia had visited Roumania the other day, the Russian Government had not talked to us about the visit as a matter of policy, or tried in any way to bring us into it as a matter of policy. I most cordially reciprocated what Herr von Bethmann-Hollweg had said, that, as new developments arose, we should talk as frankly as before, and discuss them in the same spirit as we had discussed things during the Balkan Crisis. Let us go on as we had left off when that crisis was over. I was most anxious not to lose any of the ground that had been gained then for good relations between us. The British Government belonged to one group of Powers, but did not do so in order to make difficulties greater between the two European groups; on the contrary, we wished to prevent any questions that arose from throwing the groups, as such, into opposition. In the case, for instance, of the German military command in Constantinople, which had caused some anxiety early this year, we had done all we could to ensure its being discussed between Germany and Russia direct, and not made the subject of formal representations in Constantinople by one group, and thereby an occasion for throwing the two groups, as such, into opposition, and making them draw apart.

Prince Lichnowsky cordially agreed. He said that our being in the group we were was a good thing, and he regarded our intimacy with

France and Russia without any misgiving, because he was sure that it was used for peace.

I said that he was quite justified in this view. We should never pursue an aggressive policy, and if ever there was a European war, and we took part in it, it would not be on the aggressive side, for public opinion was against that.

Prince Lichnowsky expressed, without qualification, that the view he held of our intentions was the same as the one that I had just explained to him.

In conclusion, he spoke again of the apprehension of his Government lest a new armaments scare should grow up in Germany. He added that he had frankly told Herr von Bethmann-Hollweg that there were certain things that would make friendly relations with us impossible.

I presume that he meant by this an addition to the German Naval Law, but I did not press him on the point.

I said that I realized that our being in one group, and on intimate terms with France and Russia, had been used in past years in Germany to work up feeling for expenditure on armaments, and there was always the risk that that might be done again. I sincerely hoped, however, that too much importance need not be attached to articles in the *Novoe Vremya,* for, just as he had had to read an article of which I had not heard before, an article hostile to Germany, so, as recently as last night, I had had to read an article from the *Novoe Vremya* containing a violent attack on us in connexion with the Anglo-Persian oil concession.

In the course of conversation I also said, in order to emphasize the point that Russia did not pursue a really anti-German policy, that there were three persons through whom we learnt the disposition of the Russian Government: one was Count Benckendorff, who, I was sure, Prince Lichnowsky would recognize was not anti-German; another was M. Sazonof, who was sometimes anxious, owing to attacks made on him in the Russian Press, as to whether the Triple Entente was not contrasting unfavourably with the Triple Alliance, and proving to be a less solid force in diplomacy, but who never showed any indication of desiring to use the Triple Entente for aggressive policy against Germany, and who used it solely as an equipoise; the third person was the Emperor of Russia, and, as I was sure Prince Lichnowsky would know, he did not favour an aggressive policy against Germany, or, indeed, against anyone.—I am, etc.,

E. GREY.

What reflection does the reading of this record suggest in the light of after-events? I am sure that it faithfully represented both Lichnowsky's feeling and my own at the time, and the description given by me of our relations with France and Russia was as frank and explicit as it was possible to make it to anyone who did not belong to the Entente. The statement about the pacific disposition of France was certainly right: her whole conduct in 1914, up to the very outbreak of war, proved her desire to avoid a conflict. Lichnowsky's hope and mine that if new difficulties arose in the Balkans they would be discussed between us as frankly as in the last Balkan Crisis, that of 1912-13, was genuine; so, I am ready to believe, was that of Bethmann-Hollweg at this time. It was not fulfilled. When Lichnowsky came back from Berlin after a visit there subsequent to the murder of the Archduke Franz-Ferdinand, he was no longer in the confidence of his Government. He had then nothing to tell except that he feared something very strong was preparing, and he did not know what it was. It was in fact the ultimatum to Serbia. The documents, with their marginal notes, revealed by Herr Kautsky, tell how that ultimatum was prepared. Had Lichnowsky continued to be the trusted representative of his Government, had they dealt frankly with him, and through him with us, after the murder of the Archduke, war might have been avoided.

And what about Russia? I know of nothing to alter the opinion, expressed in this conversation, about the

Tsar, Sazonof, and Benckendorff; but it may fairly be
thought, in the light of after-knowledge, that more allowance should have been made for the inherent insta-
bility in Russian Government; for the possibility that,
in a moment of great crisis and excitement, the Tsar
might be rushed into some imprudent act. It needs more
than good-will to preserve peace in a crisis; it needs
steadiness and strength. The Tsar was not strong, and
the Kaiser was not steady, and in each country there was
a military element.

The conversation with Lichnowsky took place on June
24. I am told that, in the classification of documents
in the Foreign Office, it is the last of those allotted to
times of peace; those that come after it are in the War
Series. On June 28, the Archduke Franz-Ferdinand was
murdered.

# CHAPTER XVI

## (1914)

## THE FINAL CRISIS

The Murder of the Archduke Francis Ferdinand—Sympathy with Austria—An Unproved Assumption—The Ultimatum to Serbia—Serbian Submission and Austrian Ruthlessness—The Week before the War—Four Guiding Thoughts—The Proposal of a Conference—The German Veto—Bethmann-Hollweg and the German Military Party—The German Bid for British Neutrality—A Dishonouring Proposal—The Inevitable Answer—An Inquiry about Belgium—Russian Mobilization—Difference between Russian and German Mobilization—The Position of Germany and Austria—How it seemed at the Time—Opinion in the Cabinet and the Country—The Anti-War Party—Interviews with Cambon.

THE world will presumably never be told all that was behind the murder of the Archduke Francis Ferdinand. Probably there is not, and never was, any one person who knew all that there was to know. An attempt to murder the Archduke was made on his way to the ceremony at Serajevo. It failed, and he arrived uninjured, but not unnaturally in a state of high indignation. On his way from the ceremony another attempt was made and resulted in the assassination of himself and his wife. The inference drawn at the time was that, if this attempt had failed, there would still have been others, and that when the Archduke started for Serajevo he was, as far as human calculations and preparations could make him so, a doomed man.

There was more than one quarter in which his succession to the great position of his uncle, Francis-Joseph, might be supposed to be unwelcome; it has been surmised that there was more than one plot to remove him, emanating from more than one source, each working independently of and unknown to the other. But, so far as I know, all this is surmise, and the desire to explore the dark recesses of the individual tragedy faded away in the distress and consternation caused by the world tragedy that followed.

In Austria the popular excitement and indignation caused by the crime were intense, and the sympathy of the world was with Austria. For the first weeks the attitude of the Government in Vienna was neither extreme nor alarmist. There seemed to be good reason for the hope that, while treating the matter as one to be dealt with by Austria alone, they would handle it in such a way as not to involve Europe in the consequences. When a crime of great and dramatic villainy has been committed the indignation aroused is not satisfied with spending itself upon the void and the unknown. If the real criminal cannot be certainly indicated, popular indignation insists that some direction should be indicated in which he is to be sought.

The distrust between Serbia and Austria pointed the direction in which to look. Austria regarded Serbia's policy as provocative. Serbia regarded Austrian policy as menacing. What more probable than that Serbian fanatics had planned this crime on Serbian soil? So far, what Austria's opinion seemed to regard as certain, did not, to opinion in disinterested countries, appear to be improbable. Sympathy with Austria, my own sympathy certainly, was not diminished by this assumption.

But when it began to be presumed that the Serbian

Government was itself responsible for the crime, sympathy paused. That theory did not seem to be probable; it was even improbable; a conclusion that could not be accepted without evidence.

At length, but suddenly at the last, came the Austrian ultimatum to Serbia: unexpectedly severe; harsher in tone and more humiliating in its terms than any communication of which we had recollection addressed by one independent Government to another.

The Austrian ultimatum was not supported by any evidence of complicity of the Serbian authorities in the murder, and it appeared that both the assassins arrested were Austrian subjects. One of them had already been regarded as an undesirable by Serbia; but the Serbian Government had then been informed by Austria that he was harmless and had been warned that he was under Austrian protection. All this gave rise to a strong feeling that Serbia was being dealt with more harshly than was just. Uncomfortable recollections of the Friedjung and Agram trials recurred.

Nevertheless, we urged conciliation on Serbia; the peace of Europe was at stake; even if the Austrian demands on Serbia went beyond what facts, as known hitherto, justified, it was better that Serbia should give way than that European peace should be broken. We, at any rate, could not protect Serbia, and she could not resist alone. I believed at the time, and I know of no reason to alter that opinion now, that Sazonof genuinely and earnestly, and not merely officially and superficially, urged a conciliatory reply at Belgrade. The nature of that reply confirmed this belief. It was incredible that Serbia should have sent such a submissive reply if Russian influence had not been in that direction. The Austrian ultimatum had gone even further than we had feared in the way of peremptory severity. The Serbian answer went further than we had ventured to hope in the way of submission. Yet Austria treated that reply as if it made no difference, no amelioration. From that moment things went from bad to worse.

I will now give the account of what passed in the week before the war, just as it appeared to me then, setting down what I felt and thought at the time. How far those feelings or thoughts have been confirmed or modified by after events and fuller knowledge will be considered in a later chaper. The lack of wisdom, foresight, or resource of those who have to take a hand in great affairs must be judged in the light of after events; but if a true judgment is to be formed of the part played by any individual, people must know not only what his words and acts were, but why he spoke or acted as he did; they must stand in the place where he stood, and see each incident as it appeared to him at the time. Not till they know how things happened can they form a just or useful opinion of the causes of them.

Certain things stand out very clearly in my memory of the week before the war. The general suffering and the private griefs of the war have left scars in the memory of all who experienced them; but the week before the war also left marks on those who had responsibility— marks indelible, too deep to be obscured even by the distress of what followed.

What was said or done by me will be most clearly explained and best understood by stating the considerations and convictions that were dominant in my mind throughout that week. They may be given under four heads, stated here just as they presented themselves to me at the time. If they are kept steadily in mind when reading the published account of the negotiations in the week preceding the war they will make the proceedings more intelligible.

1. A conviction that a great European war under modern conditions would be a catastrophe for which previous wars afforded no precedent. In old days nations could collect only portions of their men and resources at a time and dribble them out by degrees. Under modern conditions whole nations could be mobilized at once and their whole life-blood and resources poured out in a torrent. Instead of a few hundreds of thousands of men meeting each other in war, millions would now meet, and modern weapons would multiply manifold the power of destruction. The financial strain and the expenditure of wealth would be incredible.

I thought this must be obvious to everyone else, as it seemed obvious to me; and that, if once it became apparent that we were on the edge, all the Great Powers would call a halt and recoil from the abyss.

2. That Germany was so immensely strong and Austria so dependent upon German strength that the word and will of Germany would at the critical moment be decisive with Austria. It was therefore to Germany that we must address ourselves.

3. That, if war came, the interest of Britain required that we should not stand aside, while France fought alone in the West, but must support her. I knew it to be very doubtful whether the Cabinet, Parliament, and the country would take this view on the outbreak of war, and through the whole of this week I had in view the probable contingency that we should not decide at the critical moment to support France. In that event

I should have to resign; but the decision of the country could not be forced, and the contingency might not arise, and meanwhile I must go on.

4. A clear view that no pledge must be given, no hope even held out to France and Russia, which it was doubtful whether this country would fulfil. One danger I saw so hideous that it must be avoided and guarded against at every word. It was that France and Russia might face the ordeal of war with Germany relying upon our support; that this support might not be forthcoming, and that we might then, when it was too late, be held responsible by them for having let them in for a disastrous war. Of course I could resign if I gave them hopes which it turned out that the Cabinet and Parliament would not sanction. But what good would my resignation be to them in their ordeal? This was the vision of possible blood guilt that I saw, and I was resolved that I would have none of it on my head.

The first three of these considerations shall be examined in the light of the fuller knowledge brought by after events. This will be done in another chapter. The fourth will be amplified and explained in the course of the narrative of events in the following pages of this chapter. All four, however, combined to lead to one conclusion and to point one moral. War must, if possible, be prevented. Every one of these considerations worked in me to concentrate all my work on that one object; that was, and till the last moment remained, the motive of my action.

At this point it may be well to remind the reader that this book records what came under the personal observation of the author and what passed through his mind. It is not concerned with discussing what others have written about the war. Of war literature there is a vast amount in several languages; some of it may cover ground that is not touched upon here. To read, to weigh the value of each contribution and to collate the whole is work for the historian, who has time to read, ability to grasp, and impartiality to judge. Here I confine myself to my own part and that which was within my personal experience.

Day by day I consulted with Nicolson at the Foreign Office. We agreed that, if things became more anxious and the prospect grew darker, I should propose a Conference. In one aspect the proposal was hopeful and attractive. It would be on the lines of the Conference of Ambassadors in 1912-13. That was of good augury, and it could be set to work at a day's notice. The same personnel was still in London: Cambon, Lichnowsky, Benckendorff, Mensdorff, Imperiali, and myself; we were all loyal colleagues, who not only knew, but trusted each other. If our respective Governments would only use us and trust us and give us the chance, we could keep the peace of Europe in any crisis. And it would be an honourable peace, there would be no diplomatic scares; no vaunting on one side and humiliation on another. After the submission of the Serbian reply to Austria, how easy it would be to arrange peace with honour, at any rate to Austria!

On the other hand, I felt some hesitation about again proposing a Conference. It had been suggested to me, perhaps quite wrongly, that in proposing and presiding over the 1912-13 Conference I had seemed to one high person in Berlin to be a little too prominent in continental affairs. Was I to be always putting myself forward as the composer of Balkan troubles in which Britain had

*Photograph by Russell, London*

LORD CARNOCK
Formerly Sir Arthur Nicholson.  British Ambassador in St. Petersburg, 1905
1910, and Permanent Under-Secretary for Foreign Affairs, 1910-1916

less direct interest herself or through Allies than any other Great Power? Also I had an instinctive feeling that this time Germany would make difficulties about a Conference. If necessary, however, these considerations were to be put aside and the proposal of a Conference was to be made.

In discussing the situation with Nicolson, it had been agreed between us that at an opportune moment, or as a last resort, we should propose a Conference. It was not easy to decide which was the opportune moment. To make the proposal too early was to court refusal on the ground that a Conference was unnecessary and premature; possibly it would have more chance of being accepted if it came from some other quarter. Britain had taken such a leading part in the Conference of 1912-13; now it was the turn of someone else. On the other hand, if no one else moved, then the proposal must be made by us before it was too late.

My usual week-end was curtailed, but things were not yet so critical that it was unsafe to be out of town even for the Sunday, and I left Nicolson in charge that day, July 26. He judged it desirable not to delay any longer the proposal for a Conference, and sent it. This circular appears as No. 36 in the White Paper.

I entirely approved of what Nicolson had done, but I was not altogether hopeful about the answer we should get from Berlin. I believed German preparations for war to be much more advanced than those of France and Russia; the Conference would give time for the latter Powers to prepare and for the situation to be altered to the disadvantage of Germany, who now had a distinct advantage. I was prepared for some stipulations or conditions from Germany and apprehensive that she would not give an immediate acceptance. We must be ready, if such points were raised, to give or get guarantees that there would be no mobilizations during the Conference; but I did not think there would be substance in such points: it seemed so certain after the Serbian reply that a Conference, once summoned, must succeed and could not break down or fail. So clear did this seem that I felt that no objections of form or punctilio, no points not of real substance, should prevent any Government from agreeing to a proposal for a Conference. The way in which the proposal would be received would be a test of the genuineness and earnestness of the desire of each Government for peace. I was therefore very much surprised, even dismayed, when Benckendorff, on my telling him that the proposal had been made, expressed the opinion that the Russian Government would not agree to it. I told him emphatically, that it was from Germany that I feared objection: she was more prepared for war than Russia or France, and she might urge that the proposed Conference was therefore to their advantage and to her disadvantage. The two despatches that follow, though they were prior to the actual proposal of a Conference, will explain what was in Benckendorff's mind and what was in mine about a Conference:

*Sir Edward Grey to Sir G. Buchanan*
FOREIGN OFFICE,
*July 25, 1914.*

You spoke quite rightly in very difficult circumstances as to the attitude of His Majesty's Government. I entirely approve what you said, as reported in your telegram of yesterday, and I cannot promise more on behalf of the Government.

I do not consider that public opinion here would or ought to sanction our going to war over a Servian quarrel. If, however, war does take place, the development of other issues may draw us into it, and I am therefore anxious to prevent it.

The sudden, brusque, and peremptory character of the Austrian *démarche* makes it almost inevitable that in a very short time both Russia and Austria will have mobilised against each other. In this event, the only chance of peace, in my opinion, is for the other four Powers to join in asking the Austrian and Russian Governments not to cross the frontier, and to give time for the four Powers acting at Vienna and St. Petersburgh to try and arrange matters. If Germany will adopt this view, I feel strongly that France and ourselves should act upon it. Italy would no doubt gladly co-operate.

No diplomatic intervention or mediation would be tolerated by either Russia or Austria unless it was clearly impartial and included the allies or friends of both. The co-operation of Germany would, therefore, be essential. (No. 24 of White Paper.)

### Sir Edward Grey to Sir G. Buchanan [1]

FOREIGN OFFICE,
*July 25, 1914.*

SIR,—I told Count Benckendorff to-day of what I had said to the German Ambassador this morning as to the possibility of Germany, Italy, France, and ourselves working together in Vienna and St. Petersburg to secure peace after Austria and Russia had mobilized.

Count Benckendorff was very apprehensive lest what I had said should give Germany the impression that France and England were detached from Russia.

I said that France and ourselves, according to my suggestion, would be no more detached from Russia than Germany would be detached from her Ally, Austria. I had emphasized to Prince Lichnowsky that the participation of Germany in any such diplomatic mediation was an essential condition, and the situation was not made unsatisfactory for Russia if France and England held their hands, provided that Germany also held hers.

Count Benckendorff urged that I should give some indication to

---

[1] In the original White Paper, which was issued in great haste, a number appears with a blank under it, implying that a document had been included in the first proof and subsequently omitted. Careful enquiry has been made at the Foreign Office, and I am assured that this document is the one that was omitted.

Germany to make her think that we would not stand aside if there was a war.

I said that I had given no indication that we would stand aside. I had said to the German Ambassador that, as long as there was only a dispute between Austria and Serbia alone, I did not feel entitled to intervene; but that, directly it was a matter between Austria and Russia, it became a question of the peace of Europe, which concerned us all. I had furthermore spoken on the assumption that Russia would mobilize, whereas the assumption of the German Government had hitherto been, officially, that Serbia would receive no support; and what I had said must influence the German Government to take the matter seriously. In effect, I was asking that if Russia mobilized against Austria, the German Government, who had been supporting the Austrian demand on Serbia, should ask Austria to consider some modification of her demands, under the threat of Russian mobilization. This was not an easy thing for Germany to do, even though we should join at the same time in asking Russia to suspend action. I was afraid, too, that Germany would reply that mobilization with her was a question of hours, whereas with Russia it was a question of days; and that, as a matter of fact, I had asked that, if Russia mobilized against Austria, Germany, instead of mobilizing against Russia should suspend mobilization and join with us in intervention with Austria, thereby throwing away the advantage of time, for, if the diplomatic intervention failed, Russia would meanwhile have gained time for her mobilization. It was true that I had not said anything directly as to whether we would take any part or not if there was a European conflict, and I could not say so; but there was absolutely nothing for Russia to complain of in the suggestion that I had made to the German Government, and I was only afraid that there might be difficulty in its acceptance by the German Government. I had made it on my own responsibility, and I had no doubt it was the best proposal to make in the interests of peace. I am., etc.,

E. GREY.

Sazonof did not raise any of these objections, and was ready to stand and let the Conference have its chance, if Austria would hold her hand. France and Italy were ready to co-operate. Germany did not raise the objection I had feared, but, while agreeing in principle, vetoed the Conference. Von Jagow said at once that it would be like a court of arbitration, which could not be called together except at the request of Austria and Russia, and he would not therefore fall in with the suggestion:

*Sir E. Goschen to Sir Edward Grey*
(Received July 27)

BERLIN,
*July* 27, 1914.

Your telegram of 26th July.

Secretary of State says that conference you suggest would practically amount to a court of arbitration and could not, in his opinion, be called together except at the request of Austria and Russia. He could not, therefore, fall in with your suggestion, desirous though he was to co-operate for the maintenance of peace. I said I was sure that your idea had nothing to do with arbitration, but meant that representatives of the four nations not directly interested should discuss and suggest means for avoiding a dangerous situation. He maintained, however, that such a Conference as you proposed was not practicable. He added that news he had just received from St. Petersburg showed that there was an intention on the part of M. de Sazonof to exchange views with Count Berchtold. He thought that this method of procedure might lead to a satisfactory result, and that it would be best, before doing anything else, to await outcome of the exchange of views between the Austrian and Russian Governments.

In the course of a short conversation Secretary of State said that as yet Austria was only partially mobilizing; but that if Russia mobilized against Germany latter would have to follow suit. I asked him what he meant by "mobilizing against Germany." He said that if Russia only mobilized in south, Germany would not mobilize, but if she mobilized in north, Germany would have to do so too, and Russian system of mobilization was so complicated that it might be difficult exactly to locate her mobilization. Germany would therefore have to be very careful not to be taken by surprise.

Finally, Secretary of State said that news from St. Petersburg had caused him to take more hopeful view of the general situation.

Von Bethmann-Hollweg said that such a Conference would have had the appearance of an "Areopagus," consisting of two Powers of each group, sitting in judgment upon the remaining two Powers:

*Sir E. Goschen to Sir Edward Grey*
(Received July 29)

BERLIN,
*July* 28, 1914.

At invitation of Imperial Chancellor, I called upon His Excellency this evening. He said that he wished me to tell you that he was most anxious that Germany should work together with England for maintenance of general peace, as they had done successfully in the last European crisis. He had not been able to accept your proposal for a Conference of representatives of the Great Powers, because he did not think that it would be effective, and because such a Conference would, in his opinion, have had appearance of an "Areopagus" consisting of two Powers of each group sitting in judgment upon the two remaining Powers; but his inability to accept proposed Conference must not be regarded as militating against his strong desire for effective co-operation. You could be assured that he was doing his very best both at Vienna and St. Petersburg to get the two Governments to discuss the situation directly with each other and in a friendly way. He had great hopes that such discussions would take place and lead to a satisfactory result; but, if the news were true which he had just read in the papers, that Russia had mobilized fourteen army corps in the south, he thought situation was very serious, and he himself would be in a very difficult position, as in these circumstances it would be out of his power to continue to preach moderation at Vienna. He added that Austria, who as yet was only partially mobilizing, would have to take similar measures, and, if war were to result, Russia would be entirely responsible. I ventured to say that if Austria refused to take any notice of Servian note, which, to my mind, gave way in nearly every point demanded by Austria, and which in any case offered a basis for discussion, surely a certain portion of responsibility would rest with her. His Excellency said that he did not wish to discuss Servian note, but that Austria's standpoint, and in this he agreed, was that her quarrel with Servia was a purely Austrian concern with which Russia had nothing to do. He reiterated his desire to co-operate with England and his intention to do his utmost to maintain general peace. "A war between the Great Powers must be avoided" were his last words.

Austrian colleagues said to me to-day that a general war was most unlikely, as Russia neither wanted nor was in a position to make war. I think that that opinion is shared by many people here. (No. 71 of White Paper.)

The effect of these replies was not only depressing, but exasperating. I really felt angry with von Bethmann-Hollweg and von Jagow. They had given us to understand that they had not seen the terms of the Austrian ultimatum to Serbia before it was sent; they had been critical of it when they saw it. Von Jagow had said that, as a diplomatic document, it left something to be desired, and contained some demands that Serbia could not comply with. By their own admission they had allowed their weaker Ally to handle a situation on which the peace of Europe might depend, without asking beforehand what she was going to say and without apparently lifting a finger to moderate her, when she had delivered an ultimatum of the terms of which they did not entirely approve. Now they vetoed the only certain means of peaceful settlement without, as far as I knew, even referring it to Austria at all. For the whole presumption of von Jagow's and von Bethmann-Hollweg's language in Nos. 43 and 71 was that they turned down the Conference without consulting Austria. The complacency with which they had let Austria launch the ultimatum on Serbia was deplorable, and to me unaccountable; the blocking of a Conference was still worse.

I remember well the impulse to say that, as Germany forbade a Conference, I could do no more, and that it was on Germany that the responsibility must rest if war came. But this impulse was put aside; to have acted on it would have been to give up hopes of peace, and to make it the object of diplomatic action to throw the blame for war on Germany in advance. That would mean not only ceasing to work for peace, but making war certain, and, though the veto of a Conference in my opinion lessened the prospect of peace, there might still be some other solution. With good-will, direct negotiations between Austria and Russia might succeed; von Bethmann-Hollweg might have in mind some other means by which his influence could be used for peace. At any rate, as long as war was not absolutely certain, it was no time to show anger or load von Bethmann-Hollweg with reproaches; the issues of peace or war seemed then to depend on him more than on anyone. If we were not to give up in despair, if we were to continue to try for peace, we must not break with him, we must endeavour still to work with him. Let it not be supposed that I thought von Bethmann-Hollweg or von Jagow insincere. I have said why I felt exasperated and angry at what seemed to me their supineness and passive obstruction, but I believed them to be sincere in their desire for a peaceful solution; I accepted, without doubt, what they said to that effect. I was sure they did not want war. I was, therefore, still ready to co-operate in any other way for peace that von Bethmann-Hollweg could devise and preferred. In that sense I replied.

But now something that had always been an uncomfortable suspicion in the background came to the front and took more definite and ugly shape. There were forces other than Bethmann-Hollweg in the seat of authority in Germany. He was not master of the situation; in negotiating with him we were not negotiating with a principal.

Yet he was the only authority with whom we could negotiate at all. Earlier in the summer Colonel House had been in London, and I had seen him then. He had just come from Berlin, and he had spoken with grave feeling of the impression he had received there; how the air seemed full of the clash of arms, of readiness to strike. This might have been discounted as the impression which would naturally have been produced on an American seeing at close quarters a continental military system for the first time. It was as alien to our temperament as to his, but it was familiar to us. We had lived beside it for years; we had known and watched its growth ever since 1870. But House was a man of exceptional knowledge and cool judgment. What if this militarism had now taken control of policy? The thought of 1911 and Agadir recurred. There had then been tense diplomatic strain, lasting for weeks, but ending in peace; and precisely because it had ended, not in a German dictated decision or in war, but in peace by compromise, there had been an outburst in Germany against German diplomacy—of which the demonstration made by the Crown Prince in the gallery of the Reichstag during the Agadir dispute had been a symptom. The Emperor had been supposed at the last to have favoured the peaceful settlement of the Agadir affair; his popularity had suffered, and that of the Crown Prince had gained by the rôle attributed to each respectively. Even if the Emperor favoured a peaceful settlement now, would his position bear the strain of a further loss of popularity?

The precedent of 1870 was ominous; we all knew how Prussian militarism had availed itself of this time and season of the year at which to strike. The same time and season of the year were now approaching. From the moment that Bethmann-Hollweg vetoed a Conference, without qualification, without condition or reservation suggested on which a Conference might be agreed to, I felt that he would not be allowed to make a peaceful end to the negotiations. Nothing short of a diplomatic triumph for Germany and humiliation for us and France and Russia would be accepted as a conclusion by the military forces. Such diplomatic triumph on the German side and humiliation on the other as would smash the Entente, and, if it did not break the Franco-Russian Alliance, would leave it without spirit, a spineless and helpless thing. If Bethmann-Hollweg could secure that, then indeed he could hold his place and make a settlement, but not otherwise. There could be no repetition of 1911, and it seemed to me that, whether he would admit this to himself or not, he knew it, and that consciously or subconsciously this was what decided his veto of a Conference.

It may be well here to ask the reader to pause for a moment and to see that he has firmly in his mind what this chapter is intended to be. It is a record of how I thought and felt at the time from day to day; not a final judgment. If the reader feels the impulse to qualify or dissent, I would ask him to suspend it till he comes to the further chapter in which this one will be reviewed. He will then be able to compare his own qualifications and present judgment on men and affairs with mine, as they are now with fuller knowledge and after-reflection on the event.

After the refusal of a Conference one blow to the prospects of peace followed after another. I do not suggest that I thought them the direct consequence of the refusal of a Conference; they were rather like the deliberate, relentless strokes of Fate, determined on human misfortune, as they are represented in Greek tragedy. It was as if Peace were engaged in a struggle for life, and, whenever she seemed to have a chance, some fresh and more deadly blow was struck.

On the morning of Thursday, July 30, I was confronted by the following telegram. It appears as No. 85 in the White Paper, but it should be read here:

*Sir E. Goschen to Sir Edward Grey*
(Received July 29)

BERLIN,
*July 29, 1915.*

I was asked to call upon the Chancellor to-night. His Excellency had just returned from Potsdam.

He said that, should Austria be attacked by Russia, a European conflagration might, he feared, become inevitable, owing to Germany's obligations as Austria's Ally, in spite of his continued efforts to maintain peace. He then proceeded to make the following strong bid for British neutrality. He said that it was clear, so far as he was able to judge the main principle which governed British policy, that Great Britain would never stand by and allow France to be crushed in any conflict there might be. That, however, was not the object at which Germany aimed. Provided that neutrality of Great Britain were certain, every assurance would be given to the British Government that the Imperial Government aimed at no territorial acquisition at the expense of France, should they prove victorious in any war that might ensue.

I questioned His Excellency about the French colonies, and he said that he was unable to give a similar undertaking in that respect. As regards Holland, however, His Excellency said that, so long as Germany's adversaries respected the integrity and neutrality of the Netherlands, Germany was ready to give His Majesty's Government an assurance that she would do likewise. It depended upon the action of France what operations Germany might be forced to enter upon in Belgium; but, when the war was over, Belgian integrity would be respected if she had not sided against Germany.

His Excellency ended by saying that ever since he had been Chancellor the object of his policy had been, as you were aware, to bring about an understanding with England; he trusted that these assurances might form the basis of that understanding which he so much desired. He had in mind a general neutrality agreement between England and Germany, though it was of course at the present moment too early to discuss details, and an assurance of British neutrality in the conflict which present crisis might possibly produce would enable him to look forward to realization of his desire.

In reply to His Excellency's enquiry how I thought his request would appeal to you, I said that I did not think it probable that at this stage of events you would care to bind yourself to any course of action, and that I was of opinion that you would desire to retain full liberty.

Our conversation upon this subject having come to an end, I communicated the contents of your telegram of to-day (No. 77 in White Paper) to His Excellency, who expressed his best thanks to you.

I read it through with a feeling of despair. The document made it clear that Bethmann-Hollweg now thought war probable. We were henceforth to converse upon how we should conduct ourselves in war, no longer how war could be avoided. But even that was not the worst feature introduced into new negotiations. The proposal made to us meant everlasting dishonour if we accepted it. If Britain did remain neutral, people would expect the Government to stipulate terms for our neutrality. I had contemplated resignation if war came and we declined to stand by France, and I had therefore thought nothing as to making conditions for our neutrality. This bid from Bethmann-Hollweg was like a searchlight lighting up an aspect of the situation which had not been looked at yet. I saw how difficult the situation would be even for those who were most resolved to keep out of war, if war came. If their policy carried the day, they would be expected to turn British neutrality to account, to ensure that the conditions for it were such that the British position was not jeopardized by the war. What stipulations could they make? If it was dishonouring and impossible to accept the price and the conditions here offered, what other price or conditions could they require in British interests that were not dishonouring to Britain? The answer was clear —there were none. If it were decided to remain neutral we must, after this bribe offered by Bethmann-Hollweg, remain neutral without conditions.

There was further matter for depression in this telegram. Did Bethmann-Hollweg not understand, could he not see, that he was making an offer that would dishonour us if we agreed to it? What sort of man was it who could not see that? Or did he think so badly of us that he thought we should not see it? Every thought the telegram suggested pointed to despair. But while there is still time one does not sit down under despair, only the effort to lift it must be big and the appeal must be big.

I sat down and wrote the answer (No. 101 in the White Paper) as follows:

*Sir Edward Grey to Sir E. Goschen*
FOREIGN OFFICE,
*July* 29, 1914.

Your telegram of 29th July.

His Majesty's Government cannot for a moment entertain the Chancellor's proposal that they should bind themselves to neutrality on such terms.

What he asks us, in effect, is to engage to stand by while French colonies are taken and France is beaten so long as Germany does not take French territory as distinct from the colonies.

From the material point of view such a proposal is unacceptable, for France, without further territory in Europe being taken from her, could be so crushed as to lose her position as a Great Power, and become subordinate to German policy.

Altogether apart from that, it would be a disgrace for us to make this bargain with Germany at the expense of France—a disgrace from which the good name of this country would never recover.

The Chancellor also, in effect, asks us to bargain away whatever obligation or interest we have as regards the neutrality of Belgium. We could not entertain that bargain either.

Having said so much, it is unnecessary to examine whether the prospect of a future general neutrality agreement between England and Germany offered positive advantages sufficient to compensate us for tying our hands now. We must preserve our full freedom to act as circumstances may seem to us to require in any such unfavourable and regrettable development of the present crisis as the Chancellor contemplates.

You should speak to the Chancellor in the above sense, and add most earnestly that the one way of maintaining the good relations between England and Germany is that they should continue to work together to preserve the peace of Europe; if we succeed in this object, the mutual relations of Germany and England will, I believe, be *ipso facto* improved and strengthened. For that object His Majesty's Government will work in that way with all sincerity and good-will.

And I will say this: If the peace of Europe can be preserved, and the present crisis safely passed, my own endeavour will be to promote some arrangement to which Germany could be a party, by which she could be assured that no aggressive or hostile policy would be pursued against her or her Allies by France, Russia, and ourselves, jointly or separately. I have desired this, and worked for it, as far as I could, through the last Balkan Crisis, and, Germany having a corresponding object, our relations sensibly improved. The idea has hitherto been too Utopian to form the subject of definite proposals, but if this present crisis, so much more acute than any that Europe has gone through for generations, be safely passed, I am hopeful that the relief and reaction which will follow may make possible some more definite *rapprochement* between the Powers than has been possible hitherto.

I took this to Asquith in 10 Downing Street. There was to be a Cabinet that afternoon, but we agreed that the answer might be sent without waiting for the Cabinet. Time pressed, and it was certain that the Cabinet would agree that this bid for neutrality could not be accepted. We should be execrated here and everywhere if we assented beforehand to Germany taking French colonies and if we condoned in advance violation of Belgian neutrality —for that was what acceptance of the bid meant for us. Von Bethmann-Hollweg was careful not to say that Germany would not violate Belgium neutrality unless France did so first.

I returned to the Foreign Office and showed it to those whom I was in the habit of consulting there. It was suggested to me that the last part of the telegram might not be acceptable to France. But it had already been approved as a whole by Asquith, and what I had written represented my own feeling and my last hope. We had all of us been looking into the abyss for some days. There seemed just a chance that the sight might make possible what had not been possible before. It could not be supposed that, if others rose to the larger view, France would be an exception. The prospect of war, that was hideous enough to us, must be still more horrible and menacing to France. So the telegram was sent. In the afternoon both Goschen's telegram and mine were read to the Cabinet, and they approved what had been done.

The next day, Friday, July 31, I took a diplomatic step that contemplated the contingency of war. A request was addressed to the French and German Governments asking each for an assurance that it would respect the neutrality of Belgium, so long as no other Power violated it. The request was sent simultaneously to both Governments and without any previous arrangement with France, but it was obvious to everybody that France desired the neutrality of Belgium and would do everything to preserve it so long as it was intact and would avoid anything that might give a pretext for its violation by Germany. The step now taken in London was in close accord with the attitude of Mr. Gladstone's Government in the Franco-Prussian War of 1870. On that occasion both France and Germany agreed to respect Belgian neutrality. This time France agreed, Germany evaded the request for an assurance.

Germany ceased to talk of anything but the Russian mobilization. I could do nothing to stop that. The rejection of a Conference struck out of my hand what might have been a lever to influence Russia to suspend military preparations. If a Conference had been agreed to, if even Germany had said that a Conference could only be agreed to on condition that Russia did not mobilize more than Austria, I should have had some *locus standi* on which to work at St. Petersburg. But throughout these negotiations I had been given nothing that would help me at St. Petersburg. I felt impatient at the suggestion that it was for me to influence or restrain Russia. I could do nothing but express pious hopes in general terms to Sazonof. If I were to address a direct request to him that Russia should not mobilize, I knew his reply; Germany was much more ready for war than Russia; it was a tremendous risk for Russia to delay her mobilization, which was anyhow a slow and cumbrous affair. If Russia took that risk, in deference to our request, would Britain support her, if war did ultimately come and she found herself at a disadvantage owing to following our advice? To such a request the only answer could be that we would give no promise. If we gave a promise at all it must be to France, and my promise to Russia must be only consequential on that. The Cabinet was not prepared yet to give a promise even to France. This consid-

*Photograph by Russell, London*

THE RIGHT HON. H. H. ASQUITH
(Now the Earl of Oxford and Asquith, K.G.)

eration was always present to my mind in all communications to St. Petersburg during these critical days.

But besides this I did most honestly feel that neither Russian nor French mobilization was an unreasonable or unnecessary precaution. In Germany, in the centre of Europe, was the greatest army the world had ever seen, in a greater state of preparedness than any other, and what spirit was behind? I did not think the German Emperor counted for much, but others did, and the ring of his speeches, "Smite in the face with my mailed fist," "shining armour," "sharp sword," etc., was ever in people's ears. There was, too, the recollection of 1870 and the revelations of the Ems telegram. How could anyone urge on Russia or France that the precaution of mobilization was unreasonable? How could anyone affirm that it was safe to omit that precaution? For I believed the French and Russian mobilizations to be preparation, but not war. Indeed, the French, when they mobilized, did it with instructions that no troops were to go within ten kilometres of the German frontier. With Germany mobilization was something different. It was the last, and not the first word. The mechanism was so arranged that precaution and preparations were always taken and made. Mobilization was the word, and it was followed immediately by the blow. The Russian mobilization was therefore replied to, not by mobilization in the same sense in Germany, but by mobilization with an ultimatum to Russia that made war certain. This, too, at a moment when there seemed still some chance, even an improving chance, that Austria and Russia might come to terms direct over the Serbian trouble. It seemed to me that Germany had precipitated war. My reading of the situation at the time was that Austria had gone recklessly ahead against Serbia, believing that the history of the annexation of Bosnia and Herzegovina would be repeated; that she could humiliate Serbia and that Russia would, as in 1908, recoil before the "shining armour" of Germany and that there would be no great war. When Austria found that the parallel of 1908 was not to be repeated and that things were serious, she began to try to get out of it. Germany then precipitated war and told Austria, that as an Ally, she could not get out. This impression was confirmed in my mind by the fact that it was not till five days after Germany had declared war on Russia that Austria was herself at war with Russia. The White Paper gives all that I knew at the time of what was going on, and on that it was natural that I should come to this conclusion; it seemed impossible to come to any other conclusion. That was then, to me, the true account of how the war was brought about.

It is of some interest here to recall that, some time in the days before the war, I remember drawing a comparison between the crisis over Serbia now and that in 1908, I think, to someone in the Foreign Office; that I did this and I drew exactly the opposite conclusion that I now suppose Austria to have drawn at first. I said that no great Power could submit to a second humiliation such as Isvolsky and Russia had suffered in 1908. It was precisely because Russia had recoiled in 1908 that she was sure not to abdicate her Slav rôle now.

I have now endeavoured to give an account of what I thought and intended in negotiations with Germany during this fateful week, and I have explained the point of view at which I stood when Germany declared war on Russia and how I felt about it.

It is necessary now to turn back a few days from this

point and describe more fully what passed with France and Russia about promises of support, more particularly with France, for the question of supporting Russia was always subordinate to that of supporting France. To understand the great and most embarrassing difficulty in which the whole Government was placed in answering the French request for a promise of help, it is necessary to review somewhat fully the state of opinion inside and outside the Government. This was very divided up to the last moment; and when there is division on such an issue as peace or war, it cannot be bridged by formulas.

It is probably difficult for some of those who were strongly opposed to war to recall now what they thought during that last week of July. They felt so differently and so deeply afterwards, when they realized what Prussian militarism meant in war. Now, when the possibility of war appeared, there was an anti-war party in the Cabinet. As possibility became probability this party naturally became at first not less but more active and determined. It did not appear in Cabinet discussions, for neither I nor anyone tried to force a decision while there was still any hope of peace. Discussions in the Cabinet were restrained and reserved, for we kept to that on which we were all agreed—the endeavour to prevent war altogether. But outside the Cabinet I felt sure that the anti-war group were meeting, were arranging concerted action, if need be, to keep this country out of war or to resign if they failed in doing so. I was told afterwards, when we were united in the stress of war, that what had been assumed at the time was in fact true. This group included more than one of the names that came next after that of the Prime Minister in authority and influence with the Liberal Party inside and outside. It is needless to enquire whether the group included half, or less, or more than half the Cabinet; it was sufficient in number and influence to have broken up the Cabinet. I made no attempt to counteract this movement either inside or outside the Government. I do not remember asking any colleague to support participation in war, if war came. There was not a moment to spare from the exhausting and exacting work of the Foreign Office in that week; but, apart from this, I felt that, if the country went into such a war, it must do so whole-heartedly, with feeling and conviction so strong as to compel practical unanimity. If that came, all the workings of anti-war sections would be as if they had never been. If the country could be kept out of the war by such a division of forces, it had better keep out and stand aside. It must certainly not be manœuvered into a great war by the counter-workings of a pro-war against an anti-war group.

It was clear to me that no authority would be obtained from the Cabinet to give the pledge for which France pressed more and more urgently, and that to press the Cabinet for a pledge would be fatal; it would result in the resignation of one group or the other, and the consequent break-up of the Cabinet altogether. That was my deliberate estimate of the situation, and all I knew or heard afterwards confirms the opinion that it was at the time a true estimate. There was also more than the division of opinion in the Cabinet to be taken into account. There was division in Parliament and in the country. A section there was, no doubt, that identified Germany with Prussian militarism, and identified Prussian militarism with all that was evil and hostile to Britain. It was a concentrated and active section, but it did not express the prevailing feeling in the country. The country in

general wanted peace. Some Germans cannot understand
why we went into the war, because the motive that im-
pelled us is something outside their perception. Because
that is so, because they cannot see the real motive, they
invent reasons other than the true one, to account for
British action. One of these motives very generally
attributed to us is that of industrial rivalry and commercial jealousy of Germany. It is the reverse of the truth.
Our great industrial districts, especially Lancashire, were
most averse to war. Trade was good, industry wanted to
be undisturbed.

Some pro-French feeling there was—quite a substantial
touch of it, quite as much of this as there was of anti-
German feeling; but it was not enough to outweigh the
general desire to keep out of war. The notion of being
involved in war about a Balkan quarrel was repugnant.
Serbia, to British people, was a country with which a few
years ago we had severed diplomatic relations, because of
a brutal murder of the King and Queen; and, though that
was over, and we were now on good terms, there was no
sentiment urging us to go into a war on Serbia's behalf.
If France were involved, it would not be in any quarrel in
which we owed her good-will, as in the Moroccan disputes. It would indeed not be in any quarrel of her own
at all; it would be because she, as Russia's Ally, had the
misfortune to be involved in a Russian quarrel, in which
France had no direct interest and which did not arouse
feeling in the French people. Even on questions such as
Morocco we had carefully limited our obligation to diplomatic support only. We were not bound to give even that
in this Serbian trouble. What, it was asked, was the good
of keeping so carefully clear of alliances and obligations
if we were to be drawn into European war in such a

quarrel as this? People were sorry for France's misfortune in being involved in war by an alliance with Russia; but was that any reason why we, who had not the risk of an alliance, should be involved in the misfortune and danger of a course that we had deliberately avoided for the very reason that we thought it dangerous? Such I felt to be how the situation was viewed by numbers of people, and I knew the desire to keep out of war to be very widespread and strong. If this feeling had not been represented in the Cabinet, the Government would have been out of touch with the country—an unsafe position in any circumstances, a most dangerous one in a crisis.

It must be admitted that if there were not an anti-war group in the Cabinet there ought to have been. Some of us, on the other hand, felt that the considerations stated above did not touch the true issue. We felt that to stand aside would mean the domination of Germany; the subordination of France and Russia; the isolation of Britain, the hatred of her by both those who had feared and those who had wished for her intervention in the war; and ultimately that Germany would wield the whole power of the Continent. How would she use it as regards Britain? Could anyone feel comfortable about that question? Could anyone give to it truthfully in his heart any but a sinister and foreboding answer?

The House of Commons showed to the full this division of opinion. In the last week of July, Bonar Law, the Leader of the Conservative Party in the House, came daily to my room there at question time before I returned to the Foreign Office, to ask what the news of the crisis was. One day, about the middle of the week, as the news got more ominous, he said that it was not easy to be sure what the opinion of the whole of his party was. He doubted whether it would be unanimous or overwhelmingly in favour of war, unless Belgian neutrality were invaded; in that event, he said, it would be unanimous.[1] If Conservatives were not unanimous, Liberal opinion was still more uncertain. About the same time a very active Liberal member came up to me in the Lobby and told me that he wished me to understand that under no circumstances whatever ought this country to take part in the war, if it came. He spoke in a dictatorial tone, in the manner of a superior addressing a subordinate, whom he thought needed a good talking to. It did not seem to occur to him that if men like himself were feeling the strain of the situation, the Secretary for Foreign Affairs might be feeling it as much, or more, and the strain was very great, and the more it was controlled in official work the more apt it was to seek relief on other occasions. I answered pretty roughly to the effect that I hoped we should not be involved in war, but that it was nonsense to say that there were no circumstances conceivable in which we ought to go to war. "Under no circumstances whatever," was the retort. "Suppose Germany violates the neutrality of Belgium?" For a moment he paused, like one who, running at speed, finds himself suddenly confronted with an obstacle, unexpected and unforeseen.

[1] It has been said that I must have misunderstood Bonar Law; but the statement in the text is well within the mark of what he said to me in the middle of the week. He referred only to the opinion of the rank and file of his party; not to his own opinion or to that of other leaders. I supposed that a large majority of the Conservative Party would support action to help France; but that some opinion outside the Conservative front bench reserved its decision till later is certain.

I am ready to assume that even in the middle of the last week of July the leaders of the Conservative Party were unanimous, though it was not till (I think) Sunday, August 2, that their decision was conveyed to us. As to Bonar Law's own opinion, he never expressed it to me at this stage. Nor do I remember that I expressed mine to him. Each of us probably assumed the other to be convinced that we ought not to stand aside, if France were attacked.

Then he said with emphasis, "She won't do it." "I don't say she will, but supposing she does." "She won't do it," he repeated confidently, and with that assurance he left me.

In the Cabinet the two groups continued to work together for the one object on which both were heartily agreed, to prevent a European war; like two men who walk side by side on a straight road, but who see ahead a parting of the ways and are determined, when they come to it, to go one to the right and the other to the left. Meanwhile, one side did not press the other to authorize a pledge to support France; the other did not press for an intimation to France that we should stand aside. In that, at any rate, both were wise. Between the two groups were no doubt members of the Cabinet, who reserved their decision. Their attitude also was to be respected. It was not opportunism; it was a tribute paid to the gravity of the situation. The Cabinet as a whole knew that it was not in a position to pledge the country. Such were the conditions in which, inside the Foreign Office, the demand from France and Russia to know whether they could count on British support in war had to be received and could not be answered.

The interviews with Cambon were distressing to both of us, but must have been even more so to him than to me. The very existence of his country as a great nation was at stake, and it was vital to France to know what Britain would do. Later on, when the war had shown the forces and the real issues, it was generally understood in Britain that our existence was at stake too; but in those pre-war days it was the peril of France alone that was clear and imminent. Britain had never had an 1870, and we still thought we were an island.

It is unnecessary to repeat what has been written at the beginning of this chapter under heading 4.[1] That was always present to me; but, besides dread of the mortal error of holding out hopes to France and Russia that in the hour of need might not be fulfilled, there was the sense of responsibility to the Cabinet. At such a time, and on such an issue, he who spoke must not go one inch beyond what the Cabinet had authorized. No. 119 in the White Paper is an instance of the sort of conversation that took place, though a dictated summary of such a conversation is a bald and cold affair. It goes without saying that such answers did not and could not give Cambon what he wanted, nor indeed anything that was of any use to him. It had often since been a source of regret that he alone felt me to be lacking in sympathy. My own difficulties and anxiety to keep within the narrow limits of what had been agreed to by the Cabinet preoccupied me. And, besides that, I was myself a party to that Agreement; it was in my judgment all that could be said at the time; but there was a sense of the uselessness and strangeness of my words of sympathy, when the one thing asked for could not be said.

In these interviews, under all the strain of anxiety Cambon never once hinted that any obligation or point of honour was involved; never suggested that, in such a crisis as this, if we stood upon the letter of the written communications exchanged between us in 1912, we should be acting contrary to the spirit of them. He besought us to think, not of obligation but of our interests; to reflect what our position would be if Germany crushed France and dominated Europe. The only reply at the moment could be that this was what some of us were thinking about.

[1] See supra, p. 303.

Pressing, urgent, insistent as Cambon's appeals to us were, his whole attitude throughout the crisis was a fine example of loyalty. We each had a line that we were bound to take; he had the opportunity of making his a fine one, and he made it so. In mine there was no such opportunity; I felt that very distinctly, but there was no other line open to me. Meanwhile France and Russia urged, with undeniable force, that even if we could promise nothing to them, we should not give Germany the impression, or let her be under the impression, that we should certainly stand aside. In every crisis since 1905 Germany had been told that in my opinion, if war came, we should be drawn into it on the side of France. The warning was given again to Bethmann-Hollweg through Goschen, and to Lichnowsky by me. More than this could not be said. Bluff, even if it could be stooped to in such grave moments, would be useless: the Germans would have known that the border-line between truth and bluff was overstepped. Probably things that reached Berlin in this summer of 1914, private and secret as well as official, will never be published or known. If they are it will be very surprising, if it is found that the Foreign Office was the only source upon which the German Government depended for information about British opinion; or that Lichnowsky was the only German channel through which they derived it. If we knew how strong feeling in Great Britain was, it is certain that the Germans knew it too. What they did not understand was the difference that wanton violation of Belgium would make.

If the German Government had replied to our question with a promise to respect the neutrality of Belgium, provided that France also respected it, and if they had asked whether on this condition we would remain neutral, there would presumably have been discussion on this new feature in the Cabinet. The discussion might have been a counterpart of that on the point of giving a pledge to help France. In this case the group that thought we should stand by France would presumably have opposed giving any pledge of neutrality to Germany. The Cabinet was, in short, up to the time when violation of Belgian neutrality became imminent, unable to give any pledge to anybody, and in that it reflected the state of feeling and opinion in Parliament and the country. By August 1, after Germany had evaded the request to respect Belgium's neutrality, this period of indecision, as far as the Cabinet was concerned, was coming to an end. How decision was attained first in the Cabinet and then in Parliament will be told in the next chapter.

END OF VOL. I